W9-ANP-462

THE AMERICAN INDIAN TODAY

The American Indian Today

EDITED BY STUART LEVINE

AND

NANCY OESTREICH LURIE

PENGUIN BOOKS INC

BALTIMORE, MARYLAND

Penguin Books Inc, 7110 Ambassador Road, Baltimore, Maryland 21207, U.S.A.

—

First published by *Midcontinent American Studies Journal*, Volume VI, 2, Fall, 1965
Revised and expanded edition published by Everett/Edwards, Inc., April, 1968
Published in Pelican Books 1970
Reprinted 1972, 1974

—

—

—

Printed in the United States of America by Kingsport Press, Inc.
Set in Linotype Georgian

—

CONTENTS

FOREWORD

Stuart Levine. The Survival of Indian Identity   9

THE BACKGROUND

Nancy Oestreich Lurie. Historical Background   49

Elizabeth Clark Rosenthal. 'Culture' and the American
Indian Community   82

CURRENT TENDENCIES

Shirley Hill Witt. Nationalistic Trends Among American
Indians   93

Robert K. Thomas. Pan-Indianism   128

CASES IN POINT

Harriet J. Kupferer. The Isolated Eastern Cherokee   143

Carol K. Rachlin. Tight Shoe Night: Oklahoma Indians
Today   160

James A. Clifton. Factional Conflict and the Indian Community: The Prairie Potawatomi Case   184

Ann Fischer. History and Current Status of the Houma
Indians   212

Deward E. Walker, Jr. Some Limitations of the Renascence Concept in Acculturation: The Nez Perce Case   236

Rosalie and Murray Wax. Indian Education for What?   257

Henry F. Dobyns. Therapeutic Experience of Responsible Democracy   268

Contents

AFTERWORD

Nancy Oestreich Lurie. An American Indian Renascence?   295

About the Authors   329

Bibliography   333

Index   337

MAPS

Maps of the Distribution of
North American Indians, 1950   353

Foreword

STUART LEVINE

THE SURVIVAL OF INDIAN IDENTITY

THIS book argues that neither ignorance nor simple anger is a viable stance in matters Indian. The ignorance is widespread, and hardly needs discussion. The anger appears among well-intentioned Americans, liberal in their sympathies, but not very well informed about the peculiarities of the Indian situation. Their outrage speaks well for the soundness of their impulses, but is not in itself a constructive response. The situation is complex; one's first guess at what Indian people want and need will be wrong. Yet there are things which can be done if accurate information about Indian status and aspirations can be widely disseminated.

After a preliminary version of *The American Indian Today* was published in the Fall of 1965, D'Arcy McNickle said, in an article in *The Nation*, that it deserved 'special mention'

because its collection of articles does attempt to let the Indian stand forth as a person and a group member in our contemporary industrialized society – to give some meaning to the values that operate in Indian life.[1]

What pleased Professor Lurie and me most about Dr McNickle's praise was his acknowledgement that our contributors were trying very hard to see Indian problems from the Indian point of view. He feels that this is quite new among academic writers. It is almost unknown among the general population, and all too rare in Washington. Yet the point of view of Indian people is not difficult to understand, and the

9

people themselves are interesting. One might reasonably hope that the attractiveness of the subject would lure the intellectually curious into better understanding it. For a nation of Indian-buffs, we know pathetically little about Indians.

This book should provide, first, some basic information about Indian history and Indian relationships with our government and its colonial predecessors; second, introductions to specific problems which face Indian people today; and third, several examples, case histories, if you will, of the situation in specific places around the nation. It makes no claim to be comprehensive; there's a bibliography at the end of the volume for readers who want fuller background. But it should give even the general reader a good feel for the situation, and a sense of what Indian people and those who like them – the editors in particular – think we should be doing.

MISCONCEPTIONS

Let us begin by listing a few matters which are often misunderstood. These will seem obvious to those who do know the situation, but they do not seem well known among otherwise well-informed people.

☐ Indians are not vanishing. However you measure their population, there are at least as many here now as there were at the time of the first white contact. This is true even if you define 'Indian' quite strictly, including only those who are living, in one way or another, in an Indian manner. They are a fair-sized minority group if you include all of those who are living in the general culture but have a strong sense of their ties to Indian ancestry. They are a very large minority group if you include everyone who has at least some Indian ancestry. And even this last way of estimating the size of the Indian population, while it does deal with a very amorphous group, still has some potential force; for in our culture, there is little pressure to hide Indian ancestry, as, alas, there is in much of Latin America. People whose ancestors have for generations been living in the general culture, but who know that they carry a fractional Indian ancestry, are often proud of the fact, and are liable to feel surprising sympathy for Indian causes.

The exact size of the Indian population is hard to estimate: if you are fussy about it, and count only people living quite traditionally, in certain well-defined places, you can get the estimate down as low as three quarters of a million. Count anyone who knows he has Indian blood and it goes much higher; I've seen estimates running from five to fifteen million. It's probably best to split the difference, and say that several million people are actively interested in their 'Indian-ness'.

Real 'Indian-ness', by the way, is not necessarily measured on racial lines. There are tribesmen on reservations who number among themselves virtually no one who is a 'full-blooded' Indian. Different tribes require different degrees of 'blood' for membership; some have no such requirements at all, and among the millions of Indians living in the general population, the proportion of 'blood' runs anywhere from four-fourths to infinitesimal.

☐ Indians are not all alike. At the time of first contact, there was far more cultural and linguistic diversity in North America than there was in Europe, and much of that diversity remains today. With some notable exceptions, members of the many cultures which thrived on our part of the continent were not in very extensive contact with one another. Their individuality is reflected in their languages: for the most part, the languages even within any one of the numerous language families were mutually indecipherable, and the families themselves were as different from one another as language families in any part of the old world. Language, custom, belief, mode of obtaining food and shelter, and therefore personality, varied wildly. While it is true that we have lost many languages and that given tribes have become extinct or have been absorbed into large units, it is still true that Indian people are as different from one another as they are from representative sectors of the nation at large. Something like fifty different languages are still in use today.

Although 'tribes' themselves contain a great deal of diversity, it is possible in some cases to speak of a tribal personality. But the nature of that personality varies markedly from one tribal group to the next. Hopi people are not like Sioux people, nor Cherokee like Havasupai. There is a long history of intertribal cooperation of various kinds, dating back to long before first European contact, but tribal distinctness is still very strong. A great many Indian people dislike the word 'Indian'; they prefer to be identified by the name of their tribe.

☐ Although Indians have a great many problems and grievances, they do not, for the most part, like to be associated with the Civil Rights Movement as it is popularly understood. Some, indeed, are actively hostile to Negroes and to Negro causes. Some young Indian people put it this way: *the aims of the Civil Rights Movement are good, but seem to concern only Negro rights. There are other underprivileged groups with different, but equally urgent, problems.* The Indian case is subtly different from that of the Negro, for reasons which we will discuss shortly. For the time being, suffice it to say that the Negro, by and large, wants a fair share in the general culture. The Indian wants to remain special.[2]

The Survival of Indian Identity

☐ Not all Indians live on reservations, and not all are in the same economic boat. There are, for example, many small towns in which the population is largely Indian, and there are sizeable Indian neighborhoods in a number of large and middle-size cities, sometimes populated as a result of systematic Indian Bureau efforts to encourage people to leave the reservation and try their hand at living in the larger society outside, sometimes because people have been driven there by economic need. With the exception of those few famous 'oil Indians', most of them members of the Osage tribe in Oklahoma, it is true that by and large Indian people are quite poor. The conditions among them run a wide gamut. There are reservations in which per capita income is just a few dollars a year; there are others, such as the vast Navajo reservation, in which tribal organization, government aid, light industry, tourism, and utilization of whatever natural resources are at hand (Navajo herd sheep) have created a modest amount of capital which does filter down among the large population which lives there. Indians in the cities for the most part are very poor, but their situation is not always exactly like that of, say, Puerto Ricans or Negroes, for as we shall see later, often they do not intend to remain. They are here only to pick up some cash or to weather the winter. There is also, of course, a small Indian middle class, and there are Indians operating successfully in all the professions – as doctors, teachers, politicians and lawyers. Quite a few are anthropologists, including, I am pleased to note, several of our contributors and Dr McNickle. On the morning on which I write, an application reached me from a Ponca man, active in Indian affairs and currently president of the National Indian Youth Council, who wants to work toward an advanced degree in the American Studies Program which I administer. The present head of the Bureau of Indian Affairs is an Indian, too. And there are a few very wealthy

Indians, at least one of them the chairman of the board of a major oil company.

☐ Indian people do not form a political bloc in the way other minority groups often do. Some are politically active; some are pointedly detached from politics; some, as we shall see, are attracted to extremist positions; some after examining the history of the Indian policies of Democratic and Republican administrations, feel that one party is to be trusted more than the other. But many feel strongly that Indian people should not have to form a voting bloc to get what they want and deserve, because, unlike other minorities, they have treaty arrangements with the government. Since these generally have not been lived up to, they feel that their cause is best defined in terms of broken promises which should be fulfilled. Reliance on the ballot box alone would deny their special relationship with Washington, something older Indian people especially do not want to lose. They point out that the treaties give them special and direct access to the government.

SHALL WE ALTER THE INDIAN?

In general the anthropologists have been inclined to recommend that the social and cultural structure of a society, including its theology, be accepted without direct efforts toward immediate alteration.

Such a course has obvious liabilities as far as policy is concerned. To put it most concretely and most bluntly, it surrenders the hope of transforming the basic value systems of the great masses of people who must be our allies in the near future. It involves the incalculable risk of materially strengthening groups whose ideas are fundamentally divergent from our own, and who would therefore in the future make unreliable partners. If it is not possible to spread the notions of democracy to men brought up in a patriarchal or traditional society, have we any assurance that the collaborators our aid now brings us will ever acquire an interest in our ultimate objectives?

Without in the least minimizing the real difficulties involved it may yet be that the problem is soluble. The American experience offers suggestive clues as to the nature of an operation in the present, for the essence of that experience was the spread of a complex of ideas to large groups of men initially hostile to it.

– Oscar Handlin, *Race and Nationality in American Life*

Professor Handlin's affection and respect for the diverse cultures which have been involved in the American experience is steadily evident in his work on them. Does the position typified by this quotation represent a contradiction or a change of heart? Is he, that is, saying that pluralism is admirable, but that one cannot really tolerate too radical a departure from national norms? And, since Indian people are not 'allies' a continent away, but a 'society' living within our own national boundaries, would it not seem especially urgent that they be made to 'conform', at least to the extent of accepting our basic ideas and values?

In point of fact, the contradiction is more apparent than real. Most of us are pragmatic enough to feel, if a critical matter of national interest were involved, that the autonomy of a minority group would count less than the welfare of the nation. If we had within our borders a group which, in maintaining its essential cultural unity, identity and character, constituted a threat to the well-being of the nation as a whole, most Americans, I would guess, would feel that an attempt to alter its 'social and cultural structure' should be made, humanely, of course, but made nevertheless.

Then one would have another question to ask: Can a minority group with a sharply divergent culture accept national ideals and values and still remain itself? That sounds like the announcer's introduction to a great national soap-opera.

One's impulse, at any rate, is to answer, 'No'. Change ideals and values and you change the whole culture, probably destroying its coherence in the process.

But such melodramatic issues are really not involved in the Indian situation. Indian people, first, in no sense threaten national well-being. Indian values and ideals are not especially incompatible with national norms. And Indian cultures have always adapted extremely well to change when they have been given anything like a fair chance to make a go of the new situation. Their societies can be altered quite radically without losing their essentially Indian structure and flavor.

Indian values, when they are properly understood, are incompatible only with some of the less essential features of the dominant culture. Indian societies are traditional societies; most are less individualistic than the general society. Extended family or 'clan' ties are strongly felt; to Indian people, the American 'nuclear family' seems a lonely arrangement. But none of this differentness in any sense threatens the rest of us. Indeed, we could perhaps learn some useful psychological lessons from it. As for the problem of spreading 'the notions of democracy': one of the peculiarities of most Indian cultures is that they *are* quite democratic. Decision-making is treated so carefully that Indian 'government' processes make even a New England town-meeting seem dictatorial in contrast.

The anthropologists who helped organize the famous American Indian Chicago Conference of 1961 had faith that the Indian people they had assembled would, in the course of the conference, produce a general statement of aims and principles. Other observers doubted that they would be able to agree on anything at all. Professor Sol Tax and his colleagues intended to let the participants run their own meeting, and to let them run it in their way. This the anthropologists knew meant endless talk, utterly infuriating to observers. The participants would tend not to submit disputed matters to a vote; rather, they would try to reach consensus – and that only after letting everyone speak his piece. They would make an effort to get all points of view either reconciled or included in the final statement. Now, this Indian way of reaching consensus might be impractical as a model for governing a modern nation,[3] but, in all cases in which speed is less essential than solidity, it seems to work. The participants in the conference were, in fact, able to draft an impressive document; they were able to find large areas of agreement and far more in the way of mutual cause than had been anticipated. I would maintain that, while the institutions which we associate with democratic processes were to some extent lacking, the process used at Chicago was deeply democratic, and that, indeed, most Indian people when given the opportunity to deliberate and to reach what they feel is their best opinion of a matter will operate in a democratic manner, bargaining, compromising and politicking, but maintaining respect for diverse viewpoints.[4]

Lest this be conceded as technically true, but of not much practical importance, it is worth pointing out that Indian people tend to behave in much the same way in their relations with the dominant culture, and particularly with government agencies. Anyone experienced in government or administration knows that regardless of the institutions which are set up, a great deal of decision-making is a matter of personal conversation, give-and-take, and practical compromise. It is precisely this process at which Indian people are most skilled. Most of them have tried from the outset to deal with the white culture and its representatives in this manner.

An exception which may prove the rule is provided by an Indian organization about which very little is yet known, though its aims sound wild to outsiders. Two summers ago, as a pedagogical experiment, I gave about fifty freshmen students an assignment which involved, as part of their preparation for a longer paper, getting to know at least one Indian person. They were not to conduct interviews; rather, they were to acquire a new acquaintance, picking up only the information one would learn in the process of getting to know a new friend. One could fill a book at least this length with accounts and analyses of their experiences. The most touching, perhaps, was that of a Negro youngster who was terribly shy about the whole matter and, as he told me, had practically despaired of being able to complete this part of the assignment. Whereas many of the other students already knew Indian people, or simply walked over to the Haskell Institute campus and wandered around until they got into conversation with some of the students there, or, if they were exceedingly timid, went into the Haskell Library, and let the librarian break the ice for them, this boy could not imagine how he could go about his task. The problem solved itself in a bus station one week-end, when an Indian GI who was heading home on furlough sat down next to him and began to chat. The Negro's account of the incident is as engaging a piece of prose as any of my students has ever produced. Even more remarkable, I thought, was a report which one girl brought in of a 'very sensible seeming' Indian man who insisted to her, in dead earnest, that he was part of a group of Indians operating all over the country and secretly organized to engineer an Indian takeover! Shades of Al Capp's Kickapoo rebellion, I thought. But my reaction was naïve, for I have since been told that the organization really does exist and that people involved in it are as plausible in manner as members of, say, the John Birch Society. Some observers doubt that its membership is primarily Indian, and I have been able to learn very little about its scope. So far as it is known, however, its plans are not taken seriously by any considerable fraction of the Indian population.

I mention this group to illustrate the point that unrealistic and uncompromising attitudes are not typical or representative. The characteristic response of Indian people to a problem involves bargaining and negotiation, not plots and revolutions. Indian attitudes tend to be political in the best sense of that word: they are flexible and pragmatic.

HOW CAN WE HELP?

Custer Died for Your sins – *Bumper Sticker*
We Shall Over Run – *Lapel button worn by whimsical Indian people*
'Do you know what they call an Indian who cooperates too much with the BIA?'
'No. What do they call an Indian who cooperates too much with the BIA?'
'Uncle Tomahawk.' – *Oral gag in current circulation*

It would be presumptuous for this writer, a newcomer to Indian affairs, to offer any sort of general program or proposal for dealing with the problems and aspirations of this intriguing people. I don't know enough to make recommendations; indeed, I am not sure that anyone does. A program will have to be worked out in the years to come through the familiar processes of political and bureaucratic decision, objection and compromise. There will continue to be mistakes; incompetent as well as competent personnel will be involved; one can expect hearings, lawsuits, even an occasional scandal. When I ask 'How can we help', I mean, 'What are reasonable attitudes for laymen to hold?' 'What sort of climate of opinion will make it easier for good solutions to be worked out?' There is no telling exactly what resultant programs will be like, but they are more likely to be just if we are informed and concerned.

After they had read a good deal of material about the current situation of the Indian people, I asked my batch of freshmen what they would do if they were in the shoes of the Indian Commissioner, but had more authority, generous appropriations and firm Congressional and administrative support. One girl responded with the suggestion that not one program but three were really needed. For those Indian people really interested in achieving status within the dominant culture, she would offer all kinds of aid of the sort we currently associate with the Office of Economic Opportunity – aid to education, vocational training, work-experience, and the like. For the people who wanted to continue to feel prime allegiance to a tribal group, she proposed programs of the sort already under way among the Cherokee described in Harriet Kupferer's paper or on the huge Navajo reservation; programs, that is, designed to raise levels of income, health, education, and welfare, while allowing tribal life to go on.

But for genuine conservatives who want no part whatsoever of the great rat race out there, she could see no realistic solution, because it seemed to her that there was no way to escape some contact with the media of the dominant culture. I had explained to the class how such contact changes cultures. About all she could suggest, whimsically, was an island in the Pacific or another planet. The first two of her ideas are clearly within the range of current government and Indian Bureau philosophy and practice. All that is lacking, from the Indian point of view, is the involvement of the tribal group itself in the decision making, and the recognition that the solution it suggests may not match patterns preconceived in Washington. Indian people, again, like to talk things out thoroughly, and decide for themselves what is to be done and how. There is encouraging evidence that to some extent at least the lesson is being learned in Washington. Though a friend close to one tribal group reports that local Office of Economic Opportunity staff members are 'as intransigent as the old Bureau used to be', and doing a great deal of harm, I know also of OEO administrators eager to learn, game, flexible and imaginative. There has been increasing talk, in discussions of the operation of the OEO, of allowing groups which are benefiting from OEO aid to develop their own leadership. This is a different thing from taking someone from the group, training him, and then sending him back. Too often, with Indians as with other minority groups, he returns somewhat hostile to his old way of life and no longer trusted by his old peers. Ideally, then, the leadership should come from within, and, since Indian people generally already have a tradition of arriving at consensus, that tradition should be used and respected. The result will not be rubber-stamp approval of government schemes, but rather plans evolved through healthy give and take.

But for the really conservative people, those stubbornly refusing to deal in any way with 'what's out there', it may be that my student was being more solicitous than was necessary. We do not know a great deal about 'grass-roots' Indians. Stubbornly conservative Indian people hostile to change of any sort and suspicious of all contact with cultures other than their own may well be only a tiny minority. I have been told both that such people are 'the real Indians' and that they are exceptions to the general Indian pattern. I have even heard it put more strongly: a person who holds such views is usually regarded as a nut; he is generally not even in on tribal problems and activities; he is an outsider to his tribe. The contradictory evidence suggests to me first, that we need more data before deciding, and second, that the situation probably varies markedly from area to area or from tribe to tribe.

A more advanced student actually involved in field-work among Indian people reports the following anecdote, which rather nicely summarizes the difference between how representatives of the outside culture understand the program of economic aid and the way Indians are liable to understand it. A technical adviser was sent into a reservation area; one of his jobs was to set up a laundromat, and to train several Indian people to run it. He found three likely young men and worked for months with them until they were capable of handling every aspect of the operation themselves. His thought, of course, was to leave things in their hands so that they could go on running the place without outside supervision. At first glance, this seems a good example of encouraging local autonomy. But just before he was ready to leave, the tribal council removed the three from office and replaced them with three new and totally untrained workers. The administrator, of course, was in distress; he wanted to move on to another job. The council had understood the project very differently: here were three jobs which brought in good pay. Should they not be rotated among worthy individuals?

It is distressing to note that, while the declaration of Indian purposes produced at the American Indian Chicago Conference is available and well known, and really fulfills admirably the functions of defining all sorts of things which administrators of the OEO say that underprivileged groups should define, mistakes in dealing with Indian people continue to be made. McNickle relates a characteristic incident: Secretary of the Interior Udall speaking in New Mexico and urging more rapid action to an audience of experts, while delegates to an emergency meeting of the National Congress of American Indians, convened in hopes that 'a dialogue might develop between the government men and the Indians whose affairs were being discussed ... cooled their heels on the outside.'[5] One does not envy the administrators involved in Indian affairs, who must feel that they will displease somebody whatever they do. The situation is not made easier by the fact that there are vested interests involved nor by the fact that there is a tradition of squabbling. Anthropologists, I have discovered, are by no means entirely united in their beliefs about how Indian problems should be handled, but it is fair to say that they are more sympathetic to tribal tradition and uniqueness than are people working for the Bureau of Indian Affairs. The BIA people accuse anthropologists of being unrealistic and of befriending only the most uncooperative of Indian people. Anthropologists in turn say that the BIA is trying to turn Indians into WASPs.

In point of fact, neither accusation is really true. Anthropologists deal, after all, not merely with isolated cultures, but with cultures in contact and in the process of change. They are perfectly aware that Indian cultures have never been stable and unchanging, and are the first to point out that it is foolish to look for 'pure' examples of one or another tribal culture. They know that Indian cultures cannot avoid contact with the dominant culture, and that this contact will change them profoundly; it already has. They simply maintain that the change must never be imposed from above, that Indian patterns of life must be respected, and that negotiation among equals is the only just way to make adjustments when they are needed. The Indian Bureau is in a different fix: from above comes pressure to 'do something' quickly to 'solve' the 'Indian problem'. From Indian people comes cautious suspicion of change. The suspicion is well-grounded; in the past, most new ideas from above have ultimately hurt.

My own contacts with Indian Bureau personnel have on

the whole been pleasant. It is true that the Bureau still carries what seems to me an unwholesome missionary flavor; there are still Indian Bureau employees who think that their main job is to show the benighted savages the error of their ways. In part, this must be a carry-over from the days when religious groups did more for Indian welfare than anyone else.[6]

Certainly the BIA is exceedingly sensitive to criticism and interference, and its sensitivity is largely justified. In 1966, for example, officials at Haskell Institute in Lawrence, Kansas, were visited by a young man who presented himself as a reporter from a major metropolitan newspaper. He was hospitably received and given the grand tour; every effort was made to answer his inquiries. It turned out that he was a reporter for a college newspaper. In the series of articles that he produced, he treated the information he had picked up out of context. Now there are in fact policies at Haskell which seem arbitrary and condescending, especially when presented without explanation. Haskell was, until quite recently, essentially a technical and vocational high school, and its students were subjected to rather more restrictions than one would expect, let us say, at a private institution for students of high-school age. For many years, for instance, students were forbidden to walk on most of the streets in Lawrence, the town of 40,000 in which the institution is located. Indeed, the author made his first real acquaintance with Indian people by chatting with Haskell students in front of his house, which, because it is the one street then open to them, always had Indian students in front of it on week-ends. Haskell now operates on the junior college level, though its design is still primarily vocational and technical. (Students are not prepared to transfer into regular college after graduation from Haskell; rather, they are expected to enter jobs for which they have been trained.) The regulations which govern them today are a good deal less rigid. The principal told me that Haskell still has rather more regulations than most colleges and junior colleges, because of its students' inexperience, but that these currently place much more emphasis on the students' own judgment than was true in the past. They still strike young Indian activists as terribly paternalistic. Interestingly, many Haskell students themselves will tell you that they believe that fairly strict regulations are necessary. A girl told me some years ago, for example, that if they were allowed to go wherever they wanted to in Lawrence, the boys would all get drunk at bars, and the girls would behave immorally. To what extent such opinions are typical of Haskell students I don't know. The liberal's reaction to statements of this kind is, 'They have been brainwashed!' But youngsters from homes in which the parents are trying very hard to break what they consider deplorable habits will pick up such attitudes. Those with whom I spoke understood clearly that this was not a racial trait, but a simple cultural fact, true enough in many areas. A student of mine who is currently working with a small Indian community in Topeka, Kansas, informs me that alcoholism is a severe problem there; it is in many other places as well. (In Kansas, actually, it is fairly difficult to get physically drunk in a public bar, unless one is culturally predisposed to over-react to alcohol: the bars serve nothing but a 3 per cent beer.)

The principal volunteered the following rough figures on what becomes of the students. Only about 10 per cent drop out before graduation. Of those remaining, from 90 to 95 per cent find good jobs, and of these jobs, 80 per cent are off-reservation, because job opportunities for trained people are scarce on the reservations. I have no figures to show how many of these 80 per cent remain at their jobs for any considerable time, but it is clear enough that making

Indian people assimilable is the real goal of Haskell Institute. It continues to be a prime motive of the Indian Bureau in general. However, even if every Haskell graduate stayed at an off-reservation job, the number of people involved would still be too small to be significant in terms of the total Indian population.

Haskell provides a good illustration of the point that one often cannot predict what Indian people will make of aid which they are given. Designed to encourage 'spin-off', Haskell has instead tended to promote what Shirley Hill Witt calls 'Indian nationalism'. Tribally oriented youngsters discover that their tribe is not alone, that there is some basis for Indian solidarity. More sophisticated students from more or less assimilated families, who are at Haskell because it is a good free education to which their ancestry entitles them, become more aware of their Indian-ness. It is probably correct to say that Haskell today is a hotbed of pan-Indianism.

I would suspect that a fair number of Indian people who have the training to succeed in the larger culture return to the reservation or other tribal center. A life at home clearly seems to most Indian people the most important life, yet it is fair to say that most BIA personnel regard 'spin-off' as their real objective; they are often proudest of Indian people who have left the reservation and 'made it' in the general culture. This is one source of genuine conflict of aims. There have been periods in which government policy has been quite sympathetic to Indian traditions, but the Bureau has a continuity of its own, and it is not easy to change the thinking habits of sincere workers who see their role as missionary – especially when, in a few years, government policy generally swings back to their way of thinking.

It is clear enough that 'spin-off' does not work; if this book proves anything, it is that Indian societies are still vital, and that Indian people desire and intend to maintain them. If we are really looking for an Indian 'cause' to support, I would suggest that we work for a meeting of minds in which the efforts of BIA staff, the OEO, tribal organizations and those unofficial 'friends of the court', the academic anthropologists, would be bent together to produce economic amelioration *within* the social context of Indian societies. That would be a goal consistent with national ideas and Indian hopes. These hopes are expressed clearly in the conclusion of the Declaration of Purpose which the 1961 Chicago delegates adopted:

... the Indians ask for assistance, technical and financial, for the time needed, however long that may be, to regain in the America of the space age some measure of the adjustment they enjoyed as the original possessors of their land.

Regaining 'some measure of ... adjustment' does not mean rejecting all modern culture; it means retaining those cultural patterns which give Indian life meaning, and adapting them to contemporary economic and technological facts. What Indian people would have us do is understand first, and then act on the basis of that understanding. They do not want action based on our preconceptions, however benevolent they may be. The Declaration is both eloquent and explicit:

We ask only that the nature of our situation be recognized and made the basis of policy and action.

NAIVETE AND EXTREMISM

To me it also seems important that the Indian community develop a better sense of the culture around it. One of the sad features of the current situation is the tendency for Indian people to get involved in the kind of closed-minded and even racist thinking one associates with the extreme right wing. While it is possible that the current vigor of Indian organizations is to some extent a response to what Indian people have heard of the Negro Civil Rights Movement, Indian people on the whole do not like to have their cause associated with that of the Negro. They are right to an extent, for their case is very different and they have a right to be heard on their own. But getting mixed up with so-called conservative groups which are really racist in nature will in the long run do their cause no good. In many southern and border state areas, for example, there is an uneasy and unsavory alliance between local Indian populations and white supremacists. I find it easy to understand how this feeling has developed but consider it deplorable. This letter-to-the-editor of a Winston-Salem newspaper is a rather good illustration of its sources:

A Good Street

To the Editor of the Journal:

This is pertaining to the article in Sept. 11 morning paper, where the shaded area showed poverty. We are all working people who are making our living, paying our taxes. We also have a deputy sheriff and a policeman on this street (Bloomfield Drive). I think we have a good street. In other words, I feel you are classing us with the Negroes to get them help. They live off welfare checks. They can have 12–14 children cause we help pay for their up keep. We stop at 1–2–3 because we have to support ourselves. Take another survey. Most of your dropouts and delinquents are from the Negro section, I bet. If we are in this poverty area, why aren't you helping us some? If you get this federal grant, we will be looking for sidewalks for our children to skate on, etc.

Since living in Winston-Salem, there are many things that I would like to tell you about. A tree fell in my back yard; I called the city to haul it off. We cut it up. The answer was we haven't the facilities. An article came up about leaves. I raked a pile, called the city. The answer was we haven't the facilities. My child was to have a physical. I called the Health Department. The answer was, do you have a pink or blue card? My answer was, 'no, I'm not black'. Why did you take the Public Records out of the paper? Because the biggest majority of all the meanness was Negro. Take another look at that map; it covers the Negro area. If you're wanting to help them, help them, but get us off that shaded area or else start sending me a few dollars a week. I could use it to send my three to school.

I am an American Indian from South Dakota and feel myself equal with any of you. Don't class us with these rioting, shooting, cutting friends of yours.

– Mrs Walter B. Feezor

Winston-Salem

What is saddest about the whole business is that there are places in the country in which discrimination *is* directed quite deliberately at Indian people, not other racial groups, and where the same stereotypes to which Mrs Feezor reacts are applied to Indian folk. Even though the Indian situation is very different, in short, fellow-feeling with other underdog groups, and firm opposition to any racial or ethnic discrimination would do Indian causes no harm, and would gain a good deal of needed sympathy. There is no reason that Indian uniqueness should produce hostility to other persecuted or deprived peoples.

(Some progress, I am happy to report, has been made since the first edition of this book went to press. The young Indian leaders who worked with me to organize what they tell me was the first accredited higher-educational venture ever conceived and run entirely by Indians, The Clyde Warrior Institute of American Indian Studies, were involved at the same time in the Poor People's March on Washington in the summer of 1968. They returned speaking very favorably about many black leaders; certain aspects of Black Power struck them as analogous to positions they had long held.

One leader who returned to our campus a semester later as a guest lecturer in an American Studies course said that the combination of the Institute and the March made him realize for the first time that Indian people have an identity as a minority group, and that that identity contains a promise of political influence which could supplement the treaty-rights argument.)

In many parts of the country Indian people are easy prey for pseudo-patriotic organizations. It is not difficult to guess why they find such outfits attractive. In matters which do not affect their uniqueness, Indian people feel quite strongly the desire to demonstrate that they are good Joes who have the right ideas and attitudes. If their ideas of 'right' are naïve it is because the people who hold them are, too. In places in which Indian people are living in the general culture, and beginning to 'make it' to some extent, one can expect them to behave in the manner which sociologists tell us is typical of other people in the same situation: they will want to do what is respectable, and to hold respectable attitudes and opinions. In many places, the attitudes most available to them are those of whites whose political and intellectual backgrounds are insufficiently sophisticated to enable them to see how naïve are the positions of the extreme right wing. It is difficult, for example, for Indian people living in a rural area of Oklahoma to see that there is anything wrong with the curious mixture of the religious fundamentalism, radio evangelism, and super-patriotism ('Impeach Earl Warren') which they encounter on billboards, on the radio, in small towns, and in sections of cities settled largely by people from relatively isolated rural backgrounds. I would suppose that all such things look quite safe to Indian folks, who are happy to go along with ideas which sound 'true' and which in no way threaten their own identity. Perhaps because I have lived ten years in a Kansas town, I am one of those who hold that most people involved in movements of this sort are worthy and decent; not vicious, but merely insufficiently informed. This makes the ideas no less ugly or dangerous, of course, but it does help to explain why it seems to newcomers that nice people hold them. Certainly they are the ideas handiest to where many Indian people live, and they pick them up naturally and easily.[7]

The Native American Church provides a rather good illustration of the process. This is the famous 'peyote religion', which has spread through a surprisingly large part of the country and must be regarded as one of the most important 'pan-Indian' phenomena of our period. The nature of the services varies quite a bit from area to area, as does the 'miracle' story, which, in the versions I have been told, involves a young girl learning of Christ's message to the red man. The peyote seems universal; it is eaten and songs are sung to the beating of a little drum. All this seems very exotic and mystical in the context of other religions in America today. But the Native American Church in all other matters is fundamentalist, and quite narrowly so! The total effect seems a popular illustration of Indian willingness to adopt, compromise and yet retain Indian-ness. In those portions of the faith which do not bear on Indian identity, the position seems 'conventional' and 'respectable'. One has to add that if Indian judgment of what is respectable and conventional seems naïve, it is the judgment which peers and neighbors would also make.

A SENSE OF CONTEXT

One evening in Lawrence two Indian boys approached me at a gas station and asked me to give them a lift to a pizza parlor downtown. I had Indians on the brain at the time (I was editing these essays) and so we fell to talking. Since these were Haskell students, I was curious about whether they thought of themselves 'tribally' first or as 'Indians' first. They produced no clear answer, but got to talking about what their two tribes had in common. It was evident that they had discussed this before. Finally one of them said, 'You know what all Indian people have in common? They fight and argue all the time. Never agree on anything. Talk, talk, talk.' The other laughed in agreement.

To arrive at consensus, of course, we must 'talk, talk, talk'. The impatience of these youngsters reflects their 'modern-ness', perhaps. I doubt that they are really hostile to extended discussion; if I hadn't told them I had to get home, they would have sat in the car and talked all night themselves. But misinformation and igorance can stall or misdirect the process of reaching consensus, and this does make younger Indian people impatient. Young 'modern' Indians have told me repeatedly of how their campaigns for this or that issue – a new tribal constitution, or a govern-ment-aid project, say – were frustrated by stories which were circulated about whatever it was that they were supporting. The stories were often based on falsehood; what frustrated the people I spoke to was that there was no way to make this fact clear. It was one man's word against another's, and the constituencies involved, with the inherent conservatism of tribal people, tended, when the chips were down, to take the word of those skeptical of any change. In point of fact, of course, the skepticism is based on long and bitter experience, and is often well founded. But acceptance or rejection of new proposals should be based on a realistic understanding of the facts, and often they are not. I've heard many stories of Indian tribes rejecting things which were unambiguously beneficial to them after this sort of long, confused, and un-factual debate.

A priceless record of continuing foggy debate is provided

by a notable tribal newspaper, *The Navajo Times*, which I commend to your attention. As one reads through a file, one picks up a feel for factions, personalities, ambitions and suspicions, but is struck by the maddening paucity of facts. Sometimes one reads through six or seven numbers, trying to figure out a given dispute, before one can learn even what the issues are. It seems to me that the proper response for interested outsiders is, first, to be patient with the process, and second, to do whatever is possible to provide facts and a realistic sense of context, so that Indian people can go on deciding for themselves, but do so with somewhat less strain and somewhat more evidence.

As an outsider, neither a BIA employee nor an anthropologist, I have two suggestions. One is obvious: Give Indian groups a larger part in policy-making. Evolve new proposals only when the impetus comes from 'below', not 'above'. This does not mean 'agreeing to demands'; rather, it means working out policy through give and take. Second, to make the first work, provide as many Indian people as possible with really sophisticated information about the government they are dealing with and the attitudes of the people it represents.

If we tell Indian people, 'Look, fellows, you are in the same boat as other American minority groups – study the ways that they licked their problems and you can do it, too,' we will encounter stiff resistance. The Indian Bureau has been trying for more than a century to convince Indian people that they can make a go of it in the general society. Although there are plenty of tragic stories to show that many Indian people who tried it were given terribly dirty deals, the truth is that now, in most parts of the country, there is no particular prejudice against Indians, and that any Indian people who want assimilation have only to pick up a trade or skill, move to where the jobs are and set to work.

I would guess that most Indian people know this. The point is that this is *not* what they want. They want to go on living as Indians, and think that the nation owes them help in finding a way to 'make it' economically while still living as Indians. Their claim seems reasonable; it is the least we can do to repay what we have done to them. Our treaties promised much more.

The paper by Murray and Rosalie Wax suggests some of the complexities and difficulties of providing education for Indian youngsters. The situation they describe seems so serious – the goals of the educators do not match the students' aspirations, the students are undertrained, the drop-out rate is terribly high – that to discuss providing really sophisticated education for Indian people sounds a little foolish. There are things to be done which seem much more urgent. Teachers and administrators sympathetic to Indian values must be involved in the schools: curricular changes need to be made to help bridge the gap between 'country' Indians and their more experienced classmates, and some clearer definition of what the education is *for* needs to be derived. Yet an educational program which would give Indian youngsters a better feeling for their place in the world is highly desirable, and worth exploring at once wherever possible. This would do a great deal of good even if it reached only a small number of Indian people, for ideas do filter down when they are important to a people's identity.

One would like to be in on an experiment of this sort. I can visualize a program which might run as follows:

I. *Purpose:* To give you a good sense of why non-Indian Americans behave as they do so that
   A. You will be able to deal more effectively with them
   B. You will be able to present your case in a context meaningful to them

    c. You will understand how it is possible, in a nation which professes high ideals, for your people to have been treated so badly

    D. You can help define a continuing role for Indian people to play in American society.

It is important that 'adaptation to the general culture', 'assimilation' or 'making it in the white world' *not* be considered part of the purpose.

II. *Content:* American social and political history, with special attention to those factors which hindered the development of a consistent and fair policy toward Indian peoples.[8]

The aim here is to replace stereotypes and hearsay with fact. No attempt should be made to make the program an apology for US policy, or, on the other hand, a muck-raking attack on national greed. The truth, as always, is complex, and that complexity should not be hidden. For example, in dealing with the nineteenth century, both the pressure from frontier areas for more land and the efforts of whites sympathetic to the Indian predicament should be presented. Whenever possible, indeed, material from beyond the confines of American history should be incorporated to give better perspective: European preconceptions about aboriginal peoples change over the centuries, and do affect American actions and attitudes. Aboriginal people in other parts of the world have been placed in similar situations with varied results. Comparisons are worth making.

National attitudes toward other minority groups should be covered thoroughly, *not* to minimize the uniqueness of Indian people, but to help the students understand why their own point of view has been so consistently misunderstood even by national leaders predisposed to be sympathetic.

If properly handled, such a special program should be attractive to Indian people because it is aimed at genuine needs. One hates to over-use that cliché-word 'identity', but identity is an urgent concern for Indian folk, and training of the sort outlined here would aid thoughtful Indian people in defining Indian identity far more precisely than most can now manage.

But what people enrolled in such a program will do with what they learn can't be controlled or even predicted. Nothing much may happen, or a great deal may. More likely, the unspectacular development of Indian sophistication will be slightly accelerated. That alone would make the experiment worthwhile.

PEDAGOGICAL SPECULATIONS

Having proposed what may be a naïvely conceived program, I find myself fascinated with aspects of its content. Take, for example, the problem of relating the experience of Indian peoples to those of other minority groups. It is important in dealing with Indian people on this matter not to attempt to minimize their own uniqueness; they are different from any other minority group in the country, and, as we have already said, even within the Indian world, each tribe and culture area is unique. But it would do the Indian cause no harm to raise the issue of the nature of that uniqueness, and to try to define it through comparison with other peoples.

Uniqueness alone, of course, proves nothing. Examine any ethnic sector of our population and you find uniqueness. What a queer set of problems is posed, for instance, by those oddballs, the first English settlers. Theirs is the only immigrant group which did not encounter in the New World an established Western culture, and was thus denied the character-forming experiences of discrimination and economic exploitation. Deprived of the wholesome loneliness of the newly arrived stranger, never having been called dirty, sub-human or different, this underprivileged group even had to wait until a war and the arrival of strangers made it possible to form its equivalent of the Sons of Italy, the DAR. One wonders whether we will ever succeed in assimilating it into the texture of American society.

Nor can one define what is special about Indian people by saying that they are the only Americans who have not shared American social ideals, believed in 'progress' or partaken of 'the American dream', because those ideas have varied immensely from one group or period to another, and because not every group which came here held them. The Puritan view of the New World as a model theocracy which would inspire others is revolutionary, but not especially democratic. Peasants who came fleeing famine or persecution saw America more as a refuge than as part of a worldwide revolutionary movement; to later immigrants, the vision of America ran less to the city upon a hill than to the land of milk and honey.

Indeed, if one attempts to generalize about our ethnic groups, one runs into so many complications that one hardly knows where to begin. Each seems characterized by special peculiarities of one sort or another: Japanese who shared American ideas of effective social organization, but who had the bad fortune to be here during the Second World War; German Forty-Eighters who came with a social philosophy more radical than that of the dominant culture; Cubans who fled Castro's revolution, but many of whom were rather cynical Batista-ites; Scandinavians who went directly to rural areas and never underwent the big-city ghetto experience so formative for millions of their contemporary co-immigrants; Mennonites who came over wealthy, not poor, and who already had been immigrants in their previous homes; Jews, who lacked a 'national origin' in the usual sense; Negroes who carry the peculiarities of having come involuntarily, having been slaves, and being racially visible; groups too small to have gone through the first-generation process of generalizing their culture so as to create a satisfactory ethnic identity for themselves; people who trickled in over so many years that they hardly constitute groups at all; groups which came to escape a repressive social system; groups which attempted to reproduce the old system on the new soil.

If it is made clear that such material is not being presented in an effort to get Indian people to assimilate as most minority groups have, I would think that the training would be immensely valuable. If we think of the United States as, to borrow Henry Dobyns' image, a national laboratory, we see so great a range of ethnic experiences that almost any issue or problem which troubled or troubles Indian people confronted or confronts some other group.

In an undergraduate seminar I had occasion recently to send my students out to familiarize themselves each with one minority group or community, and to see how what they found squared with any of the analyses of the American experience they had read (they were familiar with those of Alexis de Tocqueville, Crevecoeur, Turner and Handlin; some also knew Veblen, Parrington and others). What a hard time these good students had. Without summarizing their evidence it is possible to suggest what they ran into with a simple list of some of the groups they selected to read about: a group of Latvian settlers in Wisconsin, the Boston Irish, the Krimmer Mennonite Brethren, Mennonites in Southeastern Pennsylvania, Louisiana Creoles, the Greek community of Tarpon Springs, Florida, Chinese in San Francisco. It is hard to think of anything one can say about the peculiarities of the Indian situation that does not apply to one or more non-Indian group, except that important matter of having had to leave the old country. The Indians, too, at least those east of the Mississippi, were uprooted, though it is possible to argue that they were uprooted by the dominant culture, and thus are unique in that the nation to them has been menace, not refuge. Even this, however, does not leave them all alone, for Americans at times have forcibly uprooted non-Indians (Negroes and Japanese, for instance) as well. There are, moreover, other groups which regard the nation's activities as 'menace': Mormons who fled its customs and authority, and continue to fight its attempts to impose its ways; Quakers, and the members of other pacifist churches; Mennonite groups which fight against continued education for their children. Indians are not unique among American minority groups in that they alone have not wanted to be assimilated. Almost all have wanted to maintain a separate identity, and some have wanted virtual isolation. Few have been treated as shabbily as have Indian people, but their experiences should hold valuable lessons for a people bound on the special goals defined in Chicago in 1961.

One can go even to very specialized characteristics of the Indian situations and find at least some other group which has had a similar experience. Unlike most of us, Indians seek group, not individual solutions. To retain Indian identity, they have to retain group feeling. If they seek individual solutions, they do cease to be Indians, and then become like other assimilated minorities. This is certainly a special characteristic of their culture, yet it is still not entirely unique. One thinks of the Amish, who also want group solutions, and understand full well that any individual who finds his own adjustment to the society is no longer really Amish. The small community of Hassidic Jews in New York holds related views. Its members cling strictly to all traditions, fight even what seem pragmatic and reasonable compromises, and are actively hostile to former members of the community who have adopted 'American ways' and yet would very much like to feel that they still belong to the community. The faithful do not like them, and do not consider them Jews. A Jew, they feel, is someone who is different, and lives by the Law; if he 'assimilates', he ceases to be a Jew. The issue for the Hassidim is not quite the same as for Indian people, but the fear of losing identity and 'way' is similar. Hassidim do not want to alter their dress, their visible peculiarities, their customs; Indians have always been flexible and eclectic on such matters. They want to stay together, to work out 'Indian solutions' to their problems even as they continue to borrow from the culture around them. But the two share an unwillingness to join the 'Anglo' world and the conviction that faithfulness to their own history requires a separate path.

Certainly there is a place in American culture for people who feel the way Indians do about their uniqueness and their group identity. One would think, all things considered, that they would have rather less difficult a time of it than other groups which feel the same way. Many minority groups which want to retain their own character, for example, are quite hostile to education, which they accurately recognize as dangerous. One of the reasons, for example, that Mennonite communities in various parts of the country have resisted advanced education is that they understand that it will tend to secularize the young people, and so draw them away from the community. Other minority groups have special attitudes, such as pacifism, which tend to produce friction between them and the community at large. This sort of thing is no problem at all for Indian folk, most of whom have nothing at all to fear from more education (though they may feel that much of it is irrelevant to their goals) and who have repeatedly volunteered to serve in times of national crisis.[9]

The Survival of Indian Identity

Indian cultures can absorb and assimilate anything they want from the culture among them, and they always have. I attended a small pow-wow on 30 April 1967 in Mayetta, Kansas. The occasion was a celebration. A family had been put into a severe physical and economic crisis by an automobile accident, but through community help and hard work, had gotten itself on its feet again. The pow-wow was its thanks to the community; everyone, even people like myself and a few of my students, who had known nothing at all of the matter until a day or two before, was invited to share the hospitality. There was a great feed, splendid singing and drum beating, and some of the most glorious dancing I have ever seen. Someone was also running a raffle, for a charitable purpose which never became very clear to anyone in the room. What was interesting was that the object being raffled off was a portable tape recorder. The fellow in charge recorded some of the songs being danced to and then took the tape recorder around to show how well it worked. Quite properly, no one thought that there was anything incongruous about the intrusion of so commercial and contemporary a product at such a traditional occasion. After all, the family had been injured in an auto accident, and many of the folks at the pow-wow were city-dwellers out for a day on the pow-wow grounds. For that matter, the men seated in the center of the dance floor around the big drum, were presented, about half way through the day, with brand new drum beaters, leather-tipped like the ones that they had been using but with bright blue plastic stems. They tried them out, chatted about them, and decided they were fine. And the costumes themselves were a wonderful patchwork of what these people (who happen to be Potawatomi) liked in the clothing of many different tribes from many different areas. Indian people can make things their own, picking up anything they like, without diluting the strong feeling of

41

community they all retain. 'Enriching' would be a better word than 'diluting', and the process has been going on since long before first contact with white settlers.[10]

Indians who leave tribal areas to live in the cities or in other parts of the country, unlike immigrants who came from Europe, can go home again quite easily. Indeed, they often do, and some evidently regard the economy of the dominant culture as a vast game preserve to be raided now and then when one needs money. Indians, however, are not the only group to feel and behave this way. Migrant Mexicans move into the United States to work in agriculture for a number of months, and bring the cash back home. Moreover, even among solidly established Mexican communities, people who have been American citizens for years still frequently drive or take a bus home for family occasions or for visits. The same is notably true of Puerto Rican communities throughout the nation. Puerto Ricans can't drive home, of course, but they can keep the airline terminals in New York very busy with their continual hopping back and forth. I doubt that Puerto Ricans and Mexicans retain quite the feeling for home which Indians have; Nancy Lurie says that in moving to cities, Indian people feel merely that they are expanding their perimeters, not moving from a rural to an urban location, but finding new fields to exploit. Many feel that the reservation is still the center of their lives; many go to the city just during the winter: it is warmer there. One might say that such Indian people regard the dominant culture almost as a natural resource, to be raided or exploited for a short period of time, and the spoils brought back home.

The special nature of this relationship needs to be explained to other Americans who are too liable to regard people who behave this way as simply shiftless. One would like to see the job done by Indian spokesmen who know their American culture, and can point out that not only are they not the only people who use our economy this way, but that there is a nationally respected philosophical position which urges precisely this attitude toward livelihood. I am referring of course to Thoreau's argument that gaining a living makes sense only if, having 'gained' it, one then 'lives'. Certainly his example of a metaphorical 'year' lived on the fruits of a few weeks' wages and an ordered regimen seems an almost literal call for what many Indian people are trying to do. Indian people are not transcendental romantics, of course, though their Declaration of Purpose does say 'When Indians speak of the continent they yielded, they are not referring only to the loss of some millions of acres in real estate. They have in mind that the land supported a universe of things they knew, valued, and loved . . .' But they do, like Thoreau, wonder what other Americans see in the great rat-race, and, with their traditional group and extended-family feelings, clearly have access to a more ordered life than most of us. If they want cash values to be subordinate to that meaningful life, are they not asking, with Thoreau, 'Pause! Avast! Why so seeming fast, but deadly slow?'

Notes

1. McNickle, 'The Indian Tests the Mainstream', *The Nation*, 203, 9 (26 September 1966), 275–9.

2. Recent tendencies in Negro ghetto areas suggest that the contrast may not continue to remain so clear. Negro leaders who advocate 'Black Power' and the emphasis on African heritage talk a language which many Indian leaders respond to more readily than they did to the ideas of the older civil rights groups.

3. Eldon Turner points out that explanations of Indian understanding of consensus sound curiously like recent Polish statements on the operation of their government: they stress that, while there is but one party, it selects representatives on the local level through consensus, and these in turn achieve consensus when they select national leaders. I doubt that this demonstrates conclusively that Indian people are really Polish secret agents, or that Indian rebellion, with arms from the Katowice works, is imminent.

4. In honesty I should point out that when I showed this passage to an Indian friend active in Indian political affairs he said that he had been at the conference and had stomped out, angry because the point of view which he held was not getting a fair hearing. He regards the Declaration which the conference issued as a 'fink document'.

5. McNickle, op. cit., 279.

6. The history of religious missionary activity among the Indians is fascinating and complex. Colonial Americans often held simultaneously the idea that Indian people were history's greatest opportunity for bringing souls to Christ and salvation, and that Indians were agents of the devil. One finds gentle and pious writers describing the massacres of innocent Indian women and children with undisguised glee. It was interesting to me, when the material in this volume was originally presented, to see how much of the response to it came from people associated with missions to various Indian groups.

7. Matching the naïveté of the right is a newer naïveté of the left, already apparent in the Negroes' Black Power movement and to be looked for in young Indian leaders. For example: however one may admire the attempt of Negro leaders to create a black identity of which black Americans can be proud, one knows enough social science to be skeptical of the claim they make of African traditions in the American Negro community. There are very few, even in jazz, which can be convincingly shown to be African in origin. To a sympathetic observer, it seems that it would be better in the long run to build on Negro culture as it is – it has much to be proud of – than to found one's edifice on shaky pseudo-anthropology. Similarly, one can be totally sympathetic with the young Indian's impatience with the foot-dragging of government, with conservative Indians and with 'white Indians', but one knows that some young leaders are under-informed about how one gets things done, and how one estimates attainable goals.

8. Since I wrote this, I have been asked to administer a summer institute for Indian college students which has goals fairly close to these. It places more emphasis on Indian culture and Indian problems than does my scheme, but its designers also hope to give the participants a better sense of how to operate effectively in the political situation in which Indians find themselves.

(It has now, by the time of this Pelican edition, taken place at The Clyde Warrior Institute. Courses were approved by the University of Kansas for college credit, 35 Indian college students

[25 of them 'tribal' in background] were recruited, and qualified Indian instructors hired and appointed to the university faculty. It included an academically solid pair of courses and a field trip to Chicago. Sponsored jointly by the American Studies Program of the university and the National Indian Youth Council, it received excellent cooperation from the BIA in the form of free housing at Haskell, and this despite the clear understanding of BIA personnel that its goals and philosophy were largely unsympathetic to those of the BIA. Participants felt it successful. I understand that several changes in NIYC thinking resulted, notably a desire for a broader base; the NIYC is currently attempting to organize local chapters. If funding can be found, the Institute will be repeated and enlarged. It was, incidentally, named for the University of Kansas graduate student who had been president of the NIYC until his death a month before the Institute convened.)

9. The recent participation of a few Indian people in anti-Vietnam war demonstrations is exceedingly interesting. It suggests the growth of diversity in political point of view among Indian people, and is thus probably very healthy. I don't think that it amounts to much, however.

10. One seldom experiences anything with Indian people without later being told that it's not typical. Some weeks after the pow-wow a friend who knows the Potawatomi told me that the group that runs the pow-wow grounds is a mish-mash pan-Indian collection of city dwellers practicing 'sentimental pluralism'. I would insist that there is no one kind of 'real' Indian, and that anyone who feels himself Indian is Indian, whether he lives in Mayetta or Minneapolis.

The Background

+>-<+

The Background

NANCY OESTREICH LURIE

HISTORICAL BACKGROUND

THANKS to work by generations of archeologists, ethnologists and historians, there is an enormous literature for intensive study of the prehistoric and historic cultures of the North American Indians and the effects of Euro-American influences on Indian life.[1] This paper seeks only to provide a brief and general chronology of significant phases in the history of Indian–white contact as a background in understanding contemporary Indian life.

DISCOVERY AND EARLY CONTACT

It is commonly but incorrectly assumed that Indian societies, before Europeans arrived, were stable, and that they had existed in idyllic and unchanging simplicity since time immemorial, until Europeans made their first landfall and began disrupting and ultimately destroying native life. We now know, on the contrary, that their societies were developing and changing in important ways long before first contact. Archeological evidence reveals that prior to the discovery of America by Europeans, widespread trade routes stretched over the entire continent. Many of our important highways follow trails long familiar to the Indians. Furthermore, pottery, burial practices, grave goods, earthworks and other clues uncovered by the archeologist clearly show that new ideas arose in many different places and diffused to neighboring areas to be adapted to different natural environments, further elaborated and passed on yet again. Religion, economic practices, and artistic and utilitarian productions were all subjected to the process. By the time of significant European contact along the east coast in the late sixteenth and early seventeenth centuries, a simple hunting and gathering economy was already giving way to a food-production economy in the vast area south of the Great Lakes from the Mississippi River to the Atlantic Ocean. Domesticated corn, beans, squash and possibly other food plants as well as tobacco were in a process of northward spread from the lower Mississippi valley. They had undoubtedly been introduced from Mexican sources about 1 A.D., but by a process and routes not yet fully understood.

When Europeans first arrived, tribes in the northern Great Lakes region had only begun to experiment with gardening as a supplement to a diet based primarily on hunting and gathering, while tribes in the southeast had already achieved populous, permanent settlements exhibiting marked social and material complexities as natural concomitants to the development of food production. The spread of cultural complexity was paced to some extent by the gradual selection of ever hardier varieties of what had been essentially a semi-tropical plant complex, but which now had to survive even shorter growing seasons. Warmer coastal regions permitted a somewhat faster diffusion of gardening than colder inland regions and in some cases peoples already accustomed to raising crops moved northward, displacing groups still largely dependent on hunting.

The establishment of permanent European settlements along the eastern seaboard and St Lawrence River in the early seventeenth century required assistance of Indians in providing food, information and skills to survive the first years in a new environment. As the fur trade took on importance, and with it competition among European nations for control of North America, the Indian tribes enjoyed a good deal of bargaining power and learned to use it astutely in their own interests in regard to both commercial and military activities. For many eastern tribes, it is the long period of the fur trade and not the aboriginal past which is recalled as a golden age.

Although the popular view is that a rapid demise was the fate of all Indians, generally it was the more fully agricultural and rigidly structured tribes which went under quickly and completely in the face of early European contact. Located close to the coasts to begin with and hemmed in by mountains or hostile tribes at their backs, these societies bore the first brunt of intense white competition for desirable land. Their more populous villages and accompanying social norms had developed prior to the advent of Europeans, which may have made for a certain inflexibility in adaptiveness. It should be borne in mind that in the seventeenth century, the difference in political and technological complexity between Indians and little groups of colonists was not so great as to suggest immediately to the tribes and powerful alliances of tribes that Europeans posed a serious threat to their future. Certainly, the relatively large and compact Indian villages with their gardens and stored surpluses of food were highly vulnerable both to new epidemic diseases and scorched-earth campaigns in times of open hostilities when their continued presence in the region became a nuisance to the colonists. Thus, only remnants remain of once formidable alliances of tribes along the eastern seaboard, and many tribes noted as powerful and culturally sophisticated in the early British, French and Spanish chronicles have disappeared completely.

Further inland, the tribes were less fully committed to complexities attendant upon food production. They apparently benefited from the greater flexibility and mobility of a hunting ethos as well as from the fact that Europeans were

more interested in their country for furs than for coloniza-
tion. Moreover, the nascent alliances and confederacies
which had begun to develop inland were influenced and
shaped in response to the Europeans who sought trade and
friendship. These tribes accepted, made adaptations, and
recognized as inevitable and even desirable that Europeans
should be on the scene. When demand for their land eventually developed, as had happened so quickly on the coast,
the inland Indians had established clear patterns for looking
after their own interests as societies distinct from those of
Europeans, despite their long association and extensive
trade and more than occasional acceptance of white in-laws.

Beyond the St Lawrence to the Arctic Circle, there
are still groups of people, Indian and Eskimo, who are essentially hunters. Even where ecological conditions might have
eventually permitted aboriginal plant domestication, their
contact with Europeans occurred before there was an intervening native food-producing stage. In many instances,
contact with outsiders has been so recent that the first encounters involved immediate introduction to features of
highly industrialized society. Thus, there are Indian and
Eskimo people who rode in airplanes before they even saw
an automobile.[2] Some groups are still able to subsist largely
off the land but have availed themselves rapidly and selectively of alien items to make the life of the hunter more efficient and comfortable: repeating rifles, gasoline 'kickers' for
canoes, even radios. Some are as fully committed to the fur
trade as a way of life as the Indians of the eastern woodlands
in the seventeenth and eighteenth centuries, while for others
the fur trade is in its terminal stage, and they face painful
adjustments experienced earlier by other groups living in a
market economy.

Gardening also diffused into the Prairie and Plains region
from Mississippian sources in aboriginal times, but was

largely confined to river bottom lands where bone or stone implements could turn the loose soil. The people built substantial villages of timber-framed, mud-covered lodges and settled down to the elaboration of existence permitted by food production. The open plains, where coarse grass matted the earth, were exploited in brief, organized forays to take buffalo in quantity by such means as driving herds over cliffs. Having only dogs as beasts of burden, Indian people found the Plains dangerous, with uncertain and widely spaced sources of water. Only scattered bands of hunters wandered there on occasion.

Important contact with European people occurred only after the Plains had been made habitable for many tribes by the introduction of the horse. As herds of wild Spanish horses spread north, techniques of horsemanship diffused from Spaniard to Indian. Raiding for tamed animals from tribe to tribe became an important and exciting aspect of existence. The great herds of buffalo which a hunter approached on foot with trepidation could now be exploited efficiently from horseback. The buffalo suddenly became an abundant and dependable food supply and source of housing, utensils and clothing as horses became available to more and more tribes. Some tribes were more or less pushed into the Plains as the pressure of white settlement forced one Indian group against another, but the Plains clearly attracted tribes to a new and exciting way of life as well. The gaudily befringed Indian in warbonnet astride his horse is the archetype of the American Indian all over the world, and we note with wonder the spectacular history of his distinctive way of life. It was made possible by native adaptations of an animal of European origin, achieved astonishing complexity to govern and give deep psychic and esthetic satisfaction to the life of large encampments, and collapsed with the disappearance of the buffalo in the short span of less than 200 years, roughly from 1700 to 1880. By then, the repeating rifle and commercial hunting, which hastened the demise of the buffalo, the windmill, barbed wire and the steel plow transformed the Plains into a rich grazing and grain area, no longer 'The Great American Desert' of the early maps, fit only for Indians.

In the Southwest, agriculture had diffused directly from Mexico and stimulated elaborations of social life even earlier than in the Southeast, beginning perhaps about 1000 B.C. Changes in climate and invasions of hunter-raiders from the North saw shifts of settlements, abandonment of old villages and building of new ones before Europeans first visited the pueblos in 1539. Archeological studies show that the settled peoples of the Southwest, pueblos and other gardening villagers, had long exchanged items and ideas among themselves. Although actual relations with the Spaniards were frequently strained, they readily took over from the Spaniards a host of new objects, skills, plants, animals and ideas to make them peculiarly their own. Learning early the futility of overt aggression against the better armed Spaniards, the pueblo peoples particularly have developed passive resistance to a fine art in dealing with strangers in their midst – even holding hordes of modern tourists at arm's length with bland pleasantries while doing a brisk trade in hand crafts and fees for taking pictures.

The pueblos' once troublesome neighbors, the former raiders today designated as Navajo and Apache, successfully incorporated elements of sedentary Indian cultures into their more mobile life in aboriginal times, and eventually they too made judicious selections from Euro-American culture, reworking and molding them to fit their own cultural predilections. The Southwestern Indians in general retain more obvious and visible symbols of their 'Indianness' and for many white observers these are the only 'real'

Indians left. However, their modern culture is far from aboriginal, distinctive though it may be. Like Indian groups throughout the country, the important criteria of identity rest in intangible attitudes, values, beliefs, patterns of interpersonal relations.

As in the East, native social and material elaboration in the West tended to thin out toward the North, limited by environmental factors. In the Great Basin, tiny bands of roving gatherers maintained a bare subsistence level of existence. Nevertheless, even some of the simple Basin societies were attracted by the horse-buffalo complex of the Plains and in an incredibly short time the Comanche, for example, had ventured out to become a Plains tribe *par excellence*.

North of the Basin, the relatively greater richness of the environment permitted the Plateau Indian to live much as the more favored northern hunters east of the Mississippi, even to enjoying a fur trade era, although of brief duration. Gardening never reached this region in aboriginal times, but after contact the horse became important to many of the Plateau peoples.

In the West, there were several unusual situations where nature furnished dependable 'crops' which man could harvest without first having sown. In Central California, huge stands of oak accounted for regular supplies of acorns which the Indians converted into a nutritious flour by ingenious techniques of leaching out the bitter and somewhat toxic tannic acid. On the coast, enormous shell mounds are evidence of once large permanent settlements supported in large part by easily gathered mollusks. Many of the California Indians took quite readily to the ministrations of Spanish friars who began arriving in 1769, and set up mission compounds where they introduced the Indians to agricultural and other skills. Crowded together in the new villages, the Indians proved tragically susceptible to new diseases. The eventual discovery of gold, the influx of law-less miners, and competition by the United States for control of California, in which Indian property and rights were often identified with Hispano-American interests, contributed to a rapid and widespread disorganization and decline among many of the California groups. The picture is, in fact, strikingly similar to the rapid depopulation and disruption of native life on the East Coast.

Along the Northwest Coast from Oregon to Alaska, an abundance and variety of marine life and a northerly climate mitigated by the warm Japanese Current created ideal conditions for population growth and social elaboration which could be promoted in most places only through the development of food production. The peoples in this region had regularly traded, visited and fought among themselves when first European contacts were made by sailing ships out of Russia, England and the United States in the late eighteenth century. Trade soon flourished in which sea otter and other pelts were exchanged for both utilitarian and novelty items. The Northwest Coast peoples quickly earned a reputation for sharp bargaining and scant concern for the welfare of hapless seamen wrecked on their shores as they busily plundered ships' cargoes. An impressive way of native life became further enriched. Already skilled in working cedar with simple tools and clever methods of steaming, bending and sewing boards, the Indians soon appreciated that totem poles, storage boxes, house posts, masks and other objects could be enlarged and more ornately embellished with metal tools. However, indiscriminate slaughter of the peltry animals brought a rapid close to the coastal trade. Unlike the eastern tribes which foraged further and further west for fresh beaver areas, even to pushing out the resident tribes, the Northwest Coast people had no place else to go. The arrival of Lewis and Clark in 1806 heralded the opening of overland routes of settlement from the east and encroachment of farmers, miners and loggers. The later adaptations of the Coastal Indians have tended to center in fishing both for their own support and as commercial enterprise.

If we take a broad view of the entire continent from the end of the sixteenth century until well into the nineteenth century, we find that white contact stimulated new ideas, introduced new goods and even greatly accelerated the pace of cultural change in some cases. However, whites arrived on a scene where changes, experimentation, movements of people and diffusion of goods and ideas were already taking place. For the vast majority of tribes, there was time to develop attitudes and adaptations about the presence of whites which involved negotiation and selective borrowing of items rather than absorption into white culture and society. Exposure to similar opportunities to change, furthermore, did not lead to cultural homogeneity throughout the continent, since different Indian societies in different kinds of environments made different selections and adaptations in regard to white culture. The multiplicity of languages and local cultural identity persisted. When, from place to place, the nature of contact changed to one of intense competition for right to the land, the Indians were clearly at a disadvantage. However, even as their power to bargain waned, the various Indian groups continued to adapt to maintain their ethnic integrity. Because they made massive borrowings of European material items, which tended to be similar from place to place – guns, textiles, household utensils and tools – white people generally assumed they would soon gracefully phase out their social and cultural distinctiveness. However, we are still waiting for them to vanish.

TREATIES AND RESERVATIONS

When the United States and Canada finally emerged as the national entities controlling North America, increasingly determined to remain at peace with one another, Indian societies were obliged to deal exclusively with one or the other of these governments and were bereft of the opportunity to play the familiar game of favored nation in war and trade among competing powers – France, Spain, Britain and the young United States. Both Canada and the United States derive their Indian policies from guidelines which were already being laid down in the mid seventeenth century in New England and Virginia. In the face of overwhelming defeat, the depleted and demoralized tribes in these areas were offered and accepted small parcels of land – the first reservations – secured to them by treaties. These guaranteed homelands and other considerations, in the way of goods and religious and practical teachings, were to be compensation for the vast domains they relinquished. The Indians, in turn, pledged themselves to peace and alliance with the local colonies in case of war with hostile tribes or European enemies. In Virginia, in 1646, the regrouped remnants of the once powerful Powhatan Confederacy agreed in their treaty to pay a small annual tribute in furs to the colony, an interesting portent of things to come for their Indian neighbors to the West, as the fur trade was just beginning to loom importantly to the British.[3]

As the scattered and often competitive British colonies began to recognize their common interests in opposition to the French in the north and both Spain and France to the south, Indian policy became more firmly structured. By 1755, negotiations with Indians, particularly in regard to land, became the exclusive prerogative of the Crown acting through properly designated representatives. A northern and a southern superintendency were set up to regulate trade and undertake necessary diplomacy with the Indians. After the American Revolution, the southern superintendency ceased to exist as a British concern and the northern superintendency was moved from the area of New York State to Canada.

Canadian colonial governors handled Indian affairs locally until 1860 when responsibility in Ontario and Quebec was given directly to the Province of Canada. In 1867, the British North America Act placed Indian affairs under the jurisdiction of the Government of Canada. During the ensuing years, administrative headquarters were shifted between various Offices and Branches of the Government, but policy itself tended to remain relatively consistent. Whenever possible, Canada dealt with tribes by treaty, including as many tribes under a common treaty as could be induced to sign in any particular region. Reserves were located in the tribes' homelands or in nearby, ecologically similar areas, the process being repeated from region to region as national interest in regard to allocation of land expanded west and north. Canada made its last treaty with some of the far northern Indians in 1923. A system to encourage understanding of modern principles of government provides for election of a chief and headmen in each 'Band', the Canadian term for locally autonomous Indian groups. The number of headmen is determined by population size, with roughly one headman per 100 people. For some bands, such as the Iroquois groups along the southern border of Canada, this system is an uncomfortable imposition on their own patterns of semi-hereditary leadership, while for bands in the Northern Territories, it has given a formal structure to an old system of leadership based on individual ability. The Canadian government has always cooperated with religious denominations in sharing responsibility for Indian affairs, especially in regard to education.

A few Canadian bands were by-passed in treaty negotiations and special provisions have been made for them to qualify for 'Treaty Indian' benefits as well as conform to limitations placed on full citizenship by Treaty Indian status. A basic objective has been to encourage Indian people to declare themselves 'non-treaty' as individuals and be accepted as full-fledged citizens. After 1950, most of the limitations on citizenship were lifted, even for Treaty Indians, in the hope of hastening the day when Indians would become assimilated. The Canadian government, however, has been generally more tolerant than the United States of ethnic distinctiveness and more agreeable to protecting Indian rights to their lands as defined by treaties.

Eskimo affairs, until 1966, were considered a separate concern, centering more in matters of trade and welfare than in questions of land. At present an effort is underway to consolidate and regularize Indian and Eskimo administration, stressing new experiments in economic development of native communities.

Perhaps the most distinctive feature of Canadian Indian history is the explicit recognition of old communities of stabilized Indian–white mixture, designated *Metis*. This is a sociological and not an official concept; the Metis are simply an ethnic group like Ukrainians or French Canadians, sharing none of the benefits of Indian status. They are considered different from Indians both by themselves and the Indian people who also represent some white admixture in their genealogies. In some cases, the actual kinship between certain Indian and Metis families is known to both sides. Since Metis are generally found in the western Provinces and Territories, where there are large Indian populations, and suffer the same disabilities of isolation and inadequate education and perhaps even lower social status in the Canadian class system, there is an increasing tendency to group Metis and Indians in Canadian discussions of problems of poverty, employment, education and the like. The extent to which Metis and Indians themselves are interested in making common cause remains debatable.

The picture in the United States is much more complicated. In the first place, there were and are more Indian people representing greater diversity of languages, cultures and ecological adaptations. Encroachment of whites on Indian land has always been a much more acute problem. After France ceased to be a consideration in the struggle for control of North America, many tribes allied themselves with the British against the Americans in the Revolution and War of 1812, or maintained a wary neutrality during these conflicts, waiting to see how they would turn out. Few tribes declared themselves clearly on the side of the Americans. Thus, from the start, American negotiations for land frequently followed recent hostile engagements with the tribes involved. The settlers' fears of disgruntled and warlike Indians, perhaps not yet entirely convinced they were defeated, gave added impetus to a policy designed to move Indian tribes far from the lands they ceded. In Canada, the relatively smaller populations of both Indians and whites as well as a history of friendlier relationships permitted comparatively easier negotiations for land and establishing reserves close to areas opening up for settlement.

Eventually, there was no place left to move Indians and the United States was also obliged to set up reservations in tribal homelands. Added to these many complications was the fact that in time American policy had to be adjusted to old Spanish arrangements in the Southwest where land grants established Indian title, a plan analogous but not identical to the British plan of treaties and reservations.

Following British precedent, the United States made Indian affairs a concern of the central government, but actual procedures were left vague. The third Article of the Constitution merely empowered Congress to 'regulate commerce with foreign nations, and among the several states, and with the Indian tribes.' At first, administration was carried out through a system of government authorized trading posts, reminiscent of the British superintendencies. The army handled problems of hostile Indians. Peace negotiations and land sales, including arrangements for reservations, were carried out by special treaty commissions appointed as need demanded. The idea prevailed, as it had since colonial times, that changes in sovereignty over land did not abrogate the rights of possession of those who occupied the land, and that Indians should be recompensed for land which they relinquished. This concept was enunciated in the Northwest Ordinance confirmed in 1789 and extended to cover the tribes in the Louisiana Purchase in 1804. By the time the United States acquired Alaska, we had begun to equivocate on this philosophy, and questions of Indian and Eskimo land remain somewhat confused.[4]

The fact that the United States pledged itself to pay Indians for their lands at a time when there was virtually no national treasury has given comfort to those historians who would see the founding fathers imbued with the noblest of ideals. Cynics point out that it was cheaper and easier than trying to drive the Indians out by force. The price paid across the continent averaged well under ten cents an acre, and the government expected to recoup quickly by sale of land in large blocks to speculators at $1.25 an acre minimum. Moreover the debt on each treaty usually was paid under an annuity plan extending over thirty years. On the other hand, many of the tribes were not entirely naïve and held out for payment in specie rather than the uncertain paper issued by banks in the early days of the republic.

Although successive efforts were made to establish a firm line between Indian and white holdings east of the Mississippi River, settlement continued to encroach on the Indian area, necessitating renegotiation of the boundary. By 1824, the demands of settlers, competition from illegal private traders, and the diminishing returns of the fur trade led the government to abandon the trading business as basic to Indian affairs and concentrate on the land business. The Bureau of Indian Affairs was set up under the Department of War. When the Department of Interior was established in 1849 and Indian affairs were placed under its aegis, most of the eastern tribes had become located much as we find them today.

A few tribes on the seaboard occupy state reservations or are simply old Indian settlements, legacies of the colonial past which could be ignored. Along the Appalachians, particularly toward the southern end and elsewhere in the Southeast, there are isolated communities which identify themselves as Indian, such as the numerous Lumbee of Carolina and adjoining states and the Houma of Louisiana discussed in this volume by Ann Fischer. Their tribal affiliations are vague, because these people are the descendants of fugitive remnants of many tribes driven from the coasts, white renegades, and, in some cases, runaway Negro slaves. These people are, in effect, Metis, but popular and official thinking in the United States has tended to more rigid classification than in Canada. Thus, rejected as white and reluctant to be considered Negro, the American Metis stress their identity as Indian. Those Indian societies which maintained a clear and unbroken tradition of tribal identity and stood in the path of settlement were exhorted, negotiated with and paid to move further west during the period of the 1820s and 1830s.

The United States entered into numerous treaties with these tribes and though it tried to deal with blocs of tribes as was done in Canada, this proved inexpedient. Both tribesmen and treaty commissioners tried to outmaneuver each other by devious diplomatic ploys. The Indians could play for delay in land sales by noting boundaries which had only Indian names and were unknown to the whites, so that final settlement would depend on formal surveys. The whites attempted to play one tribe off against another, and even one sub-band within a tribe against another, in the hope of leaving intransigent factions so isolated and unprotected that they would be forced to capitulate when their neighbors moved out. And then the factions would rally and claim the treaty had to include all parties with an interest to the land in question. Since treaties had to be ratified by Congress and the work of the commissioners was hampered by both budget allocations for their time and the desire to get back to Washington before Congress recessed, the Indians won compromises. The commissioners could afford to be philosophical as these loose ends could always be tied up in the next round of negotiations. There is little doubt that the Indian tribes hoped to make the best of what could only be a bad bargain, but to stick to that bargain once made, whereas the treaty makers from Washington took the treaties lightly, striving toward a final goal of general Indian removal to the less choice land west of the Mississippi acquired in the Louisiana Purchase.

Thus we find representatives of eastern tribes scattered from Nebraska to Oklahoma: Potawatomi, Winnebago, Miami, Shawnee, Kickapoo, Ottawa, Creek, Choctaw, Chickasaw, Cherokee, Seminole and others even including members of the League of the Iroquois such as Cayuga and Seneca. However, bands or small clusterings of families of many of these tribes managed to return to their old homelands or held out against removal, arguing either the illegality of the treaty under which they were to move or misrepresentation by the government as to the quality of the new land or the terms whereby they and their possessions were to be transported. In some cases, this determination led to creation of reservations for them in their homelands, as in the cases of the Eastern Cherokee and Seminoles. Others, including some of the Potawatomi and Winnebago, were granted homesteads as individuals where it was hoped that they would become absorbed into the general rural white population. Popular indignation about the injustice shown one band of Potawatomi in Michigan led to the establishment of a small reservation for them under state jurisdiction. A group of Mesquakie (Fox) picked out and purchased their land and applied for reservation status. Perhaps the most bizarre instance was the band of Kickapoo who just kept on going west and sought sanctuary in northern Mexico where they remain to this day, preserving many features of nineteenth century woodland Indian culture. In many cases, particularly in the Southeast, little groups simply managed to maintain themselves as Indian neighborhoods on property they were able to purchase, little noticed and bothering no one.

Several Iroquois tribes or portions of them who did not flee to Canada after the Revolution were granted their reservations in New York State by treaties signed during Washington's administration. Of these, the Oneida were induced to move to Wisconsin in the early 1830s along with the Stockbridge, a highly acculturated Algonkian group drawing its membership from remnants of coastal tribes, primarily the Mahicans. In Wisconsin, Michigan and Minnesota we find a number of tribes, Menomini, bands of Ojibwa and others who by various delaying tactics finally managed to get reservations in their homelands.[5]

There is no question that when it was a matter of the larger national interest, defined as the demands of settlers or speculators, the government made every effort to remove the Indians.[6] Humanitarians such as Jefferson expressed the hope that if Indian people conformed to the habits of rural whites they might remain in possession of what land they would need for this purpose, but if they would not change their ways, the only alternative was forceful persuasion and removal. The rationale for dispossession of the Indians has usually conformed to a logic summed up by Theodore Roosevelt in the late nineteenth century, 'this great continent could not have been kept as nothing but a game preserve for squalid savages.'[7] The myth of the hunter Indian, incapable or unwilling to rouse himself from the sloth of ancestral tradition in the face of new opportunities and the model afforded by civilized man, remains with us today. On close inspection, the problem seems to be less the Indian's inability to adapt than the unorthodoxy of his adaptations. Western cultures have a different history; our traditions evolved out of a stage of feudal peasantry which the Indians by-passed. So Indians react in unexpected but perfectly logical ways to our ideas and artifacts.

The essential problems which arise in the confrontation of different cultural systems, each changing and adapting in its own way, are well illustrated in the fate of the Cherokee, who became literate as a result of exposure to the European idea of writing, but hit upon a syllabary rather than an alphabet to best convey the vagaries of their own tongue in written symbols. By the early nineteenth century, the Cherokee and other groups in the Southeast had built upon their growing aboriginal commitment to agriculture with new crops and implements brought by the Europeans. They were successfully self-sustaining from small farmsteads to large plantations, with many acres under cultivation and large herds of horses and cattle. But they wished to maintain themselves as distinct Indian societies, while acknowledging allegiance to the United States.

Decisions sympathetic to this outlook were expressed by the Chief Justice of the Supreme Court, John Marshall, in 1831 (*The Cherokee Nation v. The State of Georgia*) and 1832 (*Samuel A. Worcester v. The State of Georgia*) but had little effect in protecting the Cherokee or any Indian tribes from private interests and states bent on their dispossession. Frontier statesmen, particularly during the administration of Andrew Jackson, could argue that Indians were different and therefore still clearly savage and a danger. Congress, as the body duly authorized to deal with Indian affairs, simply went around Marshall's decisions. It carried out the will of local states in regard to unwanted Indians, and provided for treaties and removals.

It must be noted that not all the proponents of the plan of Indian removal were motivated by selfish interests. There were missionaries and others who felt that removal of Indian tribes from the corrupting and demoralizing influences of frontier riff-raff would be in the Indians' best interest and allow them to establish a new and better life. However, even the kindest construction placed on this view must admit to its short-sightedness. Already resident on the land in the west were tribes whose interests were not consulted before newcomers were moved among them. They were often considerably less hospitable. Furthermore, it was becoming obvious that the Plains area would not remain forever the habitation of buffalo hunters. By the time pioneers were spreading out into the Plains, instead of by-passing them on the way to the gold fields or fertile valleys of the west coast, there was really no place left to move Indians. There was also the danger that the plan of one, and later two, large Indian Territories in the West would allow tribes to see the advantages of alliance and make common cause against the white man. Therefore, most of the native tribes west of the Mississippi were placed in reservations which are separated from one another yet in or near the original homelands. In contrast, large numbers of eastern Indians were clustered in Oklahoma.[8]

By 1849, when the Bureau of Indian Affairs was shifted from the Department of War to the newly created Department of the Interior, the eastern tribes had been 'pacified', although troops were occasionally called in to round up returnees and get them back to their western reservations. The real problem, however, was the Plains Indians, who at this time were in the very midst of their great cultural florescence and were formidable and enthusiastic warriors. The efforts of Interior to get these tribes on reservations by negotiation, conciliation and persuasion were often confounded by the outlook of the War Department, which considered all Indians hostile, dangerous and fair game. An unfortunate term, 'ward', used by Marshall in his 1831 decision was revived. Marshall only intended a rough analogy in endeavoring to explain the responsibility of the federal government to protect Indian tribes against unauthorized usurpation of their lands: 'Their relation to the United States resembles that of a ward to his guardian.' Because the Bureau 'sometimes became the uneasy and unhappy buffer between Indians and the US Army',[9] it was decided in 1862 to designate the Indian tribes as 'wards' of the Indian Bureau rather than let them be considered simply as 'enemies' over whose fate the army would have jurisdiction to make decisions. Unfortunately, and without ever really having legal sanction, the term 'ward' took on administrative connotations by which the Bureau exercised incredible control over the lives and property of individuals, much as a guardian would act for minor and even hopelessly retarded children.

Historical Background

As noted, Canada took its Indian treaties more seriously from the start and has continued to respect them. In the United States, although important hostilities such as Little Big Horn and Wounded Knee were yet to come, it was apparent by 1871 that the process of 'pacification' would continue at a rapid pace. The need to make treaties with so many different tribes and the embarrassment of making new treaties every time the demands of settlement required reduction of Indian acreage suggested to policy makers that Indian tribes were not really 'nations' entitled to the respect and formality of treaties. Treaties required the unwieldy and expensive process of mutual agreement – albeit the United States held the greater power in dictating terms and Senate ratification. Terms of existing treaties would be observed as long as the government found it practicable, but after 1871 no more treaties were made with Indian tribes. Instead, 'agreements' were negotiated which were worded much like treaties and mistaken for treaties by many Indians, but which were administratively more expedient and not as binding in legalistic and even moral terms as far as the government was concerned. Champions of Indians' rights long endeavored to pique the conscience of the nation by pointing to our bad faith in entering into solemn treaties, 'The highest law of the land', which we did not intend to keep.

It was the period from the 1870s to the 1920s during which the worst abuses occurred in regard to administration of Indian affairs. Most Indian people were denied the vote, had to obtain passes to leave the reservation and were prohibited from practicing their own religions, sometimes by force. Leadership and management of community affairs smacking of traditional forms and functions were either discouraged or ignored as proper representations of community interest. Children were dragooned off to boarding schools where they were severely punished if they were caught speaking their own languages. While these things all happened, shortage and rapid turn-over of Bureau personnel, administrative apathy and occasional enlightenment at the local administrative level meant that the regulations were not always rigorously enforced. And the Indian societies themselves took a hand in playing off administrators, missionaries and other whites against each other to keep them busy while Indian people held the line in their determination to remain Indian. The ubiquity of factionalism in Indian societies which is so regularly deplored by those people, Indian and white, who are sincerely interested in helping Indian people make a better life, may actually have acted as an important mechanism of social and cultural survival for Indian groups. No outsider could gain total dominance for his programs aimed in one way or another at reducing Indian distinctiveness. This suggestion, while admittedly speculative, seems worth bearing in mind when we turn to the contemporary scene where there seems to be a striving for common goals, in which factionalism for its own sake in avoiding undesirable goals may be giving way to what are really healthy differences of opinion based on habitual wariness in working toward positive objectives.

ATTEMPTS AT REFORM

Educated Indian people and their philanthropic white friends during the nineteenth century were generally as committed as the government to the view that the Indians' only hope was social and cultural assimilation into white society. The reservation system *per se* as well as the widespread peculation and dereliction in duty of reservation per-

sonnel were held responsible for impeding Indians in their
course toward 'civilization'. This view tended to ignore the
many non-reservation communities in the east which
remained almost defiantly Indian, even where government
experiments in granting stubborn 'returnees' homesteads
scattered among white neighbors did not automatically
result in Indian assimilation or break-down of a sense of
community. If their conservatism in language, religion and
other aspects of culture was noted at all, it was viewed opti-
mistically as inevitably temporary. Ironically, one of the
major measures of reform promoted by humanitarians
turned out to exacerbate rather than alleviate Indians' problems. This was the Indian Allotment Act of 1887. It was
actually protested by some far-seeing people who recognized
the opportunities it afforded for a tremendous Indian land-
grab, but these voices were drowned out by those who considered themselves the Indians' true friends, righteously
supported by those who stood to gain from the Allotment
Act as predicted by the pessimists.[10]

The idea of allotment was that Indians could be assimilated into the white rural population in the space of a generation by granting them private property. Each individual was
to receive his own acreage, usually coming to about 180 acres
per family unit, and land left over after all allotments were
made was to be thrown open to sale, the proceeds used to
build houses and barns and to buy stock and equipment for
the Indians to become farmers.

However, even by 1887, subsistence farming by individual
families was giving way to large scale, single crop enterprises. Although allotments remained tax free for a period
of twenty-five or thirty years, Indian people were not adequately informed nor technically prepared for managing
farms. The result was that many of the allotments were lost
through tax default or sold to pay debts which far-seeing

whites had allowed Indians to run up against the day they would gain patents-in-fee to their land. Although the necessity for more protective provisions was soon recognized by the government, an unexpected complication rendered much of the land useless to its Indian owners. Some time between 1900 and 1910, a rapid decrease in Indian population leveled off and a steady rise set in. Original allotments were divided among increasing numbers of heirs. Given American laws of inheritance, there developed a common situation in which an individual might own forty or more acres, but as scattered fractions of land inherited from a number of ancestors who had received allotments. The easiest course was for the Indian Bureau simply to rent the land out in large parcels to white agriculturalists and stockmen and divide the proceeds among the many heirs. Some people could live on their rent money alone, often supporting less fortunate relatives as well. But, in most cases, rent money brought only a few dollars a year and a living was eked out by wage labor in planting and harvest seasons, forays to the cities to work in factories, and exploitation of the growing tourist industry in terms of sale of handcrafts and public dance performances.

As regulations on Indian movement off the reservations tended to relax, especially if people left to seek work, Indian people became increasingly better informed on the myriad opportunities to earn a living in industrial America besides the drudgery of farming. However, Indian communities persisted even where the allotment process had drastically reduced the land base. Indian people seemed to join circuses and wild west shows, seek out areas where relatively high wages were paid for crop work, or find their way to industrial employment in the cities in a manner reminiscent of hunting, trading or war expeditions. They drifted back home periodically to seek help from relatives if they were broke or to share the spoils of the 'hunt' with their kinsmen until it was necessary to forage again. They took to automobiles as enthusiastically as many had taken to ponies at an earlier time, becoming commuters to cities or other places where they could find work, returning daily or weekly or seasonally or by whatever schedule was practical. Some people spent most of their lifetimes in the city, but returned home to their tribesmen upon retirement. And these patterns persist today. Unlike the usual migrants, Indian people do not seem to perceive urban work as a break with the rural past, but merely as an extension of the peripheries of the territory which can be exploited economically. It is difficult to escape the conclusion that Indian people were 'rurban' long before anyone coined the term or saw the industrial blending of city and country life as the direction in which the nation as a whole was to move.

Although Indian groups, with their characteristic close communal life, were persisting and increasing in size, the national outlook stressed rugged individualism and private enterprise. Both policy and administration of Indian affairs were oriented toward assimilating Indians as individuals into the general population. Tribal enterprises and industries were introduced only where the overwhelming argument of certain natural resources militated against allotment in severalty. Thus a few tribal forests and fishing grounds provided regular employment and income on the reservation, but even in these cases Indian people were given little voice or purposeful training in management of tribal businesses. Beyond that, a number of areas escaped allotment either because the terrain made it impractical for subsistence farming or the problems created by allotment elsewhere had become apparent and the plan was simply shelved before more remote areas were included under it.

Other efforts to reform Indian administration gradually

got around to matters of practical welfare. The Indian Bureau had always been a political pork barrel, appointments to various posts being handed out to party stalwarts. The pay was poor, but there were opportunities to shave budgets for personal gain. Allotment opened more opportunities to bribe officials to declare Indians 'competent' to sell their land. The scandals of peculation, the complaints of sincere employees that the uncertainty of their jobs made it impossible to carry out decent programs, and the clear evidence of honest but unqualified and emotionally callous personnel all led to demands for improvement. Doctors and teaching staffs were put on civil service in 1892, and by 1902 all Bureau employees were on civil service except the Commissioner and Assistant Commissioner.

At the time of the First World War most of the Indian population was still without the vote and also not subject to conscription, but a surprising number of young men volunteered for the armed services and were recognized for remarkable heroism. This stirred the nation from complacency about Indian problems and in 1924 the franchise was extended to all Indians. Significantly, one Indian view, which found expression among tribes all over the country, considered the right to vote a pretty shabby reward and no more than further evidence of national disregard for Indian rights as established by treaties. The implication was that Indians volunteered in America's defense as loyal allies as pledged in treaties rather than as patriotic citizens.[11]

However, few white Americans were aware of this reaction to their magnanimous gesture, and concerned people continued efforts to understand why Indians had not yet been granted their proper place as assimilated Americans and to search for better means of accomplishing this end. The results of extensive investigation of Indian affairs by the Brookings Institution were published in 1928,[12] setting forth in concise and depressing detail just how bad things really were among Indian people under the federal jurisdiction, and suggesting means of improving the situation.

Although committed to the entrenched view that assimilation of Indians was both desirable and inevitable, the Brookings Report noted that this would take time and the settling of many just grievances harbored by the tribes before trust and cooperation could be expected of them. Throughout the Report we begin to see indications of a changing perspective on Indians' problems in the recommendations reached by objective investigators. For example in speaking of administration as 'leadership', the Report says,

This phrase 'rights of the Indian' is often used solely to apply to his property rights. Here it is used in a much broader sense to cover his rights as a human being living in a free country. ... The effort to substitute educational leadership for the more dictatorial methods now used in some places will necessitate more understanding of and sympathy for the Indian point of view. Leadership will recognize the good in the economic and social life of the Indians in their religion and ethics, and will seek to develop it and build on it rather than to crush out all that is Indian. The Indians have much to contribute to the dominant civilization, and the effort should be made to secure this contribution, in part because of the good it will do the Indians in stimulating a proper race pride and self respect.[13]

Serious efforts to implement the Brookings recommendations were delayed as the nation entered the depression of the 1930s With the election of Franklin D. Roosevelt and appointment of John Collier, Sr, as Indian Commissioner, a 'New Deal' was also in store for Indian people. Collier's thinking went beyond the Brookings recommendations both in revising administrative procedures and in philosophy. He endeavored to set up mechanisms for self-government which would allow Indian communities to bargain as communities with the government and the larger society. He sought to teach them about a host of opportunities for community improvement and let them choose accordingly – revolving loan funds, tribal enterprises, resource development, land acquisition, tribal courts, educational programs. In many ways Collier's plan was inappropriate: too 'Indian' for some tribes, not 'Indian' enough for others, and characterized by unwarranted urgency and hard sell in some instances. For all that, Indian people recognized in large measure that Collier really understood what their grievances were about even if his methods were sometimes less than satisfactory or if Bureau personnel on the local level were often incapable of throwing off old habits of mind and behavior in carrying out the intent of the new administration. Where Collier and Indian people were in agreement was in the objective of restoring not the Indian culture of any past period but the kind of conditions and relationships which existed prior to the 'ward' philosophy of Indian administration, a period when Indian people could still select and adapt innovations to find satisfactory patterns of their own for community life. Above all, Collier understood the need to secure an adequate land base for meaningful social experimentation and development.

Collier's administration and philosophy are discussed elsewhere in this volume, but in our running historical review it is necessary to point out that they were short-lived as views Congress would be willing to support. They were in effective operation for seven years at most. The Indian Reorganization Act was passed in 1934, time was required to inform Indian people and allow them to make decisions in regard to it, and by 1941 the nation was at war. Domestic programs, including those of the Indian Bureau, were naturally made secondary to the war effort. Wartime prosperity brought temporary alleviation of economic problems for many Indian communities. Collier remained in office until 1946, but it was becoming increasingly apparent that his administrative ideas were losing popularity with Congress.[14] After the war, when servicemen and factory workers returned home, Indian population like that of the rest of the nation had increased. Programs just started before the war had not been able to keep pace with the added pressures on the still limited sources of income of the reservations. Since the 'Indian problem' suddenly loomed larger than ever, the easy explanation was Collier's revolutionary departure from the time-honored Indian policy of assimilation.

Because Indian people showed a marked aptitude for industrial work during the war, and it was obvious they would not succeed as farmers, the solution was simple. Relocate them in urban centers, preferably in each case as far from the home reservation as possible, and legislate the reservations out of existence so that Indian people could not run home when things got tough or share their good fortune periodically with kinsmen who lacked the gumption to get out on their own.

Like the grand scheme of 1887 to solve the Indians' problems by the simple expedient of allotment in severalty, the relocation-reservation termination plan of the 1950s was out of date for its time in terms of national social and economic trends. If the ideal of the Allotment Act was to ensconce Indian people in a kind of average, small-farm middle-class, which was actually disappearing, the ideal of the policy of the 1950s was primarily to get the government out of the Indian business and scant attention was paid to where Indian people might be able to fit in American life. Indian people opposed the policy of the 1950s, arguing for the alternative of community development through local industries and beefing up the long neglected educational programs. This, Indian people argued, would enable them to plant and manage intelligently in their own behalf community development and tribal enterprises. It would also make it possible for those individuals who wished to assimilate to enter the larger society at a decent economic and occupational level.

At the very time that suburbs were burgeoning, commuting was a way of life for much of the nation, and far-sighted people were anticipating greater segmentation of industrial operations and dispersing them to where the people live, Indian policy was based on models of concentrating population in large urban centers. Like the rural myth of the nineteenth century, mid-twentieth century policy promoted the myth of the 'melting pot', whereby the ambitious immigrant worked his way out of the poor ethnic neighborhood by frugality and hard work. Such thinking ignored a number of facts: (1) The agonies which such groups suffered during the period when they were exploited minorities living in urban slums. (2) The loss of a sense of community which such people suffered when, sometimes after repeated moves as a group to different urban neighborhoods, they finally 'spun off' into the larger society. (3) The special reliance of Indian people on group identity, group membership and group decisions, which goes beyond anything comparable which the immigrant communities were able to establish. Immigrant communities usually were not communities when they came; their ethnic identities were, to a surprising extent, constructed in America. (4) The increasing difficulty of 'making it' economically and socially in an economy which has much less use today for unskilled labor, and a society which sees color so strongly that many of its members still doubt that noncaucasians are really capable of achieving middle-class standards.

The trends of social reform and legislation had taken increasing cognizance of the fact that the individual could no longer hope to go it alone, saving for the rainy days and providing for his old age. Studies of crime and mental health had begun to raise serious questions about the nature of modern, industrialized society in depriving the individual of a sense of community and meaningful engagement in life. But in the 1950s, and to a great extent in the 1960s, it is considered unrealistic, impractical and perhaps even a little silly to suggest, as the Brookings Report did in 1928, that 'the Indians have much to contribute to the dominant civilization and the effort should be made to secure this contribution.'[15]

Whether or not Indian people are potential models for satisfactory community life for the nation at large, one thing became clear during the 1950s. They were not happy with the solution to their problems of poverty offered by the government. Furthermore, it was soon obvious that the policy of the 1950s, like allotment in the 1880s, tended to create more new problems rather than solve old ones. By 1960, the presidential candidates of both parties recognized the need to reassess Indian affairs and find new directions for policy. At the same time, Indian people appeared to be more vocal and concerned with exercising a positive influence in regard to legislation affecting them. The present volume resulted from interest in delineating the nature of political activity in the contemporary Indian world.[16]

Notes

1. For more intensive study of the subject: William Brandon, *The American Heritage Book of Indians* (New York, 1961; paperback: Dell, 1964): more historical than ethnological. Harold Driver, *Indians of North America* (Chicago, 1961), a scholarly reference book with useful maps. Organized according to topics rather than culture areas. Wendell H. Oswalt, *This Land Was Theirs* (New York, 1966): good treatment of ten representative tribes across the country. Robert F. Spencer, Jesse D. Jennings, *et al.*, *The Native Americans* (New York, 1965): general introductory chapters followed by culture area descrip-

tions and accounts of specific tribes within the areas, written for textbook use. Ruth Underhill, *Red Man's America* (Chicago, 1953), also a textbook, and in many ways still the best general introduction to the subject for the beginner. Wilcomb Washburn, ed., *The Indian and the White Man* (Garden City, N.Y., 1964), a fascinating compendium of documents from the period of early contact to the present day, including John Marshall's decisions of 1831 and 1832, and House Concurrent Resolution 108 – the termination bill referred to in this paper.

2. A small but revealing incident, illustrative of a kind of hunter's pragmatism, occurred in the Canadian Northwest Territories. When questioned about his first airplane ride, a Slave Indian was clearly enthusiastic but not awe-struck by modern technology – 'Good! See moose sign. Come back, go find moose.' Personal conversation, June Helm.

3. Nancy Oestreich Lurie, 'Indian Cultural Adjustment to European Civilization', in James Morton Smith, ed., *Seventeenth Century America* (Chapel Hill, 1958), 33–60, discusses the Powhatan Confederacy and notes origins of the reservation system in North America.

4. Lurie, 'The Indian Claims Commission Act', *The Annals of The American Academy of Political and Social Science* (May 1957), 56–70, reviews the question of Indian land title, with special reference to an Alaskan case, 64–5.

5. The multitude of treaties in the United States and problems of boundaries are fully set forth in Charles J. Kappler, comp. and ed., *Indian Affairs, Laws and Treaties* (Washington, D.C., Vol. 2, *Treaties*, 1904); and Charles C. Royce and Cyrus Thomas, 'Indian Land Cessions in the United States', *Annual Report of the Bureau of American Ethnology*, Smithsonian Institution, Vol. 18, Pt. 2 (Washington, D.C., 1896–7).

6. *Cf.* William T. Hagan, *American Indians* (Chicago, 1961), for a discussion of Indian rights vs. national interest.

7. Theodore Roosevelt, *The Winning of the West* (New York, 1889–96), I, 90.

8. There are exceptions, however, as a few multi-tribe reservations were set up, particularly in the Northwest.

9. *Answers to Questions About American Indians*, Bureau of Indian Affairs (pamphlet), Washington, D. C., 1965, 7. The concept of ward, an equivocal term at best, is often confused with 'trusteeship' which has legal meaning and refers to land, not people, in regard to the

protective role of the federal government in regard to Indian affairs.

10. Before the General Allotment Act was passed in 1887, an earlier 'pilot' allotment act was passed with specific reference to the Omaha Reservation in Nebraska in 1882. *Cf.* Lurie, 'The Lady from Boston and the Omaha Indians', *The American West*, III, 4 (Fall 1966), 31–3; 80–86.

11. This view of the vote is still found among some Indian people.

12. Lewis C. Merriam and associates, *The Problem of Indian Administration: report on a survey made at the request of the Honourable Hubert Work, Secretary of the Interior*, The Brookings Institution (Baltimore, 1928).

13. ibid.

14. It is an open question whether the Indian Claims Commission Act, passed in 1946, represented the last of the Collier era or the beginning of the termination era. The objective of the act is to provide restitution for Indian grievances, particularly in regard to non-payment or unconscionable consideration for land. However, as sentiment grew in favor of relocation and termination, one argument was that Indian communities would disperse once grievances were settled and only the hope of payment on old debts perpetuated Indian identity. Ideally, claims payments would give Indian people the necessary stake to begin a new life as ordinary citizens far from the reservations. In actual fact, the amounts paid were relatively small on a per capita basis, and Indian communities persisted. Many tribes are still waiting for their claims to be settled.

15. Merriam, *The Problem*, 22–3.

16. Stan Steiner, *The New Indians* (Harper and Row, 1968) documents contemporary Indian views and efforts to improve Indian life by innovative adaptations of industrial opportunities to community development. Marred by errors in spelling and dates throughout and by Steiner's polemics, the book as a whole is, nevertheless, a valuable contribution to our understanding of the Indian today in so far as Steiner includes extended verbatim quotations from Indian people across the country. These are excellent selections.

ELIZABETH CLARK ROSENTHAL

'CULTURE' AND THE
AMERICAN INDIAN COMMUNITY

THE conventional view of American Indian life in the
United States is that it is disappearing – a view so deeply
held that many who themselves are drawn by profession and
training to participation in programs of technical assistance
abroad wonder at interest in contemporary Indian affairs.

It is true that one hundred years ago, American Indian
communities were under pressure of tribal wars and in conflict with the encroaching whites. It was easily predicted that
all Indians would die out except for those few who might
manage to melt into non-Indian society imperceptibly – a
kind of random disappearance into a 'mainstream'. Looking
back, it is a little hard to understand how this was to happen
in an historical and cultural setting so sensitive to differences
of color and custom. At any rate, it is not what did happen.

Today we are suddenly aware that Indian communities
have been growing. They are centers of rapid population
increase. There are twice as many persons of Indian descent
now as at the turn of the century. And the Indian population is a young one. We see also the spread of Indian communities on the reservations and off: some rural, some migrant, some near small towns, some in the cities.

American Indians are not so much disappearing into as
they are appearing within the 'larger society'. Only by an
intellectual *tour de force* can we continue to demonstrate,
scientifically, that Indian life is dwindling away in accord-
ance with the conventional view. We may if we like cling to

an academic definition of culture which constrains the facts of movement and growth in Indian life, but it will not contain them.

It is the premise of this discussion that we anthropologists have severely limited our use of the concept of culture in the examination of American Indian societies. We are thus caught quite unprepared, intellectually, to cope with present facts. We have carried along an outdated interpretation of culture change which may be summarized in the following standard formula: 'old culture – transition – breakdown – disappearance'. There is a tendency to apply this same formula in other parts of the world as well, in other situations which, by popular consent, have been classified as 'contact between primitive and modern'. And it is increasingly evident that it fails to meet the test.

From the point of view of applied anthropology, it is clear that this kind of routine thinking plays directly into the hands of politicians and administrators who make use of anthropology to 'prove' that Indian people or others are without culture today. For with good will or evil, it is easy to argue then that the cultural vacuums must be filled, according to whatever set of values the observer has in mind, and on this basis to justify an astonishing number of plans and programs.

Anthropology was built on the strength of a unique professional ethic that requires of each of its members that he cross over into the alien and live with it until it becomes the known, the sure, in its own terms. In this process, almost without intent, each for himself comes upon a new dimension of dignity. Thus, working from field data gathered for the most part alone and first-hand on Indian reservations, anthropologists have contributed richly to our knowledge and understanding of Indian peoples. Ethnologies have been written, languages recorded, songs and stories set down. We know more now because we have these fuller descriptions of Indian life, and because our perception has been sharpened in the analysis of structure and process which inevitably enter into these descriptions. As a result of the cooperative procedure by which 'informant' and 'fieldworker' sat down together, or traveled and lived together over long periods, Indian people today have access to their own tribal tradition and history.

For many years, however, it has been proper anthropological practice to describe one Indian society after another as if it were an isolated and insulated social system. There are historical as well as conceptual reasons for this. When reservations were first established, Indian groups were drastically separated from one another, even from related bands, and from the white settlers moving in around them. This was only an interruption, not a permanent break, in the flow of social relationships. But most researchers in the years since have confined their work to the framework so conveniently established.

Working against time, with the urgency of the primitive material ever in mind, there was every reason for the anthropologist to concentrate on those aspects of Indian life which were linked most directly with the tribal tradition, and to deal with those members of the community who most fully represented this tradition. The purpose of a study might be retrospective, descriptive or theoretical; nevertheless it made sense to avoid further complications which might be introduced into the data if one tangled with local informants who were whites, or too much identified with whites, or who were members of tribes other than that under observation. The Indian community seemed, at the time, so remote that there was no reason to explore the total social field. The concept of culture came to be applied in a highly restricted sense. In practice, it meant only, 'certain aspects of the way of life of the people on this particular reservation who are really Indian.'

It is difficult to be critical of the anthropologists who worked this way, for their motives were good, and their harvest was golden. If we had it to do over again, it might be wise to make the same choice. At the same time, a great deal was left out: the world of administrators, of Indian policemen, interpreters, traders, missionaries (Indian and white), 'employees' from other tribal backgrounds, visitors from other reservations, clerks, local farmers and ranchers, blacksmiths, teachers from Kentucky, matrons in the dormitories, state politicians and reformers.

There has been, to be sure, a great deal of generalization, especially in closing chapters, about the relevance of Indian policy and about the impact of the dominant American society on Indian life. Where, one may legitimately ask, are the field notes that contain the primary data on these subjects? Policy and society do not walk around in Indian communities; people do. What did the clerk actually say in the agency office? Who got the job at the power plant? Whose grandfathers went to Carlisle on the outing system? When did you wail at a funeral? Who made up songs for the men from the state university? What town was best for trading in and why? Who always visited friends over at Wind River Arapaho? Who lived three years in Rapid City? Who said, 'Please keep these potatoes in your house, my relatives are coming'? With whom did the Norwegian rancher's wife visit?

These are questions to which I know the answers out of the shared life of a Sioux community. I also know that, off-hand, we could tell exactly what percentage Indian blood each member of the community had, officially on the record and also what he 'really' was. We distinguished full, three-quarter, half, quarter, eighth, sixteenth, thirty-second, sixty-fourth. We knew which families were 'old-timers' and which

Indians were socially white and which whites were socially Indian, and when, because that varied with the occasion. Yet this was not tribal, not racial, not even intercultural. In its own terms, this was one community, experienced by its members as a cultural whole.

We have not sensed that people are at home in the culture of their own time. As a result, there are very few descriptions of Indian life in which the total local community is taken as focus, in its own right, to be examined as a going concern, including all its members, of whatever tradition. There is little material outlining the systematics of interaction as between any local Indian community and communities neighbor to it, Indian or white.

Anthropology has recognized at most 'the changing culture of an Indian tribe', 'a modern Teton community in the light of its past', 'acculturation in seven Indian tribes'. For sixty years, the concept of tribe has taken precedence over the concept of culture and defined its content. We have been led to believe that our data were disappearing right before our eyes. And hence we have construed the on-going process of Indian community life only as 'transition'.

Under this influence, covert culture has come to mean 'hidden from the anthropologist' – translated as a function of how far one may travel in miles, not in depth. A professional social scientist gave me this example of covert culture a year ago: he was studying kinship and, at considerable trouble, managed to get to a remote corner of one of the larger Indian reservations. He was delighted to find what he had been looking for: a family in which the children still called their mother's sister 'mother'. I was not surprised. I had spent the night before in a nearby city with old friends. They have lived there ten years, owned their own home, had young children. Their children called the mother's sister 'mother' too.

In so far as an Indian community today shows overt signs of anthropologically defined traditional life, an anthropologist is comfortable with his materials. Beyond this, there is some confusion. We have so reduced our legitimate field of observation that we do not know what to look for any more.

If most of the people in an Indian community speak English, if eighty per cent are on relief, if we see alcoholism and wife-beating, if Elmer Comes-a-Flying goes to college, if the medicine bundle is in the basement of the council hall, and the tribal chairman is in town having dinner with a lawyer – what is there to see?

In this situation the major theme on which we build our analyses is 'Culture-in-Crisis'. It is a most useful notion, especially for one time around. When you live in an Indian community for any length of time, you get awfully accustomed to it. Culture-in-Crisis is rather like having a talkative relative come to visit, especially one who knows the latest psychological jargon. Your guest has been alerted to symptoms of breakdown, and points out one piece of evidence after another which indicates imminent and inevitable collapse. You thought you had a home and you have only a problem. (If you are aware of other kinds of strength, or of pressures your guest fails to note, you say nothing. If you have aspirations and hopes, you keep them to yourself.)

Using the lingo of the social sciences, an anthropologist can easily hide from himself and others that he is not seeing anything very different from what his untrained, gossipy, obviously 'ethnocentric', suburban neighbor back home might see. Let the statisticians of disorder take over. Call it 'social disorganization' – everyone else does. When the tourists shake their heads and say sadly, 'These people have no culture left', we silently agree and apply for foundation grants elsewhere.

In the tribal inventory of anthropology, there was a time

when the concept of culture was a working tool. Now 'culture' has become our sacred cow. We keep it for ritual and display purposes. In our everyday work, we use only phrases derived from it, which thus may have a certain legitimacy and a special power. We need to remind ourselves that the concept itself is not time-bound, nor bound by any tradition.

In his early work, Tylor wrote of 'uncultured races'.[1] The breakthrough came in moving beyond that – in the application of the concept of culture to all human communities. It was then that anthropologists searched for and found the internal logic in what had, quite literally, seemed wild and strange. With our particular twentieth-century sophistication (African masks on the wall, Navajo rugs on the floor, folk-music on the Hi-Fi) we forget what that breakthrough meant.

There is much that is equally strange around us now. There are the overwhelming facts of population explosion. There is poverty that goes beyond a chosen simplicity of life to poverty that means pain, deprivation and illness. There is restlessness that we sometimes describe as a baffling complex of apathy and ambition. We recognize it in many places, though it has no name. There are persistently different social forms which we cannot fully explain in terms of 'tribalism' or of ancient ways of life.

The alien societies in which the contemporary anthropologist may be required to live seem quite as 'uncultured' to many of us as the 'primitive' first appeared to our intellectual ancestors. It is hard to make sense of modern American Indian communities or of communities like them in other parts of the world – perhaps as hard as it was, 100 years ago, to discern the patterns of tribal life, to record them, to interpret them. But that is the job all the same. We may be expected to overcome our private nostalgias and any personal tendency we may have to think that 'the way some other people live is really a problem'. We may even have to overcome fear, and be reminded that many an early anthropologist found himself in frightening situations. It is the anthropologist's job to discern the pattern, not to point the finger, to interpret the present cultural scene without sentimentality over the tribal past. Yet he will not lose sight of this past as it may yield insights into the culture of today.

Anthropology is a science of the field, and the concept of culture is our key tool in the ordering of primary field data. If we continue to limit its definition in fieldwork and in the analysis of field materials, we shall not see what there is to see. We shall see only what we like, or perhaps we shall see nothing at all.

Note

1. Sir Edward Burnett Tylor (1832–1917), called the father of modern anthropology, uses this term in his classic study *Primitive Culture*, published in England in 1871. At that time, a society was thought of as 'cultured' only if it had progressed in some undefined way along an evolutionary scale toward 'civilization'. Later, through Tylor's work and that of other late-nineteenth-century anthropologists, the term 'culture' came to be used in a universal sense, as an analytic tool in the study of every society.

Current Tendencies

SHIRLEY HILL WITT

NATIONALISTIC TRENDS AMONG AMERICAN INDIANS

Radical changes in the situation of the American Indian
in the very recent past make Indian nationalism a significant force in American affairs. Modern Indian nationalism, while new in its ability to transcend tribal
boundaries, is not without historical precedent. The
paper which follows is not only a review of the historical
antecedents of Indian nationalism, but also a characteristic statement of the point of view of the highly
vocal National Indian Youth Council. – SGL & NOL

WITHIN the United States there exists 'the perpetual in-
habitant with diminutive right'[1] – the American Indian. He
is an anachronism. His persistent identity as an Indian
makes for an unique phenomenon in a country whose 'melting pot' tradition borders on the sacred. That he should retain his ethos in the midst of a culture whose vast impact
upon all peoples of the world is easily demonstrable, poses
questions which seek out the core of America's firm belief in
its superiority. Furthermore, the legal status of the Indian is
distinct from that of non-Indians and a notable exception to
the American code of equality before the law. My purpose
is to discuss those historical antecedents which may have led
to the development of American Indian nationalism, to
describe the framework within which Indians have functioned in the twentieth century, and to offer for consideration certain traits among contemporary Indians which may
prove to be nationalistic. The Indian world is a living thing,

a collection of unassimilated individuals and communities which have chosen to go their own way rather than integrate with the dominant culture. At a time when new nations all over the globe are emerging from colonial control, their right to choose their own course places a vast burden of responsibility upon the more powerful nations to honor and protect those rights. The Indians of the United States may well present the test case for American liberalism. As Felix S. Cohen observed:

> It is a pity that so many Americans today think of the Indian as a romantic or comic figure in American history without contemporary significance. . . . Like the miner's canary, the Indian marks the shift from fresh air to poison gas in our political atmosphere; and our treatment of Indians, even more than our treatment of other minorities, reflects the rise and fall in our democratic faith.[2]

THE BACKGROUND OF INDIAN NATIONALISTIC THOUGHT

Confederation among American Indian tribes was the exception rather than the rule throughout traditional and recorded history. The tendency was proliferation into more and more tribal groups. In fact, it might be said that the proclivity to separate off into autonomous tribes was the distinctive feature of Indian political development.

And yet, confederation did occur. Long before contact with non-Indians, the northeastern Iroquois founded the League of the Hodenosaunee, or Iroquois, made up of five (later six) nations – Mohawk, Oneida, Onondaga, Cayuga, and Seneca (the Tuscarora joining about 1712). The League produced the first federal constitution on the American continent, the Gayaneshagowa, or Great Binding Law.[3] It affected the nations already mentioned as well as such sub-

jugated tribes as the Susquehannocks, Hurons, Eries, Wyan-
dotts, Neutrals, Delawares, Nanticokes, Saponis and Tutelos.
Estimates as to the date of its founding range widely but investigators now tend to place its origin in the fifteenth century.[4]

But the founding date is not at issue here; the League's
main importance for this report is its example as the first
documented incidence of a strong cohesive confederation of
American Indian tribes. Other incorporations followed. The
Creek Confederacy appeared during the 1600s, and, in New
England, King Philip of the Wampanoag tribe succeeded in
fusing his tribe for a time with the Narragansetts, Nipmucks
and others in 1675. In the Southwest, the Pueblos were united
under the leadership of Popé in 1680. Pontiac, in 1763, managed a concerted effort against the British with warriors
drawn from such tribes as the Potawatomi, Chippewa,
Ottawa, Miami, Delaware, Mingo, Huron, Shawnee, Wea and
Kickapoo. The sagacious Joseph Brant envisioned a union of
all Indian tribes during the Revolutionary War and while his
messengers sought allegiance of tribes as remote as the Sauk
and Foxes, he led his Mohawks with the Onondaga, Seneca
and Cayuga into the war on the side of the English.[5] In the
years following the Revolution, Tecumseh conceived the idea
of a vast Indian confederacy and travelled from Wisconsin
to Florida in order to elicit support for this cause. William
Henry Harrison wrote that 'if it were not for the vicinity of
the United States, he [Tecumseh] would perhaps be the
founder of an Empire that would rival in glory that of
Mexico or Peru'.[6] Tecumseh's scheme for an Indian free state
or nation within the United States echoed Brant so nearly
that one might well wonder at the outcome had the two men
been of the same generation.

*   *   *

The American Indian Today

The Indian World. Throughout the report of this investigation the term 'Indian world' shall be interpreted as meaning the totality of American Indians who maintain identity with, and orientation to, their ethnic group. The definition applies equally to reservation Indians, nonreservation Indians, relocatees, and people having any degree of Indian blood who so identify.

Nation and nationalism. According to one dictionary definition, a nation is 'any aggregation of people having like institutions and customs and a sense of social homogeneity and mutual interest'. In this report, however, it will be necessary to expand the definition somewhat. Looking at the culture of the American Indians as a whole, we find tremendous diversity – in the past and the present. Even neighboring peoples or societies can differ considerably from one another. Politically, they are a conglomeration of multiple societies, often possessing their own distinct tract of land. 'Nationalism' shall be interpreted as the devotion to, or advocacy of, group interests or group unity and independence.

Termination. The unilateral withdrawal of federal services to Indians. It will further imply those related policies and legislation, such as resolutions, bills, acts and public laws, which lead to this same end.

List of abbreviations used:

BIA US Bureau of Indian Affairs, Department of the Interior

ICC Indian Claims Commission, US Department of Justice

IRA Indian Reorganization Act of 1934, also referred to as the Howard-Wheeler Act

NCAI National Congress of American Indians
NIYC National Indian Youth Council

*   *   *

In 1830, Black Hawk of the Sauk tribe attempted to enlist the aid of the Osage, Cherokees, Creeks, Potawatomi, Kickapoo and Winnebago in a final stand against American advancement. He appealed to them to lay aside their tribal animosities for the greater good of all Indians.

Another type of unifying effort was waged by Wovoka, the Paiute prophet. This was a nativistic revival movement centering on the Ghost Dance by which the spirits of the dead would be enlisted to aid the living in their eleventh hour struggle in the 1880s.

Each of these figures gives clear evidence of incipient or overt nationalism. Citing other prominent Indians as, for instance Chief Joseph, Cochise, Geronimo and Crazy Horse would confuse patriotism to tribe with the concept of an all-Indian nationalism. The leaders briefly described above shared the dream of tribal unification and a united Indian nation, although they varied in the breadth and scope of their philosophical development.

The most realistic vehicles for the attainment of Indian unity of those mentioned were the League of the Iroquois and the concepts of Tecumseh and Brant. The League sufficiently impressed Benjamin Franklin so that 'in 1754... [his] proposed Albany Plan of Union for the colonies drew direct inspiration from Hiawatha's League.'[7] In a letter he said:

It would be a very strange Thing, if six nations of ignorant Savages should be capable of forming a Scheme for such an Union, and be able to execute it in such a Manner, as that it has subsisted Ages, and appears indissoluble; and yet that a like Union should be impracticable for ten or a Dozen English Colonies, to whom it is more necessary, and must be more advantageous; and who cannot be supposed to want an equal understanding of their interests.[8]

That the League may have been the governmental key to a united Indian nation is a moot point. However, its persistence in the present-day Iroquois world clearly demonstrates its survival value throughout 350 years of envelopment by a dynamic non-Indian civilization.

Tecumseh's wisdom lay in his conception of himself as an Indian first and a Shawnee second. Like Brant, he fought for more than resistance to encroachment; he propounded a design for an Indian state built on national consciousness above and beyond tribal consciousness.

Despite the general autonomous character of Indian societies, the idea of Indian commonalty is clearly grounded in Indian history. The importance of the incidents I have mentioned lies less in any possible direct evolution to present trends than in their simply having happened. It would be difficult, if not impossible, to determine whether these concepts were consciously harbored from the historical sources or not. The point remains, however, that Indian nationalism of one form or another did exist in the past, and that precedent has been set for further development.

TWENTIETH-CENTURY INDIAN AFFAIRS

At the turn of the century, American Indians were a decimated, demoralized people. The population had sunk to its lowest ebb because of war, disease and famine. The General Allotment Act of 8 February 1887, as amended by the Act of 2 March 1889,[9] was in full force, and Indian land was being alienated at a constant, rapid pace.

The Act produced internal tribal schisms unlike any previous governmental deed. Detribalization was concomitant with personal demoralization and disintegration. Intertribal communication was slight. The struggle for continued existence inhibited political development.

One exception to the picture of detribalization and the lack of intertribal communication was the political development of the Five Civilized Tribes of Oklahoma, the confederacy established by the Cherokee, Seminole, Chickasaw, Creek and Choctaw. These tribes formed a solid bloc with an aim toward creating a separate Indian state at the time of Oklahoma's admittance to the Union in 1907. Needless to say, the attempt was unsuccessful. The supposedly inviolate Indian Territory of Oklahoma was wrested from the Five Civilized Tribes and the neighbouring tribes by homesteaders who owed their success to the Allotment Act.

This incident, as well as those to follow, shows that for the major part Indian history since the Massacre at Wounded Knee on 29 December 1890 has been written by Congressional legislation. However, its importance for this paper derives from the confederacy itself, the submergence of five tribal identities to a single Indian 'cause'.

In 1907, Congress passed the Burke Act[10] amending the General Allotment Act. Although the amendment was aimed at protecting the Indians from further land losses, it merely added more red tape to the process of alienation. Its worth lay in the fact that it was a step – and perhaps the first federal step – toward improving the lot of the Indians.

Three years later a medical division was established as part of the Bureau of Indian Affairs. This event might be viewed as the first nominal attempt to fulfill portions of provisions extant in treaties made in the eighteenth and nineteenth centuries. Educational provisions in the treaties were ignored by the government. Willard W. Beatty wrote that:

The United States Government is obligated to provide education for its Indian citizens by virtue of almost every treaty which it consummated with the Indian tribes since colonial times.[11]

This responsibility has been tacitly handed over to missionaries and anyone else so inspired.

Actions such as the 1910 medical provision served to keep the elusive dream of treaty fulfillment alive. Several tribes[12] took up collections among their impoverished members in order to hire lawyers, hoping they might be able to win a special Act of Congress allowing them to press their claims. Usually they met with defeat.

With the advent of World War I, Indians pledged their active allegiance to the United States by enlisting by the thousands although they were not subject to the draft. The Iroquois League, humiliated by this exemption, instituted 'selective service'. One might well wonder at this patriotism to the federal government only a quarter-century after the last Indian war, but the fact of its existence remains.

Following World War I, lay organizations became increasingly active in pleading the Indian 'cause'. The first such organizations had been the National Indian Association, founded in 1879, a 'society for improving the conditions of the Indians'. Although this particular group died out, others rose to replace it, such as the Indian Rights Association and the Friends of the Indians. In 1923, the Secretary of the Interior appointed a non-professional Committee of One Hundred to investigate Indian problems. John Collier's American Indian Defense Association was established in 1924 in protest of the Bursum Bill, aimed at taking Pueblo lands.[13] Such actions and publicity brought up an upsurge of public sentiment which culminated in the Curtis Act of 2 June 1924,[14] granting citizenship to all American Indians not yet enfranchised. The rationale offered for this privilege was the excellent record established by Indians during the war.

Under the provisions of the Act, the right to vote and to hold public office was guaranteed by federal stature, although state laws could and often did deny these rights.

Information appears to be lacking as to the attitudes and specific actions of the returning Indian veterans after World War I. Changes such as those which occurred among World War II veterans do not seem to be in evidence. It needs only to be said that Indian political development remained in a nascent state. One observer reasoned that:

> The development of leadership among the Indians has been nullified for the past fifty years because there was no goal for the individual to strive for. . . . The development of leaders was suppressed by the system under which the Indians were governed. There was no chance for development because there was no object in developing – no incentive.[15]

More concisely, D'Arcy McNickle remarked that 'the Indians were dying of legislatively induced anemia.'[16]

In 1926 Secretary of the Interior Herbert Work commissioned another survey which was to become the most enlightened document yet to be seen in Indian affairs. Published in 1928, the Meriam Report was a comprehensive summary of Indian problems, but its greatest value lay in its recommendations. The basic emphasis was on the need for across-the-board education on all age levels.[17] It exposed the low quality of personnel in the Bureau of Indian Affairs (BIA), particularly its field administrations.[18] Recommendations were made for the improvement of the medical service.[19] And, second only to its priority upon education was the suggestion that:

> No evidence warrants a conclusion that the government of the United States can at any time in the near future relinquish its guardianship over the property of restricted Indians, secured to the Indians by government action.[20]

Although it did not say in so many words that land alienation must cease, it did point out that 'the policy of individual
allotment should be followed with extreme conservatism.'[21]

The Meriam Report was never implemented as official
policy. Instead, a third survey was inaugurated by the US
Senate. Herbert Hoover appointed Charles J. Rhodes as Commissioner of Indian Affairs in 1928 with the designated task
of accelerating the assimilation of Indians into the general
society. Termination may have been the ultimate goal, but
the immediate steps involved the expansion of governmental
services in the areas of health, education and welfare. The
Allotment Act was officially abandoned. BIA personnel improved and great advances were made in school construction.

The depression struck the still-destitute Indians with
greater impact than many other groups. The BIA budget
was severely reduced and the recent programs were discon-
tinued.

In 1934, President Roosevelt appointed John Collier as
BIA Commissioner. Collier stood firmly behind the recommendations of the Meriam Report and went further to institute policies unequalled by any administration before or
since. In contrast to the previous BIA emphasis upon ac-
culturating individuals as the means by which to achieve
Indian assimilation, Collier's program was based upon the
assumption that Indian communities should be economically
and otherwise assisted to the point where they might choose
and develop their own patterns of adjustment.[22]

In June of 1934 Roosevelt signed the Howard-Wheeler Act,
otherwise known as the Indian Reorganization Act (or
IRA).[23] Of its many provisions, that which has had the most
lasting effect was the establishment of tribal governments
and corporations by charter. A total of 189 tribes (129,750
Indians) voted to accept this provision of the Act and to set

up tribal governments under it; seventy-seven tribes (86,365 Indians) rejected it. However, not all of the 189 tribes who voted for it actually formed up constitutions.[24] They failed to do so for many reasons, not the least of which was total unfamiliarity with government by constitution. The ramifications of this choice could not have been predicted at that time, but subsequent legislation has placed much emphasis and weight upon the acceptance or rejection of this provision by the tribes.

The policies of the Collier Administration and the Howard-Wheeler Act brought about external pressures for tribal and intertribal communication unknown to that degree in previous history. The very nature of the methods employed by the BIA produced dynamic situations. The usual procedure was to call a regional conference of tribal leaders in order to explain the Act's provisions. What for the BIA was a facilitating technique resulted, in many cases, in the first face-to-face interaction of tribes culturally and geographically remote. What was considered 'regional' to the BIA did not, in fact, correspond to intertribal relations. For example, William R. Zimmerman, Assistant BIA Commissioner, called together a regional group composed of delegates drawn from South Dakota, North Dakota, Minnesota, Wisconsin, Michigan and Iowa. Thus were bands, communities, tribes and subtribes of Sioux, Chippewa, Oneida, Winnebago, Fox, Menominee, Potawatomi, Stockbridge, Munsee and Ottawa brought together to face a mutual problem. Such a situation was theoretically unlikely in aboriginal times and occurred in historic times with such strange heterogeneity only during treaty negotiations between the government and various tribes. The delegates were faced with a proposition the implications of which affected all Indians and were not keyed to specific tribes. Although the response was tribal, the stimulus was universal.

For the first time since the subjugation of the tribes, the burden of responsibility for self-government was placed squarely upon the shoulders of the Indians. Tribal and other groups fused through internal debate. 'A surprising amount of community spirit had survived the generations of attempts to break up the tribes.[25] Leaders of different tribes compared notes freely and frequently, and latent tribal organizations awoke to meet the challenge. The record of acceptance or rejection of the opportunity is less important than the fact that 266 tribes composed of 216,115 Indians grappled with the problem and produced a vote.

Those tribes which accepted the provisions of the Howard-Wheeler Act were then required to formulate their own types of government and constitution. Less than the 189 tribes actually submitted their constitutions, but the more important benefit – that of political consciousness – had been largely achieved.

The remaining years of Collier's BIA administration were encouraging ones for the Indians. The population continued the upswing begun in the early 1900s, more and more land was brought back under trust status, and educational services and medical care reached new dimensions. Restrictive legislation upon the Indians' individual liberties was repealed or drastically modified. In 1938, Indians were granted freedom of religion for the first time.

World War II left Indian legislation at a standstill. The BIA budget was sharply reduced as were the quantity and quality of its personnel. Indians enlisted or were drafted into the Armed Services. As of 1945, 25,000 had served their country. Of these, two received the Congressional Medal of Honor, 51 had received Silver Stars, 70 the Air Medal, 34 the Distinguished Flying Cross and 30 the Bronze Star – an impressive war record for any ethnic group.

The war uprooted Indians as it did other Americans. In

addition to the servicemen, an estimated 40,000 Indians left the reservations for war industries. Others became migratory farm workers.[26] Though statistics are lacking, a certain portion of the migrating workers consisted of whole families, while a larger part was composed of fathers or fathers and mothers who had left the remainder of their families under care on the reservations. This latter group supported those at home in a fashion far surpassing the previous subsistence level they had known.

Acculturation was bound to play heavily upon these scattered Indians, and it did. Literally thousands first really learned English at this time. Furthermore, this was the first time Indians in such numbers had the opportunity to view the non-Indian world at such close quarters. Re-evaluations of personal worth, especially in the services, raised morale to new heights. The relative affluence of the war-workers accustomed them to a vastly higher standard of living. New ideas about health and sanitation were inculcated. And there appeared a renewed interest in education.

For the Indian world perhaps the most significant fringe benefit acquired during the war years was that of leadership training. This applied to both servicemen and war workers. During the years of detribalization and demoralization, there were few incentives to young men in the area of tribal politics. Those who had risen to power in IRA days and the traditional leaders did not encourage or foster the growth of leadership abilities in the successive generations. Despite the flurry of excitement engendered during the early 1930s, the older reasons for this lack of leadership training returned: general ennui, lack of goals beyond mere continued existence, traditionalism, the BIA's vacillating interests and a monolithic five thousand statutes and supplementary regulations governing virtually every phase of Indian tribal and individual life.[27] But because of the off-reservation opportunities in the war years, many young people received on-the-job and formal leadership training which was to prepare them for the problems ahead.

In 1944, the first all-Indian national organization was founded in Denver, Colorado – the National Congress of American Indians. Its membership included tribes and individuals. It chose as its task the dissemination of Indian viewpoints in Washington, and registered as a lobby. In addition, its affiliate, ARROW, Inc., operated as the financial arm and field operations unit.

At the end of the war, the war workers and the veterans returned to the reservations, at least briefly. The intervening years had accomplished more in the way of acculturation than had all previous efforts specifically designed for that purpose. Dissatisfaction with reservation conditions caused thousands to emigrate to the cities. Some reservations became so depleted of population as to leave them totally devoid of tribal organization. Other reservations were crucially overpopulated for the land base available. In the cities, Indians generally found themselves unable to compete in the depressed job market with non-Indians on the basis of skills and education. Indian ghettos developed in most major cities containing the jobless or part-time worker relocatees.

Discontented with second-class citizenship, the young reservation men fought energetically for equality in terms of right to vote, to purchase liquor, and other measures. Their efforts were rewarded when New Mexico, Arizona and Idaho revised their constitutions and statutes to provide for Indian suffrage.

With the establishment of the Indian Claims Commission (ICC) on 13 August 1946, Indians were made eligible to file suits against the government. Any 'identifiable' group of Indians within the US or Alaska could press for adjudication suits arising from (1) claims in law or equity, (2) tort claims, (3) claims based on fraud, duress, unconscionable consideration, mutual or unilateral mistake, (4) claims based on the taking of lands without payment of the agreed compensation and (5) claims based upon fair and honorable dealings not recognized by existing rules of law or equity.[28] The term 'identifiable' caused considerable problems and soon it came to mean almost exclusively those tribes who had become corporations under the IRA in the 1930s. Furthermore, the variety in types of claims under which suits could be filed devolved primarily to treaties and executive orders concerning claims based on the taking of lands without payment of the agreed compensation. Provision was made for review by the Court of Claims, and appeal on questions of law to the Supreme Court.[29] Appropriation of monies for claims adjudication was the responsibility of Congress.

In addition to the stated purposes of the ICC, there were indications that with the settlement of Indian claims the way would be considerably cleared for the withdrawal of federal trust over reservations and individuals. Furthermore, those who believed that old unadjudicated claims lent incentive to Indians to retain tribal membership and residence on the reservations felt that treaty settlements would finally sever this bond.

The establishment of the ICC keyed up the somnolent hopes of treaty fulfillment. Within the five-year period assigned for filing, 852 separate claims were included in 370 petitions entered.[30] The Howard-Wheeler Act in 1934 allowed for tribes to contract with attorneys (subject to capricious BIA approval[31]) and once again the tribes were in business. The Indians expended some $1,000,000 in preparing their claims for trial. Anticipations were high and the Indians back home waited eagerly for their leaders to return from Washington with their long-awaited payments. A few cases were treated and favorably adjudicated, such as the impressive $7,200,000 Mountain Ute recovery. But for the most part, it was a tedious and lengthy process. As of January 1961, only 128 petitions or docket numbers had been finally adjudicated. These awards totalled $37,127,116.25.[32] Hopes for quick recoveries had to be put into greater perspective and Indian patience was called for once again. The ICC, due to its ponderous operating procedures and the vast amounts of material involved, requested and received an extension to the time limit for adjudication in the form of an amendment to Section 23 of the ICC Act.[33] In addition to the above factors, a third reason for the extension was the slowness of the Indians in preparing their cases. Their lawyers were almost as much in the dark as to what they should offer in the way of evidence as were the Indians themselves. Neither did the ICC have any clear notion of what constituted evidence.[34] No real precedents had been laid for this type of action. The ICC often discounted Indian testimony as having any weight whatsoever.[35] Soon the matter was taken from the hands of the Indians and placed solely in those of the lawyers, who were free to compromise and make deals as they could. In the period 1959–60, more than $18,000,000 was awarded 'largely because of compromise settlement'.[36] Again the mysterious processes of the white man's world were closed from viewing.

The use of the anticipated treaty funds became a tribal matter, however. Each eligible tribe was to take a vote of its membership to decide how it would disburse the award. Many Indians clamored for division on a per capita basis, while tribal leaders generally urged a compromise consisting of a token per capita distribution and investment of the remainder in tribal enterprises. For landless tribes, of course, only a per capita distribution was feasible. In later years, the BIA required the tribes to prepare programs for the use of the monies before disbursement.

Another tribal matter was the preparation of the tribal roll. In theory, the tribes established their own eligibility rules, subject to BIA approval. On the other hand, the BIA's 'Patterson Opinion' sanctioned as members those who had one-quarter degree Indian blood, were recognized by the tribe, and who had tribal residence. Except for California, the tribal decisions have generally won out and such variety in distribution as the following has resulted. According to these tribes, a candidate must be:

Crow: one quarter degree blood and having tribal membership as of 23 July 1953

Fort Berthold: any degree of Indian blood providing that seven tribal council members endorse him

Pine Ridge Sioux: born on the reservation and having one parent as a tribal member

Chippewa: a descendant of the 1889 tribal roll

Ute: any degree of blood, on any roll, and having received favorable vote by the membership committee

Ottawa: a descendant of the 1853 tribal roll.

And yet no matter what the rules may be, the formulation of a tribal roll is an expensive, time-consuming task.

House Concurrent Resolution 108 was introduced to the House of Representatives on 9 June 1953, 83rd Congress, 1st Session, by Harrison of Wyoming – the controversial termination policy. It reads in part:

It is the policy of Congress, as rapidly as possible, to make the Indians within the territorial limits of the United States subject to the same laws and entitled to the same privileges and responsibilities as are applicable to other citizens of the United States, to end their status as wards of the United States, and to grant them all the rights and prerogatives pertaining to American citizenship. . . .

This initial statement was riddled with inaccuracies.[37] In actual fact, Congress was not so much interested in making full-fledged citizens out of Indian citizens as it was concerned with cutting down government spending. One of the first targets of the current budget reform was the Department of the Interior, and, more specifically, the BIA. Senator Arthur V. Watkins of Utah felt it high time to 'get the government out of the Indian business'. He sponsored and introduced the Resolution to the Senate. Both Houses endorsed it and termination became official federal policy.

Ten termination bills were introduced during the second session of the 83rd Congress, six of which passed. Senator Watkins was very prominent in most of this action.[38]

The Indian committees in the House and Senate were determined in the 83rd Congress to activate the policy established by Concurrent Resolution 108. . . . It seemed likely to some members, and most clearly to the chairman of the Senate Committee [Watkins] that, if left to themselves, the Indians might postpone indefinitely the time when they would be willing to excuse the United States and agree to go their own way.[39]

Dillon S. Myer, then BIA Commissioner, also favored the Resolution and bills, but the thankless task of scheduling the tribes for termination had fallen to the former Acting Commissioner, William Zimmerman, who had no taste for these policies. The proposed list began: all tribes in California, Florida, New York and Texas; the Flathead, Menominee, Kansas and Nebraska Potawatomi, Turtle Mountain Chippewa, and the Nebraska Omaha and Winnebago. Termination soon began in earnest with the removal of federal trust status over the Menominee, Alabama-Coushattas and the Klamath.

But it quickly became all too clear that passing bills did not necessarily make for acculturated, assimilated Indians. Instead, it threw vast numbers to the not-too-tender mercies of the local and state governments, to say nothing of the general public. The state of Wisconsin was caught with no plans for the assumption of responsibility for the Menominees,[40] and responded by creating a county of the previous reservation area. The Menominees were billed for taxes on their lands immediately and were unable to pay them. They were faced with the problem of paying further fees for fire and police protection, sanitation services, highway maintenance and virtually all the services a county normally provides – and all at once. The Klamath, in order to meet the demands of termination exigencies, lost $32 million in timber sales almost overnight. Despite a huge per capita payment in 1958, many Klamath were soon on welfare, their money spent.[41] Simply, the Klamath as well as other tribes had not achieved an economic sophistication which would allow them to function adequately without federal supervision.

The termination legislation sounded like a death knell to all Indians, reservation and non-reservation alike. It rang as the finale to the remnants of an Indian homeland, a way of life and a heritage. Alarm was universal. After its initial impact, however, the Indians went into action. The NCAI called an emergency conference and drew up a resolution wherein it requested that consent of the tribes would be required before such legislation could be enacted. Tribal and intertribal meetings proliferated. Protest after protest from Indians and non-Indians assailed the government. Finally, Secretary of the Interior Fred A. Seaton in 1958 made a statement endorsing a 'consent' clause, although he made it clear that termination would remain as official policy.

The actions of Congress compelled the tribes to analyze their ability to survive if and when terminated. Older leaders stepped aside or were replaced by young progressives whose knowledge of the non-Indian world was required now more than ever. The *modus operandi* of many of the new leaders was decidedly of different type than that of their predecessors. The earlier 'conservative' syndrome of protest-rejection—dejection was replaced; the younger men knew how to haggle, prepare alternative plans and compromise. Indian politics changed character almost overnight.

On 12 June 1961, several hundred Indians from 210 tribes congregated at the American Indian Chicago Conference, called by the University of Chicago. It became a demonstration of young dynamic leadership. A Declaration of Indian Purpose was drawn up for presentation to Congress. Simultaneously, President Kennedy called a halt to termination, at least temporarily. The news was greeted by the AICC participants with joy, then cautious relief. The presidential decision probably had at base the results of the Task Force on Indian Affairs and a summary report by the Commission of the Rights, Liberties, and Responsibilities of the American Indian, both prepared earlier in the year. At any rate, the pressure for immediate termination was gone, allowing Indian political energies to concentrate on other needful projects.

The AICC provided a valuable opportunity for Indians to meet, learn and work in seven days of intense interaction. At the outset, each tribe was prepared to do battle for its own personal aims; by meeting's end, virtually all were working as Indians first and tribal members second.

Another AICC product was the meeting of college students and recent graduates not yet in leadership positions in their tribes, who had come as observers. Several had attended the Workshop on American Indian Affairs, sponsored by the non-profit corporation American Indian Development, Inc. The Workshop, begun in 1956, provides a concentrated six-week summer study on Indian affairs keyed primarily to college students.

The meeting of the student and recent graduate group resulted in the establishment in August 1961 of the National Indian Youth Council. The NIYC was designed basically as a service organization, a forum for ideas and a site for leadership training – training which had gone into eclipse again since the war years.

In September 1961 the NCAI elected a new slate of officers mostly from the ranks of progressive AICC voices and the organization took on a more aggressive character than before. It chose Public Law 83-280 as its immediate target. PL 280 conferred upon certain states all civil and criminal jurisdiction over reservation Indians. It was viewed as another termination step. Considering it 'contrary to American principles of democracy and self-determination to impose jurisdiction on any people without their consent',[42] the NCAI pressed for an amendment or amendments to the law which would require consent of the tribes involved before such action was taken. President Eisenhower, at the time of the bill's signing, also felt the law to be out of keeping with American traditions and described it as 'a most unchristian-like approach' to the problem.[43] However, PL 280 remains on the books at this writing although several amendments[44] have been proposed and are still pending.

In 1962 new attention was brought to the problem of fractionated heirship, the result of the old Allotment Act. Now, as many as one hundred descendants can be found sharing original 80- or 160-acre allotments. Among the Kiowa-Apache, for instance, it is not rare for a set of twenty to thirty individuals to own and attempt to live off 80 acres of virtually worthless land. The shares are frequently split into strange fractions: one individual owns 2889/12150s of half the mineral rights on an 80-acre plot.[45] Several bills have been introduced into Congress[46] in an attempt to grapple with the problem but no panacea has yet been found.

The Senate Subcommittee on Constitutional Rights launched an inquiry into Indian problems in 1961 and by mid 1962 it had uncovered chaotic situations during the course of its regional hearings, particularly in South Dakota and Arizona.[47] Preliminary findings showed that Indians frequently lacked knowledge concerning even their most basic liberties as citizens. The full report was to come later, though.

In March 1963 the Pine Ridge Reservation was the recipient of 51 new low-rent homes provided by the US Public Housing Administration, and obtained mainly through the efforts of the NCAI. Learning that low-rent housing and a mutual-help housing program were also available to them, several other tribes filed applications with the USPHA. However, the process being slow and the housing problem so acute, these efforts could only begin to answer the needs. At present, the USPHA has announced that 3,300 dwelling units have 'been set aside for the reservations'.[48] As the wording implies, most of the housing is still in the planning stage.

The reservations have been in economic trouble for more than a century in spite of one scheme after another. But clearly, one answer became available with the introduction by Representative Berry (South Dakota) of H.R. 980 in the 88th Congress. The bill, 'Operation Bootstrap', provided for tax and other inducements to industry to locate on reservations. But it received an unfavorable report from the Department of the Interior and the Treasury. Many Indian people, having been alerted to this bill by the NCAI and other agencies, viewed its career with dismay.

In 1963 the matter of civil rights affected Indians as well as other Americans. Discrimination occurred in several areas, being more frequent where the Indian population was large in proportion to the whole. Both the NCAI and the

NIYC issued statements endorsing the sentiments of the Civil Rights measures.

In March 1964 the NIYC was called to the aid of forty-plus tribes in Washington State in their running battle with the Fish and Wildlife Department. The state had not only abrogated the fishing rights portions of the US-tribal treaties but had also instituted a vigorous campaign to jail and/or fine all Indians caught fishing even in their 'usual and accustomed places' as defined by treaty. This state action impinged heavily upon the livelihood of countless Indians. The state maintained that Indian fishing was depleting the streams. The Indians charged that stream depletion was brought on by the logging industries' tearing up of the stream beds, the chemical companies' dumping of waste into the streams, the damming up of the waterways and the multi million dollar sportsmen's fishing enterprise. Unofficial US Conservation Department surveys tended to side with the Indians' charges. But the issue that concerned tribes throughout America was the question, 'can states unilaterally abrogate treaties contracted between the federal government and the Indian tribes?' (PL 280 was a side issue as well.)

The NIYC with the help of the movie star, Marlon Brando, the Rev. John J. Yaryan of the Grace Episcopal Cathedral of San Francisco, the Civil Liberties Union and the NCAI, staged a protest demonstration which succeeded only in clarifying the situation concerning the fishing rights. Arrests and fining resumed shortly after the incident.

And yet, the demonstration was by no means a total failure; indeed, it was most heartening to many observers, mainly the Indians themselves, for a secondary result. It was the first time in recorded history that that many tribes in Washington (or possibly anywhere else, for that matter) had joined in such a concerted effort to resolve a specific problem. The protest received support from the Indian organizations already mentioned as well as from many tribes across the nation.

Another problem came to a climax soon after the Washington matter. The construction of the Kinzua Dam on the Allegany Reservation in New York threatened to flood out nine tenths of the Seneca land guaranteed by the Pickering Treaty of 1794.[49] With the aid of the Friends Indian Committee, the Senecas had been protesting the dam for years. Apparently unable to stop the US Corps of Engineers by any means whatever, the Senecas hoped that the government would do the next best thing: that is, pay them for the land which was to be flooded in order that they might begin construction on new homes, roads, churches, schools and other community buildings to replace those soon to be inundated. A conflict developed between the House and Senate Subcommittees on Indian Affairs to the effect that the Seneca reparation and rehabilitation bills came to a stalemate, the House version of the bill being the more liberal. The Senate Bill called for termination. The NIYC and tribes across the nation joined voices first in protesting the dam and then against the stalling of the bills and the threat of termination. They feared that termination would be revived and they also suspected that the construction of dams was to be a new means for alienating Indian land. Ultimately, in August, a compromise of the Joint Committee resolved upon a median figure plus termination.

The 'War on Poverty' certainly concerned the Indians. On 13 February 1964, BIA Commissioner Philleo Nash issued the following statements:

1. Unemployment on the reservations runs between 40 and 50 per cent – seven or eight times the national average.

2. Family income on the reservations averages between one fourth and one third the national average.

3. Nine out of ten Indian families live in housing that is far

below minimum standards of comfort, safety, and decency.

4. Average schooling of young adults on the reservations is only eight years – two thirds of the national average.

5. The average age at death on the reservation is 42 years, two thirds the figure for the national population.[50]

When the War on Poverty began to mobilize, Indians found that they were sixth on a list of six areas requiring immediate attention. The Council on Indian Affairs, an organization of Indian and non-Indian groups, called the American Indian Capital Conference on Poverty on 9–12 May 1964. Both the NCAI and the NIYC as well as many tribal organizations sent delegates to participate. They examined and made recommendations upon all phases of Indian life related to the problem, such as education, employment, health, housing and community mobilization.

'Operation Bootstrap' reappeared briefly as a proposed amendment to the Civil Rights Bill, but again it met defeat.

An interesting case of 'turning the tables' occurred when Mr Amos Hopkins-Dukes, a Kiowa, filed for an allotment under the provisions of the old Allotment Act which, though virtually forgotten, was still in effect. He and others now viewed the bill as a possible vehicle by which Indians could acquire land from public domain sources.[51] However, the Department of the Interior took a dim view of this idea and the matter will now be determined in the courts.

In recent years, the number of state Indian commissions designed to handle internal problems has increased. In 1964 Minnesota and Michigan were added to the list, the latter having been prompted primarily by the efforts of the NIYC. The roster now includes Arizona, California, Michigan, Minnesota, Montana, New Mexico and North Dakota. In September, the 17th Annual Convention of the Governors' Interstate Indian Council met in Denver to compare problems and procedures and to formulate new attacks within the scope of state jurisdiction.

The 1964 NCAI convention in September produced new evidences of intertribal and intergeneration unanimity with the election of the NIYC's Vine Deloria, Jr, as its executive director. There appeared a fusing of philosophy within the Indian word heretofore lacking. Later in the year, there were indications that further consolidations within the Indian political sphere were in the offing. Furthermore, Indian affairs took on an international flavor when, at the NIYC board meeting in December, Canadian Indians were represented by tribal delegates from every province except Saskatchewan.

The election year brought Indian political activity contrasting sharply with previous indifference. The Mescalero, Jicarilla-Apache, Navajo and five New Mexico pueblos issued a joint statement supporting the candidate of their choice. In Nevada, much interest centered upon the proposed Washo Drainage Project. Rallies were held and tribal voters turned up at the polls on 3 November in impressive numbers. The matter of PL 280 brought South Dakota Indians to vote and the issue was soundly defeated. Not only were several Indians throughout the nation actual candidates for office, but for the first time in such proportions, non-Indians actively sought the 'Indian vote'.

The issuance of the Subcommittee on Constitutional Rights' Summary Report was the final major event in 1964 affecting Indians. Its recommendations and observations brought to light such matters as denials of due process and equal protection of the law, complex legal difficulties, arbitrary decision-making by the BIA, job discrimination by Federal and State agencies and private businesses and the like. On the matter of PL 280, the Subcommittee recommended that –

the consent of the United States should be given to any State to assume, in whole or in part, civil and or criminal jurisdiction over Indian reservations, provided that the Indian tribes involved consent. The Congress should further authorize the United States to accept a retrocession by any State of any civil or criminal jurisdiction.[52]

Concerning tribal sovereignty, it noted that

although tribal power has been defined and limited by acts of Congress, the subcommittee's investigation revealed that the broad interpretation and administration of the guardianship power of the Secretary of the Interior has been used to thwart the development of meaningful tribal self-government.[53]

And, noting that 'a fundamental cause of the entire Indian problem – the lack of education – has long been evident', the Subcommittee offered the view that

until such time as the Indian does receive the education which adequately meets his needs, we cannot expect him to make an appreciable contribution to his progress and the Nation's.[54]

To close this section, a few words concerning Peyotism might be in order. The Peyote religion is the main present-day religion of more than fifty tribes from California to Michigan. Considerable difficulties have arisen for its adherents through their use of peyote (*Lophophora williamsii*), a non-habit-forming cactus product containing a mild hallucinogenic substance called mescaline. Recently, the Supreme Court of California set aside the conviction of three Navajo Indian peyotists arrested during a traditional religious ritual. The Supreme Court ruled that 'to forbid the use of peyote is to remove the heart of peyotism' and so infringes the principle of religious freedom.[55] Further litigation is pending in several states but peyotists and their sympathizers hope that the religious freedom granted to American Indians in 1938 will continue to be upheld in terms of the Native American Church and the Peyote religion.

FACTORS IN INDIAN NATIONALISM

In order to examine the morphology of the contemporary Indian world and its stage of evolution, it will be necessary to inspect some of its more complex elements.

As an economic asset, reservation land is generally too poor or underdeveloped to provide anything but meager subsistence for its users. Thus off-reservation wage work is often vital. This kind of employment provides several building blocks for socio-political development.

1. Off-reservation wage work obviously provides money, thus increasing financial stability.

2. Off-reservation wage work brings about knowledge of the non-Indian world; the most important benefits are 'learning the ropes' of white economic practices and recognizing the need for more formal education.

3. This newly-acquired knowledge when applied to reservation life usually takes the form of material items, but it is also manifested in the use of more general economic techniques and in the encouragement of child education.

4. The relative financial stability, allowing for free time away from economic pursuits, permits the growth and evolution of the socio-political consciousness.

Economic development on the reservations is increasing steadily, though slowly. Tribal enterprises provide internal cohesion as well as employment. This too leads to more tribal awareness and tribally oriented activities.

With increased family financial stability, more attention can be given over to tribal affairs, as we have seen. Tribal council members, now seldom BIA figureheads, are more integrated with, and representative of, the reservation populations and are more involved with their economic, educational, and political development. Furthermore, the councils are often assuming BIA functions. To name a few, they plan and operate tribal enterprises, assume responsibilities in education, and intervene between the reservation people and non-Indians as need be.

Individual financial stability plus tribal capital derived from ICC adjudications and tribal operations provide an economic base for the development of extra-tribal considerations. In addition, the increase in the number of educated individuals adds more trained resources to activities undertaken along these lines.

As we have seen, the socially and financially strengthened tribal councils are now actively participating in local, state and national politics. Intertribal cooperation is increasing, notably in Arizona, New Mexico and Nevada. There is also considerable political activity among tribal members not in council positions, as exemplified by the NIYC membership in general (although several have become tribal council members since 1961). Supplemental to these two groups are the large numbers of off-reservation and relocatee Indians who contribute their efforts on behalf of the Indian people as a whole. The off-reservation political group is made up of college organizations, city Indian community centers and clubs, and, of course, non-affiliated individuals.

All this collective interest and activity is encouraged as communication between tribes, groups and individuals is increased. Communication is effected in numerous ways. Individual mobility has increased considerably. Pow-wows and ceremonials bring about interaction to a significant degree, as do meetings of Indian clubs, regional and national organizations and the growing Indian sports leagues. Tribal and other newspapers, newsletters and the like facilitate extra-tribal awareness and exchange. Even the 'Indian grapevine' or 'moccasin telegraph', a highly developed institution, plays an important part in the communication network. And, not to be overlooked, the English language has provided the primary means by which intertribal communication has been made possible.

The first result of this communication has been the comparison of individual and tribal problems throughout the nation's Indian population. This plus the realization of the similarities in philosophy and goals has brought about a strong sense of commonality. Thus has Indian identity above and beyond tribal identity been evolved and fostered. A large part of the meaningful innovations in the Indian world in recent years has been initiated by intertribal unity. These successes, in turn, have encouraged further intertribal or nationalistic activities.

The general goals of Indian nationalism are: (1) increased education of all kinds on all age levels, (2) improved health and general welfare, (3) retention of land base and accumulation of more land, (4) economic development on the reservations, (5) true rather than nominal tribal sovereignty, (6) assumption of BIA functions as the individual tribes reach the necessary level of development required to do so, (7) greater political solidarity and strength in order to exert significant control over their affairs and (8) maintenance and development of Indian culture.

Certainly these goals are intimately related one to another. The sum total is no more or no less than the goals of non-Indian municipalities throughout America with which the reservations should be equated. The one, and perhaps only, important difference between the two is the desire of the Indian people to maintain and develop their own culture. It can be argued that with the acquisition of the first seven goals, acculturation will have negated (8). The possibility of this happening has occurred to many participants in Indian nationalism. No final answer can be offered, but the persistence of the traits next to be discussed may provide the threads for cultural continuity within an evolving framework.

One constant within the Indian world is the importance placed upon the extended family as the basic social unit. In this, it contrasts strikingly with the 'typical American' nuclear family, which consists of independent couples and their offspring. The extended family is a major and persistent cultural difference between Indians and non-Indians.

As the economic level of the Indian people rises, the extended family is strengthened despite the loss of some members through relocation. It has withstood countless small- and large-scale attempts to destroy it. Furthermore, the extended family constitutes the basic building block of tribal organization and its strength is directly related to tribal viability. Today family and tribal organization reinforce each other as they have in the past.

As a second factor of cultural persistence, no little importance must be placed upon the role of Indian land itself. It is both a tangible and intangible base for Indian uniqueness within the surrounding non-Indian world. As a physical entity, it constitutes a habitation site and an economic source. Its intrinsic value is that of providing a focal point for Indian culture and identity – to all intents and purposes, a homeland – for both reservation and nonreservation Indians.

Given the elements of land, extended family system and tribal identity, what can be said about the future of tribalism? John Provinse and others at the Conference on the American Indians Today agreed that:

Despite external pressures, and internal change, most of the present identifiable Indian groups residing on reservations (areas long known to them as homelands) will continue indefinitely as distinct social units, preserving their basic values, personality, and Indian way of life, while making continual adjustments, often superficial in nature, to the economic and political demands of the larger society.[56]

Alexander Lesser has stated that:

It has become increasingly probable that many of the communities that have endured are likely to be with us for a long and indefinite future unless radical or brutal measures are taken to disorganize and disperse them.[57]

The changes that have occurred are of a highly selective nature. Tribes and their individual members have chosen elements of non-Indian material culture and technology but have retained their Indian orientation to the world in the realm of values and philosophy. What might seem to be cultural ambiguity or dual-culturalism appears to result in a reintegration, an evolved political development described by John Collier as 'emergent social-economic political forms which are predictive of a future world not totalitarian and not ravenous-capitalistic'.[58]

The survival and florescence of tribalism ultimately fosters and encourages the development of Indian nationalism. In the recognition of intertribal commonalty which only tribal stability can truly accord, Indian political development will warrant and perhaps demand the right of self-determination. But neither tribalism nor nationalism are of themselves the philosophic goal of the American Indians. What is distinctly Indian and its most annealing factor has been best drawn by John Collier who said,

These ancient men in their ancient societies are striving with concentrated and confident will *toward physical survival and victory only as a means to an end*; the end is spiritual survival and victory, and 'spiritual' means that mystical fire which the universe, they believe, entrusted to them in a past time which must not die. The fire, they believe, even contains the inmost significance of the universe.[59]

Notes

1. C. T. Loram and T. F. McIlwraith, eds., *The North American Indian Today* (Toronto, 1943), Introduction.

2. Felix S. Cohen, 'The Erosion of Indian Rights', *The Yale Law Journal*, LXII, 3 (February 1953), 348.

3. US Department of the Interior, Office of the Solicitor, *Federal Indian Law* (Washington: Government Printing Office, 1958), 407.

4. ibid.

5. See Howard H. Peckham, *Pontiac and the Indian Uprising* (Princeton, 1947), 320, for an additional evaluation of Joseph Brant, Little Turtle, Pontiac and Tecumseh.

6. Henry Adams, *History of the United States of America during the First Administration of James Madison*, II, 67–89. Quoted in Wilcomb E. Washburn, ed., *The Indian and the White Man* (New York, 1964), 363.

7. Alvin M. Josephy, Jr, *The Patriot Chiefs* (New York, 1961), 29.

8. Benjamin Franklin, 'Smiths Instead of Jesuits', in *The Papers of Benjamin Franklin* (New Haven, 1961), IV, 118.

9. 24 Stat. 388–91, c. 119; 25 Stat. 890–99, c. 405.

10. 34 Stat. 1018, c. 2285.

11. Willard W. Beatty, 'Indian Education in the United States', in Loram and McIlwraith, op. cit., 275.

12. e.g. *Phineas Pam-to-pee, et al vs. US*, No. 21, 300 (1904).

13. D'Arcy McNickle, *They Came Here First* (Philadelphia and New York, 1949), 287–8.

14. 43 Stat. 253, c. 233.

15. William V. Woehlke, US Bureau of Indian Affairs (mimeographed text of speech delivered at Hayward, Wisconsin, 23 April 1934), 11.

16. McNickle, *They Came Here First*, 300.

17. Institute for Government Research, *The Problem of Indian Administration* (Baltimore, 1928), 21.

18. ibid., 23.

19. ibid., 25.

20. ibid., 47.

21. ibid., 41.

22. Edward H. Spicer, *Cycles of Conquest* (Tucson, 1962), 584.

23. 48 Stat. 984–8, c. 576; 49 Stat. 1967–8, c. 831.

24. John Collier, 'Politics and Problems in the United States', in Loram and McIlwraith, *Indians Today*, 144.

25. Alvin M. Josephy, Jr (ed.), *The American Heritage Book of Indians* (New York, 1961), 409.

26. Harold E. Fey and D'Arcy McNickle, *Indians and Other Americans* (New York), 149.

27. *Federal Indian Law*, 1.

28. ibid., 357.

29. ibid.

30. Arthur V. Watkins, et al., 'Recent Data on Indian Claims' (Report to the US House of Representatives, Washington D.C., 18 January 1961).

31. US Congress, Senate, Committee on the Judiciary, *Constitutional Rights of the American Indians*, Summary Report of Hearings and Investigations before Subcommittee, 88th Cong., 2nd Sess. (Washington: Government Printing Office), 18–20, 23.

32. Watkins, 'Recent Data'.

33. 'Sec. 23. The existence of the Commission shall terminate at the end of Ten years from and after April 10, 1962, or at such earlier time as the Commission shall have made its final report to the Congress on all claims filed with it. . . .'

34. See *Hannahville Indian Community v. US*, Dockets L, M, O, P (Testimony taken in ICC hearings, Washington, D.C., 6–12 May 1963).

35. ibid.

36. Watkins, 'Recent Data'.

37. McNickle, *They Came Here First*, 137.

38. See US Congress, Senate and House, Committees on Interior and Insular Affairs, Joint Hearings before Subcommittee, 83rd Cong., 2nd Sess., on S. 2745 and H.R. 7320 (Washington: Government Printing Office), Parts 4, 4-a.

39. Fey and McNickle, *Indians and Other Americans*, 141.

40. William T. Hagan, *American Indians* (Chicago, 1961), 163.

41. Fey and McNickle, *Indians and Other Americans*, 139–47.

42. *Congressional Record*, 21 September 1962, 19161.

43. ibid.

44. S. 143 (Metcalf, Mansfield; Montana) and H.R. 2104 (Olson; Montana).

45. Unpublished field notes extracted from BIA records, Anadrako Area Office, Oklahoma, 1964.

46. S. 1757 (Mansfield, Metcalf; Montana) and H.R. 5464 (Haley; Florida).

47. *Constitutional Rights* (see note 31), 10 ff.

48. J. Wagner Carruth and Erwin S. Rabeau, *Indian Poverty and Indian Health*, US Department of Health, Education, and Welfare (Washington, 1964), xxix.

49. US Congress, House Committee on Interior and Insular Affairs, *Kinzua Dam (Seneca Indian Relocation)*, Hearings before Sub-committee, 88th Cong., 1st Sess., on H.R. 1794, H.R. 3343 and H.R. 7354, 18 May–10 December 1963 (Washington: Government Printing Office, 1964), 16 ff.

50. US Department of Interior Press Release, 14 February 1964.

51. News item in *Indian Voices* (The University of Chicago), April 1964, 1.

52. *Constitutional Rights* (see note 31), 23.

53. ibid., 1.

54. ibid., 22.

55. Weston La Barre, 'The "Diabolic Root" ', *The New York Times Magazine*, 1 November 1964, 96.

56. John Provinse, et al., 'The American Indian in Transition', *American Anthropologist*, LVI, 3 (June 1954), 389.

57. Alexander Lesser, 'Education and the Future of Tribalism in the United States', *The Social Service Review*, XXXV, 2 (June 1961), 4.

58. John Collier, *Patterns and Ceremonial of the Indians of the Southwest* (New York, 1949), 23–4.

59. ibid., 30.

ROBERT K. THOMAS

PAN-INDIANISM

PAN-INDIANISM, as we use the term in anthropology, is an extremely complex and ever growing social phenomenon. It is seen differently by different people in different parts of the country. As an anthropologist, I feel comfortable dealing with social process which is firmly rooted in the small community, but such a complex social movement as Pan-Indianism, which takes in so much territory spatially and temporally, is a little beyond our methodology in anthropology and my competence. The best I can hope to do in this paper is to pick up the main threads of this social movement, to present fleeting vignettes of its historical development and to offer some ideas about its present breadth and direction.

The basis for this paper is field work done in a Sac and Fox community of central Oklahoma in 1956 and among the Pine Ridge Sioux of South Dakota in 1958. Field work in the Southwest and among the Oklahoma Cherokee has added significantly to an understanding of the limits and spread of Pan-Indianism. However, much of the material in this paper comes from more impressionistic contacts with American Indian groups – intimate involvement in Indian affairs for quite a number of years, extended visits to many American Indian communities, participation as a member at the Chicago Indian Center and the like. In a sense, this paper is an attempt to systematize many impressions, experiences and insights. Needless to say, there are many gaps in my knowledge of the Pan-Indian movement.

One can legitimately define Pan-Indianism as the expression of a new identity and the institutions and symbols which are both an expression of that new identity and a fostering of it. It is the attempt to create a new ethnic group, the American Indian; it is also a vital social movement which is forever changing and growing. But first let us look at its historic roots.

At contact, most American Indians lived in small closed tribal groups. In terms of Robert Redfield's folk urban continuum, which provides cultural criteria along a range of 'ideal types' from simply organized, isolated, preliterate societies, to complex, literate societies, one could say that most American Indian tribes were very close to the folk end of the scale.[1] They conceived of those outside of their group as a different order of being, almost a different species. Most American Indians who still have a closed, bounded tribal outlook refer to themselves as 'people', not 'The People', as many anthropologists have translated this term. They mean simply 'persons'. Other tribes are referred to by specific names, but the name for their own society and the name we could best translate in English as 'human being' is the same.

By the time of first contact with Europeans, certain tribes of North America seemed to be widening their conception of who they were in relation to others. This was particularly true in the Southwest and the East. In the Southwest the evidence is not conclusive, but one would suspect from the level of technology and social organization that these tribes were not so closed and bounded, and that particularly in the Pueblo area the extensive trade between peoples had produced a widening of their conception of themselves.

In the eastern part of North America by the 1600s the evidence is fairly conclusive that people in these tribes were beginning to conceive of those from other tribal societies as at least half-way human beings. At contact there was wholesale institutional adoption of captives from other tribes, and, at the very least, incipient confederacies were forming which included tribes which spoke different languages. One can get a clue to this widening conception by looking at the terms tribes apply to themselves and to others. For instance, the Iroquois call themselves by a term which is best translated, 'men of men', implying, of course, that there were other men although they were the best. The Cherokees refer to themselves as 'real human beings', implying at least that there were other human beings in the world, although the Cherokees were the 'realest'. In Cherokee the term for 'European', at least as early as the 1730s means simply 'white people' or 'white human beings'.

Although tribal groups in the East were coming to define others outside their groups as human beings, there was as yet no conception of 'Indian'. To the Cherokee, Englishmen and Creeks were, although human beings, simply different kinds of outsiders. As one examines the historical record in the 1700s, it is clear that tribal groups in the East were beginning to see themselves as having something in common together as opposed to the Europeans. In speeches chiefs would comment on the general style of life in common among tribal groups in that area as opposed to Europeans, and more and more Indians began to have a common interest in opposing the white man. The final outcome of this trend was the political alliance of midwestern tribes in 1763 and the accompanying Pan-Indian religious movement. Later, in the early part of the 1800s, a similar movement led by Tecumseh involved even a larger number of eastern tribes.

In the mid 1800s when the eastern tribes were pushed to the edge of the Plains into what is now Kansas and Oklahoma, even larger political alliances came into being. Great inter-tribal councils were held constantly in this period, and included not only the recently displaced eastern tribes but the native Plains tribes as well.[2]

However, it is on the Plains that we find the historic roots of modern Pan-Indianism. The horse not only enabled Plains Indians to become extremely mobile in hunting and 'warfare', but also increased inter-tribal contacts. Even a sign language developed in the area to provide communication across linguistic boundaries. In the 1800s not only had intensive 'warfare' and very mobile hunting developed, but tribes were beginning to ally with one another, camp together and intermarry. Most significant for the later development of Pan-Indianism, the Plains style of life was extremely attractive to tribes on the edges of the Plains area. Plains traits and institutions were spreading to other areas even at the time that Plains Indians were becoming pacified and settled on reservations. Indeed, the Plains style of life was very attractive to American Indians completely outside of the Plains area. This is one of the historic sources and causes of what is generally referred to as 'Pan-Indianism' which I am suggesting now is in some degree an extension of the Plains culture area.

By 1870 Indian policy had entered what is referred to as 'the reservation period'. By then, most of the Plains tribes were settled on reservations and were undergoing an intensive forced assimilation program. Further, Plains Indians had closer, more intensive contact with whites than other American Indian groups. The majority of young Indians in boarding school came from the Plains area. Whites were defining Sioux and Cheyenne on the reservations and in boarding schools as 'Indians', and, as most of you know, the white conception of Indian is the feathered Plains Indian. The reservation system was at its extreme among these tribes, and pressure for assimilation was very strong. Indians began to find comfort in each other's presence in order to bolster their identity, not only in boarding school, but in inter-tribal visiting. The extreme spatial mobility of the

Plains Indians is a very important factor in the rise of Pan-Indianism. Plains Indians think nothing of traveling hundreds of miles to attend celebrations at other Indian communities. In modern times, this mobility has fostered Pan-Indianism. And because Plains Indians come in contact with many social groups other than Indians in their travels, they have become urbane and sophisticated tribal people. In this process not only is their identity as 'Indians' strengthened, but a conception of themselves as generalized human beings, in particular American, has developed.

I am suggesting two things: first, that modern Pan-Indianism had its roots in a developing commonalty that American Indians began to conceive of particularly in the Plains area; second, that this commonalty was brought to a head by the reservation system, in the way whites related to different tribes as 'Indians' and by the pressure for assimilation which pushed Indians closer together.

The result of all this was a Pan-Indian religion, the Ghost Dance, which swept the Plains area in the nineties. Somewhat later, the Peyote movement followed the same course. Both of these movements were paradoxically spread by the institution of the boarding school.

By 1900 the Sioux Indian was a Sioux and he was an 'Indian'. Further, the symbols of being a Sioux and being an 'Indian' were consistent with one another. By the mid part of the twentieth century, there had been a general cultural leveling in the Plains areas. Almost every tribal group has pow-wows, a pow-wow committee, a women's club and a veterans' organization. There is much visiting among tribal groups, intermarriage, and fictive kin relations across tribal lines. In western Oklahoma, for instance, there is so much intermarriage and inter-tribal activity that Indian languages are ceasing to become the daily language, and English, as the *lingua franca*, is fast replacing the native tongues.

Pan-Indianism

These Plains institutions and trails spread east and west, particularly into the Plateau area and into the Great Lakes country, having reached out to these bordering tribes even in the 1800s. With the advent of the new identity of 'Indian' that was developing all over the country, these institutions and traits spread more rapidly and were acceptable symbols of 'Indianness' to many groups.

In some tribes such as the Sac and Fox of Iowa and the Yakima of Washington, Plains traits and institutions as symbols of Indianness came to exist side by side with older local aboriginal institutions and traits. In other areas, such as northeastern Oklahoma and New England, where local aboriginal traits had disappeared, Pan-Indian, or 'Pan-Plains', as one could call them, institutions and traits became *the* institutions and traits of the community. In some of these latter tribes, as in New England or even in some of the Paiute groups, Pan-Indian traits and institutions which in fact conflict with the basic ethos of the tribes are taken on because they are of such symbolic comfort and reinforcement for identity as Indians.

Even national Indian organizations such as the National Congress of American Indians are in flavor Pan-Plains. It is from the Plains that the National Congress of American Indians gets most of its support, and if one attends its conventions, one sees that the symbols of Indianness are Pan-Plains symbols. There are 'Indian Dances' nearly every night.

I think, in short, that Pan-Indianism consists of two complementary processes. On the one hand, traits and institutions of the Plains area have come to symbolize a new identity of 'Indian' for many aboriginal tribal groups in the United States. In the Plains area itself, where this conception of 'Indian' is possibly the strongest, a general exchange of traits and institutions and a cultural leveling has taken place. Plains tribes are coming to look more and more alike, in so far as specific traits go. These Plains traits and institutions have diffused to other tribal groups outside of the Plains area because they express this new 'Indianness'. In some tribes these traits exist side by side with older aboriginal forms. In other tribes where aboriginal traits have disappeared, these new symbols of 'Indianness' are *the* distinctive traits of the community. On the other hand, I am suggesting that this new identity sets up a new structure of interaction among individuals of differing tribal groups. Although local identification may be as strong as the new conception of being 'Indian', social consequences follow from this structure. The disappearance of the native language, except for ceremonial occasions, in small tribes in Oklahoma is just such a consequence. Secularization may yet be another social and cultural consequence.

In the last decade, American Indians have moved to urban centers and Pan-Indian communities are forming around Indian centers in some of our larger cities. In most cases, the tone for the activities at these centers is set by people who have had previous experiences in Pan-Indian – that is, Pan-Plains – activities, and these symbols become symbols of a forming Indian community in the city. This causes many of the members of the tribes from the Southwest and from eastern Oklahoma to avoid these Indian centers; in some cases, the center breaks into factions on this basis. Many of the people from these tribal groups outside of the Pan-Plains area do not see these symbols as 'Indian', but as in fact 'Plains', and these symbols are unacceptable to them as expressions of their new Indian identity. They tend to be less pragmatic than their fellow tribesmen in the National Congress of American Indians.

There are two very large concentrations of Indians who, as whole social groups, still have a modified closed tribal outlook. They are found in the Southwest and in eastern Oklahoma, but modern urban influences are pressing in on these tribes very fast, especially in the Southwest. The few marginal people from tribes in eastern Oklahoma who begin to get a conception of themselves as Indian tend to leave the tribe at least socially and move into urban centers, to interact with other Pan-Plains Indians or at least functionally to become part of the western Oklahoma Indian community. In this area of eastern Oklahoma, it is the children of Indian people from small towns, and the children of recent intertribal intermarriage, who follow this route.[3]

The Southwest seems to be more complicated. (For one thing, there has been a kind of 'Pan-Puebloism' in the Southwest for many years now.) Young people with a conception of themselves as Indian in this area can join modified Pan-Plains urban communities in the Southwest, become involved in a local nationalistic movement such as we see among the Navajo, or become part of the Pan-Traditional movement. This last is a recent alliance between the traditional factions of some of the Southwestern and Eastern Woodland tribes.[4] For many years now tribes in these two areas have been split into two opposing factions, one oriented toward the traditional way of life, and the other toward the outside. Membership in these factions has almost become hereditary; family names many times indicate whether a person is a member of one or the other. Over the years the traditional factions, in their resistance, have become very conscious, very aware and very ideological. In recent years the traditional factions of the Seminole, the Iroquois and the Hopi have joined forces, and now there is a new social type arisen on the American scene, the 'traditional Indian'.

So far this paper has dealt very little with the nationalistic flavor of Pan-Indianism which is becoming so evident in recent years. More and more of American Indian leadership is becoming nationalistically Indian. Nationalism has not yet affected the local Indian community, but it is certainly strong among the tribal 'elite'. There seems to be a general disillusionment among American Indian leaders regarding their own personal acceptance in the general American society and doubts about the kinds of relationships their people can have with that society. Nowhere is that attitude more pronounced than among Indians, particularly young Indian college students, who are actively organizing. Indian Clubs and Indian Youth Councils are very much part of the campus scene at those colleges where there are appreciable numbers of Indian students. And they are very angry young people. They see colonial peoples all over the world emerging as nations and they see many of the minorities in the United States being granted concessions by the general society, but when they look at the American Indian situation they see poverty, a low rank position for most, the destinies of their home communities controlled by forces outside of the community, and what they perceive as an inert Indian leadership is doing nothing about the problem. Furthermore, they are angry at the general society for threatening their home communities with social oblivion. Talk of Indian identity is very much in the forefront of their conversations about Indian affairs. Now the American middle class has an annoying habit of absorbing the talented leadership of social movement, and even of incorporating the ideas of a critical social movement, as witness the recent 'beat' absorption. However, there is an added dimension to these young people's attitudes about the general society. Some of them are very sophisticated young men and women. Their peers are American college students, the children of the middle class who are in the 'center' of the system. Indian students, like other American college students, read *Playboy* magazine, Vance Packard, David Reisman and Jules Pfeiffer's cartoons. They are well aware of the loss of community and the loss of identity in American urban life. Their concern with Indian identity is not only a wish to preserve themselves and their home communities, but also a rejection of this frightening aspect of American society. This movement among Indian youth is the growing tip of the Pan-Indian social movement.

Of course, it would be a serious omission not to mention another important factor in Indian nationalism, rank deprivation. In the process of becoming 'Indian', aboriginal tribal people in the United States have also become 'American'. Pan-Indian ceremonies not only act out the solidarity of the local group and the new 'Indian' identity, but also a new commitment to America. Most Indians in the Pan-Indian area conceive of themselves as, let's say, Sioux and Indian *and* American. (A minority think of themselves only as Indian and American.) The assignment of Indians as a social group to a low rank position by the general society then becomes a problem, to marginal Indians particularly. Many younger Indians violently reject such a definition on the part of the general society. In fact, many Indian college students find to their surprise that the general society is not open to non-whites as they have been led to believe, and some have a strong feeling of betrayal. Although they may reject this bad definition and verbally defend 'Indian culture', the rank dilemma remains, and most younger Indians, who are cued to their local white neighbors in matters of rank assignment, are fearful of becoming associated with other minorities who may have an even lower rank position than Indians. Thus, many young Indian nationalists express what seem to be very anti-Negro sentiments.

As Pan-Indianism has grown over the years, I have changed my mind about the direction of American Indian acculturation. What quite a few of us in anthropology thought we saw regarding American Indian acculturation can be stated as follows: We saw American Indian tribal groups remaining as small societies, integrating into the matrices of their cultures various traits and institutions from western civilization while at the same time retaining much continuity with the past. We saw many individuals, however, leave those small societies and become part of the general American milieu. It is the process of individual acculturation that is being changed by the Pan-Indian movement. For one thing, the marginal people are not leaving Indian communities as it seemed they would. The Pan-Indian movement has formed a healing bridge between factions. For instance, it is possible now for a very marginal acculturated Indian from a Pan-Indian area to be accepted in his community by even the more conservative Indians if he participates in the institutions and symbols of this Pan-Indian life. Even if a marginal person leaves the community he can go to an urban center and become part of a more general Pan-Indian community. These urban 'Indian' communities may, of course, be only temporary stopping places for individual Indians who will later become part of the more general middle class. However, many ethnic communities are old in American cities and are still very much alive. Further, the general problem of loss of identity and community in America may militate against even very urban Indians cutting their ties with other Indians altogether. One could even imagine a resurgence of local tribal identity in response to these conditions.

The Pan-Indianism we have so far discussed may be very productive, as nationalist movements often are, in literature and the arts, but it is also developing institutions which deal with people outside the community. Pan-Indian institutions such as Indian centers in cities, pow-wow committees and so forth are institutions through which Indians can have some productive relationship to the general society. Indians in Indian communities are beginning to learn more about the nature of American society, and are more able to deal with it in its own terms.

Pan-Indianism is the creator of a new identity, a new ethnic group, if you will, a new 'nationality' in America. The twentieth century seems to be the century for pan-tribal movements all over the world – in the New World, Asia, Australia and Africa. Research on the Pan-Indian movement would not only tell us, as anthropologists, a good deal about social and cultural process generally, but it could also give us some understanding into the 'causes' of these types of movements among tribal people. Pan-Indianism is the oldest such movement and perhaps could tell us what lies in the future for parts of Africa and Asia.

Redfield has suggested that civilization has been built upon and spread by the slow incorporation of tribal groups; either these tribal groups became enclaves or they were incorporated as peasant villages.[5] However, this pattern does not seem to apply in the twentieth century, for the nature of the numerous pan-tribal movements around the world is, as far as we know, new on the scene of world history. I would like to suggest a hypothesis. The older civilizations were agriculturally based and in the nature of the case incorporated tribal groups as whole social units and at a leisurely, non-threatening pace. Modern industrial civilization, through the vehicle of the bureaucratic nation-state and its institutions, demands not only the incorporation of tribal peoples but immediate incorporation and individual assimilation. Industrial civilization individuates and attacks the solidarity of the social group. A tribal group cannot tolerate such an attack. It is, furthermore, doubtful if the individual tribal person could survive as a personality under these conditions. The first reaction of tribes under this kind of stress is the banding together of tribal groups and a widening and bolstering of this new identity, in self-defense. Even when tribal peoples desire to be incorporated into an industrial civilization, they are unwilling to break up as social groups, and therefore try to come to some kind of compromise, such as partial incorporation while retaining the solidarity of the social group.

Perhaps the struggle we see in the world today is, in some sense, a struggle about how communities with a strong sense of social solidarity, particularly tribal groups, will enter the mainstream of industrial civilization.[6]

Notes

1. Robert Redfield, 'The Folk Society', *American Journal of Sociology*, LII, 4 (January 1947).

2. Grant Foreman, *Advancing the Frontier, 1830–1860* (Norman, Oklahoma, 1933).

3. James Howard, 'The Pan-Indian Culture of Oklahoma', *The Scientific Monthly*, XVIII, 5 (November 1955), 215–20.

4. Ernest L. Schusky, Unpublished Field Notes (Observations on Pan-Indians in Northeastern United States), 1956.

5. Robert Redfield, *The Primitive World and Its Transformation* (Ithaca, N. Y., 1953); Robert Redfield, *Peasant Society and Culture* (Chicago, Ill., 1956).

6. Martin Orans, 'A Tribe in Search of a Great Tradition: The Rank Concession Syndrome Among the Santals of Chotonagpur', unpublished Ph.D. dissertation (Chicago), 1962.

Cases in Point

HARRIET J. KUPFERER

THE ISOLATED EASTERN CHEROKEE

As the author makes clear, Isolated Eastern Cherokee are relatively prosperous and relatively aloof from intertribal and pan-Indian activities directed toward raising the Indian standard of living. To other tribes, however, they are an important model: they have succeeded in maintaining Indian identity while bettering themselves economically. Other tribes which are more intimately involved in intertribal activities frequently allude to the Cherokee example. – SGL & NOL

SOME observers of the American Indian scene suggest that there are changes in the collective comportment of the American Indians. These changes include an increasing awareness of 'rights' and of real or perceived treaty violations; recognition of shared goals and mutually held feelings; and the communication of these sentiments to the larger society in various ways. The fact that Indians have become vocal has led up to the contention that there is a collective movement[1] among native Americans.

The characteristics of this movement are, however, difficult to categorize. To apply it to the familiar labels of 'nativistic movements' or 'revitalization movements' appears to be imprecise. For example, there is no resemblance between current Indian behavior and the Black Muslim cult. The militancy which is a trait of the Black Muslims is absent, and so is the aim of uniting all Indians under one banner.[2] The familiar irrational thought and behavior associated with the Melanesian 'Cargo cults' past and present is not apparent. Neither does this contemporary Indian resurgence resemble the messianic movements such as the Prophet dance, Ghost dance or the Indian Shaker church which figured so prominently in the Indian past.

We seem to know what this phenomenon is not, but we are not sure what it is. I am inclined to agree that Nancy Lurie's term 'Indian Renascence'[3] is appropriate and is descriptive of the events which are occurring. The specific goals, however, seem to be somewhat ill-defined, and are possibly related to a particular problem or particular tribe. Although there is a great emphasis on permitting an 'Indian way' of life to continue in, or in juxtaposition to, the larger culture, the movement – if movement it is – is not explicitly opposed to acculturation. I find no public statements which exhort Indians to return to 'Indian ways' or to refrain from taking on 'white man's cultural trappings'. Indeed, there is an explicit desire to maintain separate tribal identities. On the other hand, there does not seem to be a drive for assimilation either, although there is a demand for a larger 'slice of the pie' in regard to education and higher standards of living.

In addition to these problems there is another. How pervasive is this movement? Are all or most of the 'tribes' participating in it with equal fervor? I submit that they are not. For example, I know of no evidence demonstrating that the Eastern Keresan Pueblos are a part of it. The reasons for their lack of participation are a function of, among other things, a deliberate effort to maintain cultural identity and to disassociate themselves from the white world. It is not with them, however, that I am concerned, but with the Eastern Band of the Cherokee.

There is only scattered evidence attesting to Cherokee participation. In March 1963 the then band chief and two council members attended a meeting in Washington of the National Congress of American Indians. The year prior to the Washington meeting the NCAI met in Cherokee. Participation in this gathering was also confined to the late chief and a few selected council members. The personnel of the Agency assisted in the organizational details. The presence of a few Cherokee elected officials at these meetings, I think, does not negate my contention that the Cherokee are not actively caught up in Pan-Indianism. While I was a resident in Cherokee I found almost no communication between the council and the tribe. The 'facts' that were in circulation were, as best I could discern, somewhat distorted. This observation was reconfirmed early in 1967 by an informant saying that the people are quite unaware of these 'official' meetings and that there is no mingling between them and the delegates.

The declaration of the war on poverty has called federal attention to the plight of the Indians. Consequently several meetings have been held by the Office of Economic Opportunity, focusing on Indians. In March 1967 the vice-chief of the Cherokee attended one in Kansas City. Affairs like these are initiated by agents outside of the Cherokee social system and do not represent a ground swell of Cherokee sentiment toward 'Indians Unite'.

Either through oversight or the absence of an official Cherokee correspondent, there is no mention in *Indian Voices* of Eastern Cherokee acting collectively or individually to promote generalized Indian goals.

CHEROKEE COUNTRY

The Eastern Band of Cherokee occupy a 56,572 acre reservation in western North Carolina about equidistant between Asheville, North Carolina, and Knoxville, Tennessee. The area is mountainous. A main highway climbs the mountains forming the eastern boundary of the reservation and winds its serpentine way down through the business section. Much of the reservation land borders on Great Smoky Mountain National Park. Although there are good bottom lands, most of them, over 46,000 acres, are in timber. The remaining acreage is agricultural, pasture or waste. Qualla Boundary is the main reservation. Separate from it and about fifty miles away is the Snow Bird section consisting of 2,249 acres. Still farther west in Cherokee County about 5,000 acres are held in fragmented tracts. Qualla Boundary has five townships within it: Wolfetown, Paint Town, Cherokee, Big Cove and Birdtown. Each of these has distinctive ecological, demographic and cultural characteristics.

Elevation on the reservation varies from 1900 feet to 4700 feet. The mean temperature for a year is 54.9°F. February is the coldest month, with an average temperature of 29°F., and July, with an average of 80.5°F., is the warmest. In general the climate is relatively mild, except at the highest elevation, and there is abundant moisture. Numerous mountain streams flow into the rushing Ocunaluftee River which courses through the reservation on its way into the Tennessee River system.

THE PEOPLE[4]

The 1960 census of the band revealed 4,494 members. There was a roll taken in 1924 listing a population of 2,540. From these figures it is evident that the population has nearly doubled in thirty six years. The genetic composition of the band is mixed, but accurate data exist for the 1924 enumeration. John Gulick in 1960 made an estimate based on the composition of school enrollment for 1956–7.[5] However, in the case of children with ½ or less Indian blood, there is the possibility that the child's inheritance may differ markedly from that of either or both of his parents. 'One-half Indian blood' might result, for instance, from one white and one Indian parent, or two ½-blood parents, or one ¼- and one ¾-blood parent. Table I compares the Indian inheritance of the 1924 roll with the figures obtained from the schools in 1956–7.

Table I. Percentage Comparison of Indian Inheritance

1924[a]			1957[b]		
Blood Degree	No.	%	Blood Degree	No.	%
4/4	525	20.67	4/4	197	22.89
3/4	326	12.83	3/4–4/4	223	25.90
1/2	183	7.21	1/2–3/4	172	19.97
1/4	180	7.09	1/4–1/2	140	16.26
1/16	613	24.13	Less than 1/4	129	14.98
Less than 1/16	713	28.07			
Total	2540	100.00	Total	861	100.00

a. Tribal file data, 1960.

b. Based on school enrollment data only.

The band is governed by a chief and a vice-chief elected every four years. The council is comprised of two members elected from each township for two year terms. This organization, like those of many tribes, is a function of the BIA's need to administer tribal affairs. It does not necessarily reflect aboriginal political structures. Typical council activities are arbitrating land disputes, the operation of tribal business enterprises, establishing policies on leases, and disbursal of tribal funds to needy members.

ECONOMY[6]

The economy of the Cherokee can be described as mixed. The major sources of earned money are the tourist industry, three factories, miscellaneous wage labor, and, to a limited extent, timbering. Full-time farming is practiced by so few that it can hardly be considered a significant source of cash. The major crop is tobacco, but allotments are very small.

The tourist trade is probably the most important single contributor to Cherokee income. In addition to the profits accruing to business owners, many people are employed as waitresses, sales personnel and motel maids. The craft work also owes much of its existence to the visitors.

To operate a business of any type in the reservation, a trader's license, for which there is no charge, is necessary. White entrepreneurs not married to an Indian must hold a lease. Between 1950 and 1963 there was a trend away from white lessees. In spite of this phenomenon, most Indian owned or operated businesses are not controlled by 'full bloods'. In May 1963, 134 licenses were granted in the following categories: Indian owned and operated businesses, 63; Indian owned but leased to white operators, 11; non-Indian owned, 60. There were 33 motels, 39 craft shops, 11 restaurants, 9 groceries with picnic supplies and 9 combination craft, restaurant and grocery businesses under one roof.

Gross income figures posted for three of these Indian owned and operated establishments are: $428,213, $175,072 and $151,538. We have been describing large businesses. There are other very small ones, such as a one vehicle taxi service. Figures for such endeavors are not recorded, but the net is probably less than $1,000 per year. All businesses except taxi services pay 3 per cent tax on their gross to the tribal treasury. These levies make possible assistance to needy individuals. Of even greater importance, they have enabled the tribe to solicit industry through sharing a portion of the investment.

By itself tourism is not enough to support the people. Together with the Indian Bureau, the tribal council has induced three industries to locate on the reservation. Saddlecraft, the oldest, manufactures moccasins plus a few other items, and has a yearly payroll of about $200,000. Harns Manufacturing Company, which makes quilted products and padded infant accessories, is housed in a modern plant erected with tribal funds. The company holds a twenty-five year lease with an option for renewal. Its yearly payroll is over $500,000. The Vassar Corporation, a manufacturer of women's hair accessories, has constructed a 45,000 square foot building on the reservation. Financing for it came from both the tribal treasury and Jackson County Industries. Inasmuch as the tribe assumed the major financial burden, about 70 per cent of the employees are Indians.

It must not be assumed on the basis of the foregoing review of the economy that all Cherokee are economically secure. Many of them still just eke out an existence, aided in many cases by welfare funds coming from the country in which they live. Other assistance derives from the federal Indian Welfare Department. In 1963 federal Indian Welfare expenditures totaled $55,303.

CHEROKEE CULTURAL AND SOCIAL GROUNDS

Just as there is genetic diversity among the Cherokee, so is there social and cultural diversity. It is, however, somewhat doubtful that all the Cherokee see the subtle differences. Although everyone knows his degree of Indian inheritance, the most frequent distinction made among the people is 'full blood' and 'white' Indian. A 'full blood' is one who looks like an Indian; a 'white Indian' is one who usually has less than ¼ Indian inheritance and who looks white. People also distinguish among the 'white' Indians. Some of them are scornfully called Five Dollar Indians. Allegedly these folk had themselves enrolled in the band in 1924 by bribing the registrar. The term 'full blood' tends to imply people who are traditionally oriented. This is not entirely accurate, although there is a tendency for more of the 'full bloods' to be conservative, and for those of mixed ancestry (particularly those under one-half Indian) to be more 'progressive'. But the differences among the Cherokee are not such that they are subject to simple dichotomizing. It is not a matter of 'conservatives' and 'progressives'. Nor can the people be placed into categories ranging from like-Indian to like-white in order to explain the disparateness. At Cherokee there are two categories of people based upon acculturation.[7] There are the Conservatives, people far from aboriginal Cherokee, but who retain to one degree or another a core of inter-related covert and overt traits which set them apart from others. They continue to speak Cherokee; they cling to 'Indian' doctors and native medicine, although not always exclusively. Their belief system includes witches, omens and contagious and sympathetic magic. Probably the most telling indicator of a Cherokee is his value system. The Conservative guides his behavior by the 'Harmony Ethic'.[8] Acting in accord with it, he attempts to maintain harmonious relationships with others by not offending them and by responding to their demands upon him. Conservatives abhor 'stinginess' and esteem generosity. Through various devices they avoid overt aggression or situations which might produce it.

Modern Indians comprise the second category. These are people who, while not necessarily like one another, are very different from the Conservatives. They may or may not speak or understand Cherokee, but if they do they seldom use it. There is almost no resort to 'Indian doctors', although some may practice self-medication with herbs. Their most outstanding characteristic, however, is their lack of adherence to the 'Harmony Ethic'. Indeed, their behavior is largely predicated on the 'Protestant Ethic'. To be sure, there are degrees to which it is followed, but these folk are the business owners or managers, the few farmers remaining and the skilled or semi-skilled laborers. However, many of them qualify for public assistance or federal Indian Welfare Aid as a consequence of lack of education, illness or other misfortune. Ideally, they still cherish the idea of independence and individualism. Within this category of the Modern Indian a continuum with regard to standard of living, education and adherence to the 'Protestant Ethic' is visible. The differences among those in this category suggest that a class system is emerging. Those who are economically successful, and whose style of life reflects it, comprise the Cherokee middle class. Those whom circumstances have kept impoverished or nearly so compose a lower class. Genetically, Modern Indians range in their degree of Indian inheritance from 4/4 to 1/32 or 1/64 Indian.

The formation of these cultural and social groups is a consequence of complex historical events beginning with contacts with early settlers and continuing to the present. This is another story and it cannot be told here, but these events are important in that they resulted in the maintenance of the Cherokee as the single largest group of Indians in the east. This fact also has a bearing on the place of the Cherokee in an Indian renascence.

THE CHEROKEE AND THE RENASCENCE

When Nancy Lurie called the idea of an Indian renascence to my attention in regard to the Eastern Cherokee, I responded by saying that I thought most of her generalizations held for them.[9] I did qualify my response by stating that my agreement was largely contingent upon the socio-cultural orientation of the particular segment of the heterogeneous Cherokee population one was discussing. Upon further reflection, however, I have concluded that they are neither individually nor collectively participating in inter-Indian gatherings with the purpose of bettering the lot of Indians. Two subsequent visits to the reservation have reinforced my conclusions.

Let us examine the behavior and attitudes of the disparate aggregates of Cherokee for the evidence to support our contentions. The Conservatives provide the first data.

CONSERVATIVES

For the most part Conservatives live apart from the business center of Cherokee. Their homes are usually found in mountain coves some distance from the main highway. Some live as far away as fifteen miles. It is true that many of them come to town to watch the local scene during the tourist season or to go to the agency or to the hospital. Their social life is, nevertheless, largely confined to other Conservatives, or to the lower class. I do not mean to suggest that Cherokee is *not* still a folk society. It is, and most of its residents know or recognize each other. Nonetheless, Conservatives are a group apart. They tend to be socially as well as physically isolated. Many of them have been no farther away from the reservation than Asheville. Those who can read see only the

Asheville or Knoxville newspapers, which carry little or no news of other Indian groups.

Conservatives have only vague knowledge of other Indian tribes. They are familiar with the Catawba, for at one time some Catawba lived in Cherokee. Some have heard of the Choctaw and Seminoles. Their children who have attended Indian schools in Oklahoma have mentioned others to them, but they have had no experience with them. Many of the Cherokee have relatives in Oklahoma – a consequence of the Removal – but few Conservative adults have ever been west. When questions are put to them in regard to other tribes, they indicate that they know that there are others in the country but they disclaim anything in common with them. When a Conservative refers to himself as an Indian, he means two things: (1) he is an Indian and the 'white' Indians are not, and (2) he is a Cherokee.

Conservatives know that periodically some of the tribal council members and the chief go to Washington. They are not just sure why, except possibly to get something for the Indians. They tend to be quite suspicious of any chief the band might have. He is either working for himself or the 'white' Indians. They occasionally demonstrate a subtle hostility toward whites. In their summer outdoor drama, 'Unto These Hills', for instance, there is an ever present if not entirely accurate reminder of the harsh treatment accorded the Cherokee in the period leading up to the Removal.

Some of the more sophisticated of them suspect that the Indians are not being employed by the manufacturing plants. They do not realize that in many cases their educational levels are too low. They know too that their lot is not as good as others', but they credit this to 'stinginess' or land theft on the part of the wealthier people.

Despite their occasional discontent – this also includes

real or fancied maltreatment at the hands of government personnel – the Conservatives have no real conception of uniting to correct the situation as it obtains locally. Due to their isolation from all other Indians, they have no knowledge of a movement to make explicit generalized Indian goals.

MODERN INDIANS

An analysis of Modern Indians shows for somewhat different reasons an equal lack of participation in a larger world than Cherokee.

Lower Class Cherokees: The lower socio-economic class of the Modern Indians exhibits much of the same sort of physical isolation that the Conservatives do. Few have travelled outside of western North Carolina or eastern Tennessee. Some of the younger adults have attended Indian schools in the west, but so long ago that they do not identify with people or places other than Cherokee. Their educational achievements are also limited, and consequently they read very little. The 'white' Indians among them, although they recognize their Indian inheritance, do not really identify themselves as Indians. Still, few of them have ever considered living elsewhere. They are very much like so many of their white mountain relatives. The mountains are home; 'the water does not taste right' in other places; they have rights to their land regardless of what the 'full bloods' say.

When asked about Indians elsewhere, they reply that they 'don't know nothing much about them'. Neither do they know about the various meetings held in other parts of the country by numbers of different tribes. They do think that Indians – and here they regard themselves as Indians and Cherokees – have been mistreated and that something should be done. They do not get excited about it or the prospects of rectifying any conditions. Very few know anything about the much-publicized Seneca case or other recent treaty violations. It is difficult to predict with certainty what they would do if they did know. I suspect that they would be sympathetic but would not become so incensed as to lend active support unless they were individually canvassed. They live their lives out as marginal farmers, employees of the industries or the Indian Bureau.

Although degree of Indian inheritance has little to do with culture or class, those Modern Indians in the lower socio-economic bracket who look like Indians do demonstrate a difference based on their genetic composition. They do identify with Indians racially, although they do not identify with them culturally. The fact, however, that they regard themselves as Indians does not necessarily make them any more aware of national events affecting Indians. What knowledge, if any, the people of this category have is acquired from contact with the Indian agency. When they do have some information, they are perhaps more in sympathy with the plight of the beleaguered groups than the poorer white Indians. But at present, they exhibit little tendency to become involved in a national movement. Like the Conservatives and the white Indians of the lower socio-economic class, their general lack of sophistication militates against it.

Middle Class Cherokees: The middle class is numerically the smallest of the socio-cultural categories. In general the people in it are nearly white, with several notable exceptions. As I indicated, they are usually the business people, although some are school teachers, nurses or employees in responsible positions at the Indian Bureau. Their educational attainment is much higher than that of others in the tribe, but apart from the teachers, only a few have attended or completed college. Many of them graduated from federal institutions such as Haskell, Carlisle or schools in Oklahoma. They are better read and better informed than any of the others. They agree that Indians are becoming politically active. The business people in particular feel that termination of federal control would be the best thing for Cherokee, and probably for all Indians. Their attitudes toward the Conservatives tend to be ambivalent. On the one hand they regard them with tolerant affection but on the other they accuse them of being superstitious, not quite clean, lazy and wasteful. They have heard of most of the events affecting the better known tribes and agree that the treaties have always been violated and probably always will be. When asked whether they are conversant with the various meetings held with the aim of making Indian goals public, only a few answer in the affirmative. With one exception, most of these people – particularly the entrepreneurs – are not interested in participating. In general the latter are motivated by self-interest. This is not meant to be a derogatory evaluation. They are in business: their concern is that which affects their businesses. To this extent they make themselves heard at the tribal council, through the Cherokee Chamber of Commerce, or perhaps the Lions Club. Their attention is focused on the tourists and the facilities and attractions which will increase the number of annual visitors.

The Indian agency employees and the teachers are more aware of events affecting other tribes, and more interested, too, in the outcome. This is especially true of those who are decidedly Indian in physical appearance. Their identification is, however, Cherokee first and Indian second. None of these people has attended any national or regional meeting.

There is, however, one nearly full blood family which is much more alert to the national scene. Among the men, one brother was an Episcopalian minister to the Seneca, another is a superintendent of a reservation in the west, a third has traveled extensively. One sister has a responsible position in the Cherokee agency and another is working for a national Indian organization. This family, while a respected one in the community, has not influenced the attitude of others in regard to an all-Indian movement, although it is vitally interested in the outcome. With this exception the Cherokee middle class is quite uninvolved, either emotionally or physically, in any national collective action.

I feel, then, that the eastern Cherokee are not identified with a renascence as I have defined it. What are the reasons for the absence of their participation?

First, and perhaps most importantly, the location of the reservation isolates the Cherokee from other Indians. Unlike the Indians of the southwest or others who are in close proximity to each other, the Cherokee are seldom in contact with other tribes. As far as I know, there have been only two occasions when any of them attended the Gallup pow-wow. A woman, who is a professional sculptress, and her brother went to exhibit woodcarving. The Cherokee have no native dances left, and so have no impelling need to go. In fact, only a few realize that there are these summer affairs. Their knowledge of other Indians, as I have said, is quite hazy. They emphatically disavow any relationship with the Pembroke and Lumbee Indians[10] who have on occasion claimed Cherokee status. These are the only other Indians in North Carolina. Their ancestry seems to be mixed – white, Negro and Indian – and the Cherokee want no affiliation with them.

A second reason which may explain the Cherokee situation can be found in the fact that since their reservation was established, there have been no major problems associated with it.[11] They have not been threatened with the loss

of any of their land. To date there have been no mineral resources discovered which might generate such a problem.
Their land is not coveted by local whites. In fact the latter
recognize full well that the presence of the reservation and
the national park brings money to the entire area.

The third reason, I think, is a consequence of the burgeoning Cherokee economy, which has affected in one way or
another most of the members. In fact, I suspect that the
reservation is in a financially healthier state than many of
the surrounding white communities. A comparison of the
federal Indian welfare expenditures for the fiscal years 1960
through 1963 reflects this, at least in part. In 1960–61 the
total expenditure was $114,405. Monies spent in 1961–2
totaled $101,684, and in 1962–3 the figure was $55,303. I have
no comparative data for public assistance issued to the Indian by the counties, but suspect that these funds have either
remained constant or have decreased.

It is true that there are some folks who are discontented
for personal or business reasons. In general, however, it
seems plausible to suggest that the Cherokee have no compelling need at present to join forces with other Indians in
the pursuit of mutual goals. Indeed their isolation has made
them unaware of the plight or needs of Indians in other
parts of the country.

Notes

The initial research on which part of this paper is based was supported by a grant MF-9222 from the National Institute of Mental
Health. Dr M. Elaine Burgess and Marguerite Felton read drafts of
this paper and I am grateful for their comments.

1. The phenomenon of collective movements has received considerable attention in sociological literature. It is postulated that necessary
pre-conditions for it are a deep dissatisfaction with current conditions,
damaged self conceptions and frustrations. See, for example, Arnold
W. Green, *Sociology* (New York, 1960), 622–3.

2. There is some scattered evidence to the contrary. For example, the

following is excerpted from a letter appearing in *Indian Voices* (April 1964): '. . . no longer does each one picture himself as Sioux, Navajo, Cherokee or Mohawk. First and foremost he is Indian!!'

3. Nancy Lurie, 'An American Indian Renascence?' This is quoted in full in Nancy Lurie's article in *Midcontinent American Studies Journal*, VI, 2 (Fall 1965), 25–50.

4. These data come from Harriet J. Kupferer, 'The Principal People: A Study of the Social and Cultural Groups of the Eastern Band of Cherokee'. Unpublished Ph.D. dissertation (University of North Carolina, 1961).

5. John Gulick, *Cherokees at the Crossroads* (Chapel Hill, North Carolina, 1960).

6. The material in this section derives from a revision of Kupferer, 'The Principal People', Bureau of American Ethnology, Anthropological Paper No. 78, 1966.

7. Harriet J. Kupferer, 'The Principal People'. See also her 'Health Practices and Educational Aspirations as Indicators of Acculturation and Social Class among the Eastern Cherokee', *Social Forces*, 41 (December 1962); 'Material Change in a Conservative Pueblo', *El Palacio*, 69 (Winter 1962); and 'Cherokee Change: A Departure from Lineal Models of Acculturation', *Anthropologica*, 5 (December 1962).

8. The term 'Harmony Ethic' was suggested by Robert K. Thomas, who asserts that it is central to the Cherokee way of life. For a more complete description of this ideology see John Gulick, *Cherokees at the Crossroads* and Harriet J. Kupferer, 'The Principal People'.

9. Some of the characteristics of the movement as identified by Nancy Lurie are: gathering momentum to disseminate widely Indian opinion; increased participation in inter-tribal conferences; reactivating or encouraging the perpetuation of tribal languages; and increased articulateness of Indians in general.

10. For a description of these ill-defined groups see Brewton Berry's *Almost White* (New York, 1963).

11. Six years after the 1838 Removal, the Cherokee purchased their land through an agent. This land comprises the bulk of the reservation, although additional tracts have been purchased by federal funds.

CAROL K. RACHLIN

TIGHT SHOE NIGHT: OKLAHOMA INDIANS TODAY

The author's conviction perhaps makes the paper which follows less a scholarly article than a primary source, a document, if you will, of the attitudes of a devoted worker in the field. We have chosen to include it not in spite of its editorializing, but partially because of it, and partially because it contains an impressively authoritative survey of conditions in one of the most important – and difficult to understand – centers of Indian population and culture. – SGL & NOL

SATURDAY night was 'Tight Shoe Night' for country people, a time to dress up in 'store bought'n clothes', and head for town. For the central and western Oklahoma Indians Tight Shoe Night began when they arrived at government boarding schools, and the freedom of moccasins gave way to the rigidity of stiff government shoes.

Today Tight Shoe Night in central and western Oklahoma is not confined to Saturday night. The Cleopatra make-up, the bouffant hair style and the Jacqueline Kennedy voice are necessities to young Indian women as the button-down collar, the striped tie, the four-button jacket and tight-fitting trousers are badges of achievement for young Indian men. The Indians, in short, like their non-Indian neighbors, are conditioned by television, style magazines and the 'image' of the corporation man.

Who are these modern Indians? 'The Congress has not given a general definition by legislation nor have the Courts by interpretation.'[1] Identification, therefore, rests with each group, to be defined in its tribal constitution.

This paper will be concerned with individuals who possess one-quarter or more of Indian blood, and who belong to the following tribes: Arapaho, Caddo, Cheyenne, Comanche, Delaware, Iowa, Kaw, Kiowa, Kiowa-Apache, Omaha, Osage, Oto, Quapaw, Pawnee, Ponca, Potawatomi, Sac-Fox, Shawnee and Wichita.

The problems the paper will treat will be: the general organization of Indian society in central and western Oklahoma, the interrelations between urban and rural persons, the position of young people and the checks and balances which make Indian life a cultural continuum. The general situation will be viewed without considering the individual exceptions which do exist.

The Indian population in Oklahoma City is between 12,000 and 16,000. Oklahoma City, the largest metropolitan community in the state, was created on unassigned lands. The city had no native Indian inhabitants at the time the land was opened for settlement. Oklahoma City is not designated as a relocation center by the Bureau of Indian Affairs. Therefore, Oklahoma City offers the best available example of self-relocated contemporary Indian life, and serves as the urban focus for this study.

Oklahoma has an Indian population of 64,000 (US Census 1960), but has no legal reservations. The Indians live scattered among the non-Indian population, in both rural areas and urban centers. Lack of reservation lands puts central and western Oklahoma Indians in a precarious position with relation to the Bureau of Indian Affairs, and to the city, county and state governments. The eternal question is: Who will be responsible for aiding the Indian? At present it is a question in flux. The answer in the long run will inevitably be *the Indian*.

Electricity in the rural areas, increased telephone service and super-highways have made the 'country cousin' a symbol of the past. Tight Shoe Night for the Indians is everywhere. Friends and relatives from the urban centers visit the rural areas for family gatherings, tribal activities, religious functions and just for the pleasure of returning home. Rural Indians come to Oklahoma City for socializing, seasonal jobs, specialized medical treatment, education, shopping and just for the pleasure of being in the big city.

Rural Indians live either on inherited or allotted land, or in small towns. Land sales, heirship cases and tenant farming have resulted in non-Indian people living scattered throughout what were formerly Indian lands. There are in Oklahoma towns like Andarko or Pawnee which are considered by the Indians to be Indian towns because the tradespeople cater to Indian needs. The stores stock shawls, Pendleton blankets, beads and so forth. Indian towns are usually places that have some government offices, and where the Indian people have become accustomed to visit on business and errands. Non-Indian towns are those that offer no special inducement to the Indians. However, no Oklahoma community is without Indians, and in no Oklahoma community do Indians live in any special section of town.[2]

RURAL AND URBAN INDIANS

Rural Indian communities have more old people and more children than urban communities. The old folks like to stay at home where they grew up and earned their livings. The children in rural houses often are grandchildren, either biologically or by traditional kinship, who have been given to or left with the older people. The young adults and middle-aged individuals who remain in the rural areas work for the federal government, have private businesses or farms, are employed by the State or are those people who 'just can't make it'.

Indians living in urban centers are spread throughout the non-Indian population. There are, however, very few Indian people living in predominantly Negro neighborhoods. In Oklahoma City there are certain sections of town which are more desirable to the Indians than other sections, but there is no Indian neighborhood as such.

The urban Indians range from middle-aged people to veterans or wives of veterans of World War II or of the Korean War, and either own no land in the home rural area or share in small portions of heirship lands. Many young married people are also present in the urban Indian community. They are usually individuals who came to the city with their parents, and have remained for reasons of employment and attachment.

The organization of Indian society in rural and urban communities is the same. Indian society, now as in the past, has many checks and balances. Factions interact to create Indian culture. This is not a pan-Indian culture. Tribal identification remains the predominant theme of Indian society. Ethnic personalities are very pronounced, despite inter-tribal marriages, inter-tribal activities and relocation.

RELIGIOUS AFFILIATIONS

After tribal identification, the rural and urban Indian communities make a distinction between 'Christian' and 'non-Christian' Indians. Each group, of course, feels superior to the other. Objectively, the Indians belonging to Christian faiths with international scope and more centralized leadership are those individuals who will obtain the highest objectives in the non-Indian world.

The Christian Indians belong to the Baptist, Catholic,

Episcopal, Mennonite, Mormon, Nazarene and other Christian faiths. Tribal groups reflect the proselytizing of the early missionaries. The Methodist and Baptist faiths are strongest in central and western Oklahoma among the Kiowa, Kiowa-Apache, Comanche, Sac-Fox and other groups; their mission activities began in the 1850s and have continued to the present. The Catholic faith is strong among the Osage, Ponca, Kaw and related north-central groups. The Mennonites are found among the Arapaho and Cheyenne, where German immigrants settled in clusters at the end of the nineteeth century.

The Methodists and Baptists maintain Indian mission churches in the greater Oklahoma City area, and in rural areas throughout the state. These churches can, and often do, give service to the non-Indian community. The ministers, in most cases, will be of Indian descent. Both faiths have a separate 'conference' for the Indians. Each conference sets the standards for its ministers, and for their interpretation and presentation of the faith in question. These Indian conferences have different educational standards for the ministry from those observed in non-Indian conferences. Thus, Indian ministers in these faiths usually have much less formal education than ministers of the same faith serving churches in educated white communities, or in some Oklahoma City Negro churches.

There is great rivalry between the Methodist and Baptist churches in central and western Oklahoma. The Methodists consider themselves the more liberal of the two faiths. Each considers itself the more influential in the social fields, and both look down on other faiths, both Christian and non-Christian. There is no cooperation between the two churches, or between these churches and other Christian or non-Christian beliefs. Dogmatic religion rather than Christian tolerance is the rule in their preaching.

The same conditions are present in Christian churches now that were noted over forty years ago in the Meriam Report:

The outstanding need in the field of missionary activities among the Indians is cooperation. Cooperation is needed both in the relationships between the government and the missionaries and in the relationship among the churches and the missionaries themselves. Positive action looking toward improvement, therefore, must take the direction of improving the mechanism through which cooperation can be effective.

Unless funds are available satisfactorily to maintain all stations in operation, the question should be raised as to whether more effective results could not be secured through concentration of the resources on a smaller number of stations.

The missionaries should consider carefully a material broadening of their program and an increase in the number and kinds of contacts with the Indians. Their best work has usually been in the field of education. For adult Indians their main offering has been church activities similar to those conducted in white communities, and those activities apparently make little appeal to the Indians. [In 1964 these activities have more appeal.] The missionaries need to have a better understanding of the Indian point of view, of the Indian's religion and ethics, in order to start from what is good in them as a foundation. Too frequently, they have made the mistake of attempting to destroy the existing structure and to substitute something else without apparently realizing that much in the old has its place in the new.[3]

The non-Christian Indians are those individuals who practice the old native religions, or are members of the Native American Church. The inclusion of the Native American Church in this category is an Indian colloquial classification, which shows the attitude of the Christian Indians towards the Peyote religion. Objectively, the Native American Church should be included as a Christian belief.[4]

All non-Christian Indians have had some training in

Christian ideology. Most Indians in central and western Oklahoma have been exposed to the Baptist and Methodist faiths, and the concepts of these churches furnish the Christian foundation for the teachings of the Native American Church. Similarly, the Osage and neighboring tribes use Catholic teachings as the Christian concepts basic to their Native American Church services.

The non-Christian Indians generally are more conservative about tribal traditions than are Christian Indians, and they usually represent conservative factions within their own tribes. In Oklahoma City they are the people who have the greatest struggle in adjustment to new conditions because they have no place in which to center their social life. They often belong to the lower income group, have less education and fewer skills than the Christian Indians. Generally, they look for and find employment, and are industrious, but they are handicapped by functional illiteracy and consequent difficulty in communication with employers and others outside their own group. They tend to help each other and to support at least the social activities of most Indian Christian Churches.

Christian and non-Christian Indians vacillate in their religious thinking. Many individuals profess Christianity but in reality cling to their native beliefs. There are others who experiment with religious concepts, and still others who cling dogmatically to their belief, whether Christian or non-Christian, as the only means of keeping sanity in a complex world.

EDUCATION, EMPLOYMENT AND INCOME

Education, employment and income create other strata in the urban-rural social structure. These strata will dominate the religious stratum in some situations.

Education, employment and income usually go hand in hand, although this depends upon the kind of employment and the wage scale it pays. Oklahoma has, within the past year, legally accepted union shops which will result in wage increases for certain kinds of work. Until now, the white collar worker has held the more advantageous social position. Economic advances within the jobs previously considered socially inferior may change the strata of Indian society, as union jobs pay union wages.

Most Indians over forty-five years of age in central and western Oklahoma have been educated in some type of government school. There is, however, great variation in the quality of education among government schools, and the time period when such an education was received. Government policies, teacher training and school facilities all have left deep marks on Indian adults. Those born since about 1920, in contrast, have usually attended a public educational institution. Today, except in unusual cases, all Indian children attend public primary and secondary schools. But among all the Indians at all age levels there is a high rate of functional illiteracy. The causes for this condition require intensive study in order that corrective measures be developed and applied.

College and specialized education seem to be more readily achieved by members of some tribes than by members of others. The reasons for this may be in the ethnic personalities involved, and in tribal or individual readiness to accept acculturation.

There is little doubt that all groups considered in this paper have always had class-structured societies. Structure varied from tribe to tribe and was more pronounced in some tribes than in others. Persons occupying honored positions – band chiefs, war chiefs, medicine men, priests, drum keepers, makers of songs – have continued to exist within extended family groups for many generations. It is in this upper class of Indian society that educated Indians will be found today, and from this upper class will doubtless come the future leaders and administrators of Indian culture.

The educational aspirations of the present primary and secondary school youngsters remain in harmony with the old class structure. Children born into upper-class Indian families anticipate college educations, terminating in advanced degrees. Children from the middle classes of Indian society usually anticipate training in skilled jobs. Those from the lower economic and social strata have little to anticipate. Naturally, the economic positions of the family and the home environment will influence the educational ambitions of the children. Poverty and ignorance, for the Indian and the non-Indian, go hand in hand from generation to generation.

A recent trend among Indian parents in the urban centers is to examine their children's aptitude for college. This trend has resulted from the efforts of counselors in public schools. Literature available to Indian parents, through the Bureau of Indian Affairs, stresses scholarships for college students, rather than funds for those who enter vocational schools. This may be due to the greater availability of funds for higher education.

Rural and urban Indian children frequently drop out of secondary school. Some parents are able to persuade their children to return, while others are not so lucky. Frank Moore, Director of the Legislative Study Committee for the Oklahoma Mental Health Planning Commission, said, 'Statewide, we had 23.6 dropouts per 100 ninth-grade pupils.' Moore's report also showed that one child in seven had some kind of emotional or physical handicap.[5]

The newspaper account of the report did not show a breakdown of the distribution of handicapped children among minority groups. If one considers the general health of the parents of Indian children, it becomes a certainty that a large percentage of Indian children must fall into the classification of handicapped. Tuberculosis, diabetes, obesity and coronary disorders are present today in every Indian family in central and western Oklahoma.

Many Indians desire adult education. The principal problem of obtaining adult education in Oklahoma lies in the policy of the Bureau of Indian Affairs. The Bureau has not considered any Oklahoma metropolitan area of sufficient size to qualify as a relocation center. Individuals wanting to learn such skills as cosmetology, typing or electronics go to Denver, Dallas or Los Angeles. But most Indians do not want to leave their friends, families and homes. Since Oklahoma Indians do not live on reservations, they cannot understand the attitude of the Bureau. 'That's all right for them reservation Indians but not for us.' Often an Indian tries to earn his own school expenses, or applies for a tribal scholarship, but most often these ambitious people give up in despair.

Oklahoma City's capital funds for economic growth have tripled since 1951, reaching over $3 million in 1963. Oklahoma City's percentage of unemployment has risen slightly in the same period, but remains very low in terms of the national average, and no time has been lost through labor disputes. The Help-Wanted Index of the National Industrial Conference Board places Oklahoma City in ninth position nationally, just below Dallas and above Denver and Los Angeles.[6] The local telephone directory for 1964 lists 14 business colleges, 9 schools of cosmetology and 4 schools for electronics in Oklahoma City. One cannot help but wonder, therefore, about the basis for the decisions of the Bureau of Indian Affairs.

Opportunities open to Indians in the President's War on Poverty do not seem to have been adequately utilized. These programs apparently suffer from poor communication between the local, state and federal personnel and the Indians. Many Indians do not possess the basic skills or the command of English required for the more advanced training being offered under the program at this time. Many other reasons for the failure of Indians to participate in new programs exist, and a careful study of the situation would have to be made before any conclusions could be reached.

Employment creates another type of social stratum which sometimes transcends tribal, religious and social groups. The largest employers of Indians in Oklahoma are the various civilian and military branches of the federal government, including Fort Sill, Lawton; Tinker Air Force Base, Oklahoma City; the Federal Aviation Administration; the Bureau of Indian Affairs, which employs agency, educational and administrative personnel; and the Division of Indian Health of the US Department of Health, Education, and Welfare.

There have been many criticisms leveled at federal employees. Some may be justified, but some must be considered personal grudges. There is no doubt that government employees form a sub-culture of Indian culture, with its own standards and its own hierarchy. This sub-culture is generally composed of Christian Indians who have received some portion of their education in government Indian schools. The faction breaks down into smaller groups, based on the employing federal agency, the division within the federal agency and the type of employment. Today we are beginning to deal with the third generation of individuals who have been born into 'government service'.

Among government employees many different attitudes exist, all stemming from the administration of a given agency. Indian personnel at Tinker Field, Oklahoma City, are insecure in their jobs. Changing military requirements and budgets lead to a turn-over in employees. On the other hand, individuals working for the Division of Indian Health of the Department of Health, Education, and Welfare and for the Bureau of Indian Affairs are so secure that they tend to develop a characteristic smugness. At a meeting of the State Health and Welfare Workers in 1962 at Concho, Oklahoma, an Indian administrator of the Bureau of Indian Affairs said, 'Once an employee of the Bureau of Indian Affairs has established his seniority, he has no reason for anxiety about his job.'

Other work of various sorts is considered respectable: manual labor in the construction industry, truck driving, work as pressers, white-collar work in offices, cosmetology and a wide variety of work within state agencies. But it is in employment that Indians are most often discriminated against. Many non-Indian employers feel that Indians are not reliable or intelligent workers. The myth that all Indians are lazy drunkards still prevails in Oklahoma. An Indian administrator in the personnel department of a large manufacturing firm stated: 'I won't hire Indians, 'cause you can't depend on them.' However, to offset this, there is a considerable number of employers who like Indians and who find them intelligent and willing workers. There are many Indians in Oklahoma City, both in federal and private employment, who have held their jobs for twenty to thirty years, and who have excellent employment records. Many private firms are on their second generation of Indian employees.

While discrimination against Indians exists in central and western Oklahoma, it is not one of the major problems. Many times it is discrimination against an individual rather than against his group. In some sections of the state, however, discrimination is very severe. It is to be regretted that the Sub-committee on Constitutional Rights did not conduct hearings in the Cheyenne-Arapaho country where discrimination has reached its peak. The Bureau of Indian Affairs would be well advised to undertake more and better public relations work in central and western Oklahoma. The situation could be considerably improved, for example, if the suggestions of the Task Force for Information Officers were actively implemented.[7]

A curious form of discrimination against Indians by Indians themselves is the subtle manipulation of Indian society to bring influence to bear in the employment of government personnel. Recently, in a Bureau of Indian Affairs office in western Oklahoma, a vacancy was announced. An examination of candidates for the position was given. Prior to the announced examination date, word went out on the 'Moccasin Telegraph' that a certain individual would get the job and that there really was no use for anyone else to take the examination. The position went to the individual who had been announced on the Moccasin Telegraph as the likely recipient. Other applicants took the examination, but the Moccasin Telegraph probably discouraged still others.

INDIAN TRADITIONS

Indian life does not fall into rigid categories. It is, rather, a complex of interlocking circles, each exerting pressures and control upon the others. An individual functions in different capacities in these circles or groups. The family is the central unit of Indian society now, as it has been in the past. Ostensibly a senior man is the head of each family group, but one must never discount the position of the older women.

The Indian family today retains its old balance, though increase in the life span generally has raised age levels. An old person today is someone sixty years or older. These are the sages of Indian life. The active 'doers' range in age from thirty to sixty years. Individuals under thirty are either getting an education, starting a new career or making it quite clear 'they won't make it'.

Tribal politics, while publicly dominated by younger men, is inwardly controlled by the elder members, through the restraints imposed by family ties. The desire of the older members of a tribe to hold on to the past, the need of middle-aged and young persons to hold a continuum and the attractiveness of feeling that one belongs to an in-group have enabled many tribal traditions to survive, though often in altered forms.

Tight Shoe Indians 'play Indian', as they say, when they put on their moccasins and participate in tribal and inter-tribal gatherings. The annual summer tribal pow-wows are the culmination of a year's social activities. These three- to four-day events usually occur at the approximate time a tribe would traditionally have held a midsummer or harvest dance. Pow-wows follow a similar pattern, but are different from each other in many ways. The Sac-Fox hold their pow-wow to honor their war veterans, and to remember the dead. The Pawnee have a 'Home Coming', a time to meet old friends and to be reunited with a family for a few days. Pawnee come home from all over the United States for this occasion. Tribal pow-wows are usually financed by the sponsoring tribe from tribal funds, money donated by tribal clubs, private gifts and sometimes by a small grant from the State of Oklahoma Planning and Resources Board.

Most of the tribes in central and western Oklahoma hold some native religious ceremonies. The Kickapoo and Sac-Fox hold their spring squaw dance with its accompanying dog sacrifice. The Cheyenne and Arapaho perform the sun dance, and the Pawnee their traditional war dance. Religious ceremonies are sometimes supported from tribal funds, but most often they are 'put up' by individuals. No ceremony stopped for longer than a two-year period, even at the worst period of federal suppression of native religions. The rituals simply went underground and re-emerged when excitement had died down.

Ceremonies and philosophies have, of course, undergone change. Change will affect any dynamic religious tradition. But the recording of religious procedures insures a more consistent presentation of the ceremony, even though the philosophy may have undergone considerable change. The Cheyenne sun dance today is more like that of the 1890s because of the work of 'Mr Mooney', that is, James Mooney, the anthropologist, whose publications on ceremonies are consulted by the Indians. The individuals who participate in socio-religious activities usually have inherited their positions as priests and leaders.

Pow-wows are usually managed by a person locally elected to the office of President. In most cases this individual belongs to a family that has held tribal leadership for many generations. The keeper of the drum, maker of songs, the cooks and holders of many more positions have, as I noted earlier, often inherited their duties. Religious ceremonies have the most rigid pattern of inherited positions. But if events make it necessary for the tribe to choose a new person for a particular position, the choice usually falls within the extended family of the previous incumbent. Individuals who hold these prestige positions in socio-religious events may not always hold prestige positions in other areas of Indian life. Their standing in other fields depends upon family lines. Prestige held in one area of Indian life extends often to all areas, however.

The traditional Plains custom of the 'give-away' is the most conspicuous example of continuum of a culture trait and a prestige symbol. The give-away is usually held at a large public gathering such as a pow-wow. A give-away is held to honor a young member of a family who has achieved something that will reflect credit on the tribe. This may be dancing for the first time, coming of age, joining the armed forces, excellence in traditional crafts or accomplishments in education or employment. The family sponsoring the give-away presents old people and friends from other tribes with gifts of cloth, money, shawls, blankets, and, even today, sometimes a horse. This public expansiveness will increase the prestige position of a family, even though it may leave the family financially crippled for several years.

The Woodland tribes have adapted their traditional custom of 'Gift Friends' and 'Smoking for Horses' to resemble the Plains give-away. However, among the Woodland tribes, the restrictions on those to whom a person may give things are much less stringent. Smoking for horses is the old Sac-Fox custom of forming tribal alliances, when the Sac-Fox would entertain a visiting tribe with a big feast and dance. The Chief would smoke the pipe and give horses to the visiting chief and the Sac-Fox people would ceremonially exchange gifts with their visitors. Individuals who exchanged gifts became 'gift friends'. This exchange established the brother relationship between giver and receiver. Men would give to men and women would give to women; thus sister or brother friends were established for life. Today, as in the past, for all the tribes of central and western Oklahoma the custom of giving away goods at funerals, religious gatherings, weddings and other important events continues. All these traditional Indian customs follow prescribed historic lines and have been a part of Indian life for as long as recorded history can trace.[8]

A word must be said about two innovations in Plains Indian life in Oklahoma: the Kiowa Gourd Dance Clan, and the Kiowa and Kiowa-Apache Black Leggings Societies. Alice Marriott says that today these organizations bear little resemblance to the original societies, although each group has taken its name from traditional men's societies. Many old Kiowa and Kiowa-Apache customs have been incorporated into the rituals of these societies. The members of these groups are usually well educated and in the upper economic brackets of the tribe.

The Native American Church in Oklahoma, while pan-Indian in ceremony and music, has become very diverse from tribe to tribe in its philosophy. Groups with hunting traditions emphasize the male fertility role, while the agricultural tribes place emphasis on the woman's part of reproduction. Each tribe adds to the basic ceremony ceremonies from its own culture. Each tribal group holds its own meetings, although friends from different tribes are invited, and often are given leading positions in the ceremony. The official spokesmen for the Native American Church are chosen at state meetings of the group. Today in Oklahoma about one third of the Indian population belongs to this faith. The activities of the Native American Church form a large part of the winter social life of the Indian community. Even non-believers come to eat the noon meal, which follows the ceremony, with the members of the church. Thus, the Christian and non-Christian groups of a tribe participate together in one more activity.

The traditional Plains 'Hands Game' is played throughout the winter months. This is a guessing game on the order of 'button-button, who's got the button', in which each of two players from one team hides an object in his hands to be guessed by a member of the other team. Singing to drum accompaniment, formalized gestures of guessing with an eagle-feather pointer, special scoring of right and wrong guesses, and wagers make for a pleasant and exciting pastime. Tribes, clubs within tribes, intertribal groups and just plain hand game lovers play somewhere in the state each week. Groups challenge other groups and the excitement and music of the past become joys of today. The Oklahoma Indian Council sponsored an all-state hand game tournament in the spring of 1964, at the close of the hand game season. Seven tribal teams played and 2,000 Indians attended. The tournament started at 1 p.m. Dinner was served at 5.30, and the game was followed at night by an Indian dance.

The rules of the hand game vary from place to place, usually reflecting the playing rules of the sponsoring tribe. The Woodland Indians have adopted this game to replace their traditional moccasin game. Intertribal alliances are made and Indian politics conducted at these winter gatherings in the same way that they are at the summer pow-wows. Both Christian and non-Christian Indians participate in hand games, although the Baptist Church officially frowns on this activity. The Methodist Church does not prohibit the hand game, but will not permit its being played in the recreational rooms of a church.

The urban Indian participates in these tribal and intertribal activities with his country brother. Although Indian social manners prevail, they have been altered and shaped by government boarding schools, mission activities, television and the movies to such an extent that there is little distinction between good manners in the Indian and the non-Indian worlds, although Indians still observe a formality that is not usually found in non-Indian culture.

Authority usually follows traditional patterns of tribal life. Families of influence in the past are families of influence today. The old people are the sages, as they always were, and hold the power to make final decisions for their tribes. The middle-aged people are the spokesmen and public-relations personnel. If they do not carry out the wishes of the old people, become too personally ambitious or assume too much authority, they will be verbally whipped at a public gathering, and shamed into obedience by the old people.[9]

Indeed, perhaps one of the greatest problems in settling the old tribal difficulties of the Kiowa, Kiowa-Apache and Comanche tribes is the struggle between leadership and authority; or between the old people and the middle-aged people. 'What about the old people? They won't like it,' is the inevitable question of the spokesmen-leaders. Today, as always, unanimous vote must be recorded before any action can be taken. A majority vote is not a vote at all. The only thing the majority vote accomplishes is to divide the tribe into factions. The division further complicates tribal affairs, already riddled with historic feuds.

The leaders, or spokesmen, for a tribe are elected by a majority vote of a tribe. Their authority is limited and very often they would not be able to make any innovations were it not for the pressure put on the tribe by the Bureau of Indian Affairs. If a middle-aged man has become the head of his family group then his authority will be recognized by the tribe. One of the present Arapaho hereditary chiefs has such a position today. He has become a middle-man between authority and leadership, bridging the gap which separates the old people from the middle-aged.

Leadership or authority are seldom given to a young individual. Today, as in the past, a man must prove he is A Man. Recently a young man who has participated in many youth conferences and has had an unsuccessful college career, ran for the tribal council of his tribe. He was not elected. The tribe chose a man who had proved his ability to conduct himself in all phases of life as A Man, rather than electing a perennial student who professed leadership but had never demonstrated his ability to be A Man.

Tight Shoe Night

The Moccasin Telegraph, modern highways, and fast cars unite the Indians into a cultural group within the state. Yet we do not have a pan-Indian society. Each tribal gathering is distinctive and old tribal conflicts are still apparent. Intertribal relations exist and still take the same pattern they did many generations ago. Tribes live today in Oklahoma in the same geographical relation to each other as they did before removal; socially and politically the same regional alliances can be made. All Indian people have daily relations with non-Indians. Thus, the Indians remain a minority in the complex culture of Oklahoma, rather than an isolated segment of its population.

What are the effects of national Indian movements upon the Oklahoma Indians? The Youth Conference, which is held each year at the University of Oklahoma, is attended by many young people. The thrill of spending a day at the University plus the Indian dance that follows the meetings are the main incentives for the attendance. The papers presented to this conference do not seem to influence the young people. The politically articulate youth is usually the coffee-cooling Indian whose parents hung around the Indian Agent's office in the old reservation days. He is an opportunist who is viewed with distrust by other Indians. The serious, capable young man or woman goes ahead with life and leaves the talking to his parents and grandparents.

The National Congress of American Indians has little influence on the general life of western and central Oklahoma Indians, though tribal leaders are always interested in hearing about the activities and services of the Congress. The general attitude is that it is better to listen to the other fellow than not know what he is up to. The activities of the Congress have been directed toward reservation problems, and do not focus on the problems of central and western Oklahoma Indians.

There are several intertribal groups throughout central and western Oklahoma. Some of these groups are purely social, like the Oklahoma Intertribal Pow-wow Club. Other groups which have wider programs are the Oklahoma Indian Council and the Oklahomans for Indian Opportunity, located at the University of Oklahoma. The 'Indians for Indians' radio program on Station WNAD, Norman, Oklahoma, every Saturday morning serves as a medium of Indian communication. Tribe, intertribal groups, government, church and individual announcements are read; Indian music is a feature of the program.

Although Tight Shoe Night is every night in Oklahoma, the Indian community remains a separate segment of the population which participates in two sub-cultures. Indian people live scattered among the general population, work with non-Indians and have social intercourse with all areas of Oklahoma culture. Yet Indian ceremonies continue, and Indians want to identify with Indians. Indian education advances, Indian aspirations and achievements increase, but to all appearances at present the Indians will always be *The Indians.*

The plight of the Indian people of central and western Oklahoma has been little changed by the present administration. Indians without reservations, they remain the forgotten children of 'Wooshinton'. The Welfare Officer of the Bureau of Indian Affairs for western and central Oklahoma stated at a meeting at Concho, Oklahoma, in 1962, 'The function of the Bureau is service to land, not to people.'

The 'Fact Sheet on BIA Programs and the American Indians' for January 1963 states:

A 'New Trail' for Indians leading to equal citizenship privileges and responsibilities, maximum economic self-sufficiency, and full participation in American life became the keynote for administration of the Bureau of Indian Affairs of the Department of the Interior shortly after June 30, 1961. The major effect was to shift emphasis in Bureau programming away from purely custodial functions toward greater development of human and natural resources on Indian reservations.[10]

The following article by Mark Brady, 'Official Outlines Indian Problems', appeared in *The Daily Oklahoman* on Tuesday, 17 November 1964. It illustrates the tendency to generalize a highly complex problem largely from the perspective of the reservations system.

'The disease of poverty is chronic and endemic among American Indians,' a top US Indian Affairs official told the Oklahoma Health and Welfare Association Monday.

Leslie P. Towle, area director of the Bureau of Indian Affairs, outlined problems of the Indian and the possible solution at a luncheon of the 22nd annual conference of the association which is meeting at the Sheraton-Oklahoma Hotel.

'At the root of the Indian's problem is a psychological factor,' Towle said. 'Penury is not the most important matter, although the Indian lives on an average income of less than $1,500 a year.'

Towle outlined the history of the white man's treatment of the American Indian. 'The Indian had a vital existence and a self-supporting life,' he said. 'He lived as a warrior and a hunter and he had to have great mobility.

'When he was put on a reservation with nothing to do he languished and suffered in despair,' Towle said.

Towle blamed a 'destructive and excessive federal paternalism in the early days, and a continued lack of community understanding of his problems for the present-day plight of the Indian.'

Citing his earlier experience as plains Indian administrator Towle described what he said was a frequent situation:

The child comes to the white man's school without any knowledge of the English language, and often without knowing the basic things he must know to cope with a white man's society;

Because of his earlier training in the hunter-warrior values of the Indian society the Indian child becomes confused by the conflicting codes of the two societies;

When he reaches adolescence he must chose between the white man's road which leads to ostracism and banishment by his family and tribal relations, 'or he must follow the Indian way which is a dead end'.

To ease these problems Towle urged a program of greater federal action and increased community participation. He urged the establishment of adult-child schools, where parents and their young children would be brought into schools together to begin giving the children the basic tools of the white man's culture.

'The final solution must be to place greater responsibility on the individual Indian,' Towle said.

Towle, whose headquarters is at Anadarko, was one of several welfare and social workers who spoke before the various institutes and workshops at the conference.

More than 600 professional and lay welfare workers registered for the three-day meeting. A staff of 75 directed the various meetings and more than 30 exhibits by state, local and federal agencies.

Where do the Indians without reservations fit? Do they keep on going to Oklahoma public schools and colleges? Do they keep on being administrators, teachers, judges, missionaries, truck drivers, leaders in PTA groups? Or do they stop and attend school with their children?

The time has arrived when the administrators of the Bureau of Indian Affairs and anthropologists should stop talking about 'The Indian' floating around in time and space. Today we have enough knowledge to state, administratively and scientifically, what we are talking about temporally, geographically, legally and humanely.

Indian culture in western Oklahoma never died. Missionaries, government personnel and do-gooders changed and altered Indian life on the surface but not beneath the surface. Basic Indian philosophy and ceremonies, like the sun dance of the Cheyenne and the Arapaho or the dog feasts of the Kickapoo and Sac-Fox, never stopped. Horses gave way to automobiles, buffalo to beef, hunting to office work, tipis to houses, braids to hair curlers, but Indians remained Indians. Tight Shoe Night is every night and every day in central and western Oklahoma.

Notes

1. 'Fact Sheet on BIA Programs and the American Indians' (Department of the Interior, Bureau of Indian Affairs, January 1963), 1.

2. Alice Marriott and Carol K. Rachlin, 'Urbanization Problems of Oklahoma Indians' (Distributed by Oklahoma Health and Welfare Association, 1962); see also Marriott and Rachlin, 'No Reservations – The Oklahoma YWCA's Intertribal Indian Center', *The YWCA Magazine*, LVIII, 8 (November 1964), 11–13.

3. Lewis Meriam, *The Problem of Indian Administration* (Baltimore, 1928), 48–50.

4. Carol K. Rachlin, 'The Native American Church of Oklahoma', *The Chronicles of Oklahoma* (not yet released at time of publication; available through Oklahoma Historical Society, Oklahoma City).

5. '1 in 7 Pupils Handicapped', Oklahoma City *Times* (12 November 1964), 37.

6. 'Oklahoma City – Growth at a Glance. 1963 Economic Development Report. First Six Months' (Industrial Division, Oklahoma City Chamber of Commerce, 1964).

7. 'Report to the Secretary of the Interior by the Task Force on Indian Affairs' (Department of the Interior, Bureau of Indian Affairs, 10 July 1961).

8. Carol K. Rachlin, 'Powwow', *Oklahoma Today*, XIV, 2 (Spring 1964), 18–22.

9. cf. Alice Marriott, *The Ten Grandmothers* (Norman, Oklahoma, 1945).

10. See note 1. See also the BIA pamphlet 'Answers to Questions About the American Indian' (1963), 1.

JAMES A. CLIFTON

FACTIONAL CONFLICT AND THE INDIAN COMMUNITY THE PRAIRIE POTAWATOMI CASE

KNOWLEDGE of man does not always grow according to the orderly deductive logic of cautious scientific probing. Instead, reasonably valid social science understanding often accumulates out of, and perhaps in spite of, a history of theoretical fits and starts, each punctuated by sometimes unaccountable speculative and methodological fads. However, occasionally, as with the efforts of anthropologists to build knowledge of social and cultural processes among American Indian peoples, we find rich systematic thinking linked meaningfully to well-defined problems and carefully described aggregates of fact. This is true, for example, of our understanding of such phenomena as the nature of messianic or cultural revitalization movements, the processes of innovation and inter-cultural transfer of novel traits, and the antecedent cases of cultural disorganization and decay. In recent years anthropologists have produced exciting contributions to science in these and similar areas of cultural change. One purpose of this paper is to suggest that the phenomena of factionalism is, perhaps, another place where valid understanding is now being created.

The connection between this intention and the contemporary Prairie Potawatomi community is that this human group provides one of many available laboratories for the study of factional and other socio-cultural processes. But if this group is a testing-ground it is not the only one. The study on which I am basing this article might well have been conducted within most if not all other contemporary reservation Indian communities. I am using the Potawatomi, then, as a kind of sample at least partly representative of a larger universe. This group of Indians is by no means the only one which has experienced or is experiencing the effects of persistent, uncontrolled conflict, for the causes of factionalism are much too generally distributed among modern Indians to allow this case uniqueness. Our conclusions should thus, in part, apply to many contemporary American Indian populations.

In a sense my comments here must be construed as a progress report, for the factional conflict I have been studying among the Potawatomi is as yet unresolved, and my monitoring operation continues. The aim of the study has been to obtain a natural history of the antecedents, course, character and outcome of this particular factional situation. On the one hand this contributes to special knowledge of the Potawatomi, while on the other it provides one kind of test of an existing set of ideas purporting to explain and to allow comprehension of factional conflicts in general.

SOME DEFINITIONS

The conceptual scheme I have been using to guide my research comes primarily from the recent efforts of Alan R. Beals and Bernard J. Siegel, and of David French, to formulate a coherent body of propositions concerning factional conflicts.[1] Because the word 'factionalism' comes straight from the standard English vocabulary, let me first specify what I do not mean. In ordinary speech 'factionalism' marks the opposition of parties to some sort of conflict, while 'faction' refers directly to a group of persons bound together by common interests or purposes. However, in most instances the idea involves groups which work through their conflicting interests according to some set of rules, so that while they may remain contentious over the long run, conflicting objectives may be compromised, issues resolved, and the conflict somehow regulated. But in the technical sense used here, I mean by factionalism something rather different.

In this special sense factionalism is one of several types of conflict, but the reference is to a condition of a socio-cultural system rather than to a special interest group. Indeed, as we shall see, in case of prolonged factional conflict such as among the Prairie Potawatomi, it may be extremely difficult even to specify the boundaries or membership of the conflicting groupings, which proliferate and interlock in quite complex ways. Factionalism thus is characterized as a type of overt conflict within a given social system, a type of conflict which persists long enough so that traditional control mechanisms can be brought to bear. Factionalism differs from other types of conflict in that these control mechanisms fail, so that the dispute continues unresolved and unregulated. Moreover, although initially such conflicts operate on a single structural level (for example, within the political arena, the conflict may be restricted to a council of local leaders), as they persist their effects may be diffused, felt and acted out on other levels or in other parts of the total social system.[2] Finally, factional conditions are defined as one sort of consequence of the stresses of culture contact situations, for the kinds of issues and disputes which lead to persistent unregulated conflicts seem to be especially frequent at the intersection of different cultures, particularly when the representatives of one attempt to manipulate and modify the nature of the other. In brief, the view taken here of factional conflicts holds that they are overt, unregulated disputes resulting from the stresses of acculturation situations.[3]

This kind of a model neatly fits the Prairie Potawatomi and most other reservation Indian communities, where factional disputes are often an endemic problem. In the instance of the Potawatomi, as far back as adequate ethnohistorical materials take us, there have been multiple acculturative stresses, considerable conflict, innovative responses to these situations and socio-cultural changes. In summarizing this history of the Prairie Band of Potawatomi we must necessarily oversimplify, but let us examine the last one hundred and thirty years of Potawatomi reactions to the press of American civilization.

I

The modern Prairie Potawatomi are no longer a single, homogeneous cultural population; they occupy no common territory, for the total membership is widely dispersed, although a cluster of approximately six hundred of the total of twenty one hundred members lives on or about the old reservation in Kansas; their common language is English; and they are marked by great diversity in habits, values and beliefs. They are not, in any technical sense of the terms, a single geographic community, a nation, a tribe or a band. Rather they constitute a federal membership corporation under the terms of a constitution granted them by the Department of the Interior. As we will note, there are several nodes of socio-cultural homogeneity included within this membership corporation, and there is included as well a local community, but diversity and dispersal of population are the rule. It is this membership corporation within which the factional conflict currently operates.[4]

This modern Prairie Potawatomi Corporation includes within its membership as one node of cultural homogeneity the ideological successor of the staunchly conservative and nativistic elements of the old United Band of Chippewa, Ottawa and Potawatomi who were shipped out of the Chicago region in 1833.[5] But as I will show, the membership corporation also includes several other elements with diverse antecedents, while at the same time exhibiting the results of the acculturation and assimilation of many members into the larger white society. The movement of the old United Band from Chicago in 1833 was the consequence of the removal policy, which was aimed at clearing eastern lands for white settlement. One feature of this removal policy is of special interest, for it included the notion that scattered segments of linguistic or cultural groups should be brought together in one place, where the 'Nation' could be united. Thus the United Band moved first to the Platte Purchase in Missouri, and then in 1837 to a reserve near what is now Council Bluffs, Iowa. In the same years the other major Potawatomi group in the East, a group made up of Indiana and Michigan elements and called the Mission Band, was moved to a reserve on the Osage River in Kansas. Eleven years later the United Band – now known as the Bluffs or sometimes the Prairie Band – and the Mission Band were persuaded by government officials to leave their separate reserves and come together in Kansas on the old Kaw river reservation, where they were, according to the plan of the removal policy, to be a single nation.

For predictable and obvious reasons, this experiment in nationhood was foredoomed to failure. To begin with, although they shared communalities of culture, ecological adaptation and social structure, these several bands of Potawatomi, during the years when they lived in the east, had no tradition of or experience with joint occupation of a common territory, and little experience of large-scale organization for collective enterprises. In addition, their experiences with European and American contact agents had been quite different: the Chicago (or Bluffs) Band was highly conservative and resistant to cultural change, while the Mission Band was living up to its name by attaining a semblance of literacy and some mastery of agricultural skills. It included an increasing number of christianized persons in its membership. Moreover, during the period when the Mission Band was located on the Osage River reserve, the Bluffs Band was adapting itself to large-scale hunting of the plains buffalo and the techniques of plains warfare. Understandably, the leaders of the Mission Band were none too pleased with the prospect of too close an association with their wild cousins from Iowa. The two local groups were very different in terms of the degree of acculturation of their members. Thus the Potawatomi Nation was an artificial construction, a product of the imperatives of the American frontier. It would probably have collapsed even if left in isolation, much less while being overrun by streams of immigrant trains, or caught up in the free state fracas, the Civil War and a deluge of land-hungry sod-busters and railway promoters.

The experiment failed in 1861 when the major portion of the old Kaw reservation was parcelled out in individual allotments to descendants of the Mission Band. In the years just preceding 1861 the pressure to accept allotments had been intense, and although this change was couched in terms of promoting the civilization of the Potawatomi, the important motivation was to free more Indian land for white settlement. The leadership of the Bluffs Band – now becoming known as the Prairie Band – were adamant in their rejection of the program for sectionalizing their communally owned lands. In the end, they were successful in obtaining a compromise, and managed to retain a diminished eleven-mile square of the old reservation as undivided corporate property. A few members of the Mission Band joined forces with the conservative Bluffs Band-Prairie Band, but the great majority of these more acculturated Indians elected to accept individual allotments of land. The remainder of the former reservation was homesteaded or otherwise acquired by Americans. Thus a conflict engendered by the demands of whites was resolved by a cleavage of the young 'nation' into the Prairie and Citizens Bands.[6] This is a clear instance of schismatic factionalism, and although the split did not neatly divide the descendants of the old United-Council Bluffs Band from those of the Mission Band, it very nearly followed those lines.

The resolution of this conflict over allotments and assimilation has implications which go beyond the predictable division into conservative and acculturated components. One of these implications is the fact that fourteen years of additional acculturation and co-residence had produced a small group of dissident Prairie Band members who allied themselves with the assimilationist faction. Similarly, there were a few Mission Band members who elected the nativistic style of life. The point is that even though a strong core of conservatism marked the majority of Prairie Band members, the band was regularly producing a minority of white-oriented members. The second point of significance is the use of schismatic split and emigration as a way of resolving conflict. It was a favored solution, and still is one which conservatives today generously recommend to the contemporary white-oriented faction in the Prairie Potawatomi corporation. But free lands have long since been very limited and, as we will indicate, there are several other factors which now prevent a schismatic division and out-migration.

With the Citizen Potawatomi out of their system,[7] the Band since 1861 has made constant attempts to maintain something approximating a conservative way of life in the face of vastly increased acculturative contacts and persistent efforts by contact agents to discourage or eradicate conservatism and to encourage assimilation. Pressure from local white settlers and from the government to allot or sectionalize the Prairie Band reservation never really ceased, but came to a head with the passage of the Dawes Allotment Act of 1887. The form of Potawatomi resistance to – and the methods used by Indian Agents to secure – acceptance of allotments are instructive, for they exemplify the nature of Indian resistance to forced change and the selective rewards and punishments of acculturative stress. Under very able leadership, the conservative elements of the Prairie Band bitterly and successfully resisted allotment of their lands until nearly the turn of the century.[8] After repeated inducements, threats of force and imprisonment of conservative leaders, the Indian agent finally hit upon a solution to his problem of securing acceptance of allotments. The agent offered a double allotment to each member of any family who would accept one. The response came, of course, from disaffected Prairie Band members, those most highly acculturated, but included in this group of acceptors were a number of persons with quite dubious claims to the status of Prairie Potawatomi, or for that matter Potawatomi Indian. Some of the earliest allottees were probably not even Indians, including a number of persons who claimed to have been adopted into the tribe. An undetermined number of others seem to have been drawn from wandering fragments of other populations, a misplaced Munsee or an itinerant Sauk, for example. Whether or not they were Potawatomi, or even Indians, these early allottees were understandably cooperative when offered double portions of the choicest pieces of Prairie Band real estate. It is difficult to read the intentions of deceased representatives of the Office of Indian Affairs, and the correspondence of this period is vague on the rationale of this procedure, but if we may perhaps gauge purpose from effect, the agent was applying significant pressure on the conservatives, by punishing them for resistance and rewarding their opponents for cooperation.

The conservatives drew appropriate conclusions, capitulated, and hastened to secure their own allotments. But the enmity aroused by this action and the effects of the forced adoption of non-Prairie Band persons persist to this day as major ingredients of the current factional conflict. It is of critical importance to this modern conflict because of the possibility that the Bureau of Indian Affairs may approve the distribution of Potawatomi land settlement or claims case funds to the descendants of all persons who received allotments on the reservation, and because a large part of the leadership of the current assimilated faction seems to have some difficulty in tracing its ancestry prior to the period of allotments.

Now we must abbreviate the events of thirty years. Following forced allotments came the mechanization of Kansas agriculture, the industrialization of nearby Topeka, World War I, the economic boom of the 1920s and finally the great depression of the thirties. During these decades dissident acculturated elements frequently married out and moved away from the reservation, converting their allotments into cash or rental properties. In this fashion some of the strains of cultural heterogeneity – produced by in-group variations in level of acculturation – were partially relieved. But by the late 1920s the attractiveness of the local community was increased for many of those who might have moved away earlier. There was, for example, a stable group of successful, christianized farmers living alongside the numerically dominant conservatives, and the members of this culturally progressive group were, so far as we have been able to determine, especially successful in cultivating good relations with the Indian agent and the Office of Indian

Affairs. It was, for example, the progressive farmers who were most likely to be appointed to the Tribal Advisory Board, the chief functions of which were to validate agency decisions, to communicate these decisions to the membership and to report community reactions. This tame council was chosen in the same manner in which cooperative appointed chiefs had been selected in an earlier year. It certainly was not representative of the diverse interests of the reservation community, whose membership seems to have been dominated by conservative or nativistic elements, as is evident from the frequency and the extent of participation in the Drum (or Dream Dance) religion, the Peyote religion, clan ceremonials, sorcery and shamanistic practices.[9]

II

We have fixed on this period of the early 1930s as the baseline for our study of the contemporary factional conflict, while accepting a certain arbitrariness in this date, for some of the antecedents of the conflict clearly have historical roots which go back much earlier. But it was in this period that the conservative faction got organized and emerged as a reform movement. It was in this period that the conservative reformers, by obtaining the good offices of Superintendent Baldwin of Haskell Institute, secured and adopted a constitution, the so-called Baldwin Constitution, which established a temporarily viable and more representative elected Business Committee. It was then that these reformers concentrated conservative support behind a crude nativistic-political revival, campaigning on a program of absolute, unswerving opposition to Agency rule, a program which they (perhaps too effectively) carried into effect. In brief, it was in this period that factional lines were clearly drawn, when a series of overt conflicts became prominent in reservation life, when repeated efforts at control were tried and failed, and when the dispute began to ramify into various aspects of community life, disrupting collective activities and placing increased strain on the social fabric. Further, it was in this period that the Indian agent began calling one conservative leader the 'Pendergast of the Potawatomi'. Finally, it was in the early thirties that the conservatives accepted the idea of prosecuting a claims case, thus providing a central economic issue for later factional developments.

The course of all human events should, if possible, have a dated origin point, and we cannot allow the Potawatomi factional conflict to be an exception. Let us select the summer of 1932 for this purpose. At that time a group of conservatives were in Topeka at a country fair, beating on drums and generally acting like Indians so as to earn a little spending money. One day at the fair several of these young conservatives were approached by a man who claimed to be a Cherokee, but who at first looked suspiciously like an American Negro, a suspicion which declined appreciably as he became more helpful to the conservative cause. As closely as retrospective accounts of this event can make clear, this party said something like, 'Take me to your chiefs, I have a message for the Potawatomi tribe.' As nearly as we can determine, when he was later brought before an assembly of reservation conservatives, his message contained two themes and ran something like this: 'You Indians have been badly mistreated by the US government, your treaties have been violated, and you deserve justice.' Apparently, the conservatives were quite willing to entertain this notion. The second part of his message may be reconstructed as follows: 'There is a pot of gold in Washington which belongs to the Potawatomi, and I know how to get it for you.' The conservatives seem to have found this idea equally appealing.

Fragments of Past Glory. In the same Pow-wows, a few old-timers show up dressed in the few remaining bits of their old finery; a headdress captured by Grandfather in a raid against the Pawnee, or an old silver medallion or comb.

The Peyote Ritual. Jack Forty, of the Prairie Potawatomi, is shown seated at the low table used for Peyote religion ritual meals. The ritual implements of this religion are laid out before him.

And Christ Struck the Drum. The late Curtiss Pequano shown acting out his role of *Pakokwanni* (Staffman), symbolic of the action of Christ, who put power into *misho*, the sacred drum of the Dream Dance Religion. This action, and worship around the drum, is believed to have provided relief from white oppression.

The Water Drum. Johnson Wishteyah playing the small water drum used in the Native American Church (or Peyote rite) rituals. Note the position of his left hand: the tone of the drum is controlled by the pressure of his thumb.

Polyethylene Indianism. When Pow-wow day comes around, representatives of the assimilated, off-reservation faction appear in costumes which bear little resemblance to authentic, traditional Potawatomi wearing apparel. Conservative Potawatomi refer to these plastic and nylon outfits as 'Santa Claus' suits.

(Above) *Squaw Dice Counters.* Ideally, the counters should be carved from Buffalo bone, but recently beef has had to do. This is one of the last few recreational games of chance still played by old-timers of the Prairie Potawatomi reservation.

(Left) *Squaw Dice.* Pkuknokwe shown playing Squaw Dice. The dice are thrown in the wooden salad bowl and points are made according to the number of dark sides which come up.

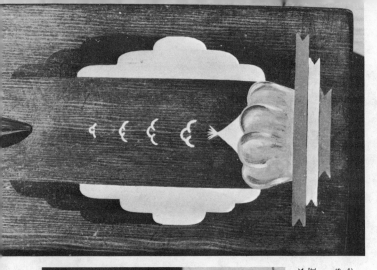

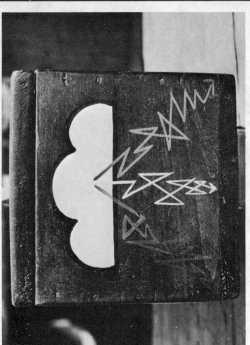

(Above) *The Peyote Prayer* (a). Design on one end of the Peyote box showing prayers – represented by blue, red and yellow bolts of lightning – returning from heaven.

(Right) *The Peyote Prayer* (b). Top of Peyote box, with wing motifs attached to a representation of the peyote button, the ritual tepee atop the button, and prayers ascending to heaven.

Viewed from the perspective of the conservative Potawatomi, this person was a godsend who could only have been improved on had he arrived in a vision. Seen through the eyes of the local Indian agent, he was patently a subversive agent and, in the spirit of the times, possibly a wobbly. And even the more acculturated Potawatomi were at first attracted by the promise of a windfall, for times were hard on Kansas farms in 1932. Viewed from the perspective of social science, he loses something of his luster, but none of his interest, for he was in fact a very special sort of culture-contact agent, a self-made inter-cultural go-between, a technical specialist in the early Pan-Indian movement, a man immensely knowledgeable concerning Indians and Indian affairs and wise also in the ways of American culture. He had read Indian law, memorized every treaty and studied all available historical documents concerning the Potawatomi. In addition to his knowledge and obvious sympathy for the situation of the Prairie Band's conservatives, he began acting as an advocate for their case, pleading for them, and arguing a course of action aimed at putting large sums of money at the conservatives' disposal. The conservatives immediately adopted him, accepted his counsel and assistance, and started the long train of events leading to the successful prosecution of several substantial claims cases involving settlements for treaty violations and for inadequate payment for their former lands.

The reasons for selecting this date as an original point are three. Although the conservatives had already begun marshalling their opposition to the appointed tame-council, they had no focal issue around which to rally their forces. The possibility of securing a claims settlement gave them just such an issue. At the same time the status of Prairie Potawatomi immediately increased in importance for all concerned, whether progressive, conservative or indifferent.

I believe that without the promise of a cash settlement, many dissident progressives, especially those settled at remote parts of the country, would simply have continued their drift away from an identification with the Prairie Band community. But given the promise and possibility of a cash windfall, they could not afford to do so. The third reason, therefore, is that the conservatives' action contributed to the maintenance of the Potawatomi group as one social system, within which the factional conflict developed further, and within which it now prevails. Thus while serving the conservatives as a rallying point, the claims issue also reinforced the importance of remaining Potawatomi in the thought of assimilated persons. The resurgence of interest in community affairs on the part of absentees, in turn, intensified the factional conflict, which, we shall see, grew to such proportions that although claims cases have been won and the funds appropriated and placed in the Federal Treasury, they have never been paid out. These monies have not been paid out because of the effects of the continued conflict situation.

While they were developing the claims case issue, the conservatives were also successful in obtaining considerable freedom from Agency domination, and simultaneously they began ignoring the demands of progressives for a hand in Potawatomi community government. The history of this aspect of community life during the 1930s and 1940s is a series of victorious jousts with their agent and with other representatives of the Bureau of Indian Affairs. For a long time, the conservatives' principal adversary was a man who served them first as chief clerk of the Agency, and then as superintendent of the local Indian office. This superintendent was himself an assimilated Indian and a man firmly raised in and devoted to the old Indian service policy of total paternalism. He was convinced of and always acted on the premise that the business committee elected under the Baldwin Constitution was no more than a powerless board of advisors, while the committeemen were at least partially convinced that they represented continuity with an ancient line of Potawatomi Chiefs. When the idealistic ferment and the fervent humanism of the Roosevelt Administration's Office of Indian Affairs in 1934 produced the Indian Reorganization Act, and action manifestly intended to function as a means for promoting community self-government and economic uplift, the Potawatomi's local superintendent interpreted that legislation as an instrument of assimilation, and began a series of maneuvers designed to secure acceptance of the IRA at all costs.[10]

Thus it developed that the Prairie Band never adopted an Indian Reorganization Act constitution, although following systematic research into community conditions by Indian Service Personnel several tentative ones were drawn up, constitutions which would have put the weight of power into the hands of the residents of the reservation. Part of the reason for the conservative's rejection of this social-structural novelty lay in the character and actions of the local advocate of change, their superintendent. Another part was a considerable suspicion of anything unrequested coming out of Washington, in which instance the Indian Reorganization Act was interpreted as a further instrument of assimilation and was identified with the Dawes Act of forty-seven years earlier. Yet other conclusions were drawn by the conservatives: that the IRA would largely benefit the Catholic, farmer element, and that it was a threat to their own power. But their rejection was firmly decided when they became convinced that the costs of the Indian Reorganization Act – if applied to the Prairie Band reservation – would be deducted from any future claims case judgments. By the mid 1930s the conservatives were apparently convinced that if they could avoid reorganization and secure a substantial judgment against the government, they could then obtain unrestricted control over such funds and parlay this into a device for limiting the influence and rewards going to the more highly acculturated Potawatomi.[11]

Because of the parallel they afford with the means of securing adoption of the earlier Dawes Act, and because they further illustrate the selective rewards and punishments applied by white contact agents, a few examples of the superintendent's efforts to secure Prairie Band acceptance of the IRA are in order. Never an ingenuous man, after direct persuasion and negotiation had failed him, this superintendent called a meeting of all tribes under his jurisdiction – the Iowa, the Kansas Sauk and Fox, the Kickapoo and the Prairie Potawatomi – for the purpose of voting on the reorganization legislation. The trick here was that the other three tribes were highly acculturated and heavily in favor of reorganization, and their votes combined with those of the dissident Prairie Band progressives could easily have carried the day, especially if the superintendent's proposal, that the votes of all present be applied to all participating tribes, were accepted. In a stormy public revolt in which threats of overt violence against the body and person of the superintendent were prominent, the conservative Potawatomi leadership upset this move.

On another occasion the superintendent, exercising powers he did not enjoy, simply fired the conservative Business Committee. A protest telegram from the conservatives to Washington pointed out the illegality of this action, and brought a reversal from the Commissioner's Office. Shortly thereafter, the agent stage-managed a meeting in an off-reservation setting which he publicly and pointedly announced was not concerned with the IRA issue at all.[12] This meeting was well attended by the progressive farmer

Potawatomi and technically boycotted by the conservatives.[13] After a brief opening speech the superintendent was surprised to find the meeting developing into a spontaneous demonstration against the conservatives. A motion to throw out the conservative council was made and seconded. The motion was made by one of the men the superintendent had earlier appointed to the committee after firing the conservatives; it was seconded by another such; and when it passed, the meeting promptly elected the same progressive council which had just been deposed by the Commissioner of Indian Affairs. Again a protest from the conservatives to Washington caused a reversal, this time on the basis of a technical foul – the agent had not given the requisite thirty-day constitutional notice for a special Business Committee election.[14] These were only a few of the devices open to the superintendent, for on other occasions he attempted to have the children of conservative leaders separated from their parents and placed in boarding schools on the grounds that they were insanely fanatic in their political activities. He also tried to make political use of the economic rewards he had at his disposal. But conservative opposition was unceasing, and thereafter the superintendent gave up the battle. When the country entered World War II the reservation was largely, if temporarily, depopulated, and with men away in service and families off at defense jobs, the factional fight simmered down.

Earlier I suggested that perhaps the conservatives were overly successful in their efforts to seize and hold the reins of power within the reservation community. While their short-run tactics were nearly impeccable, they committed strategic blunders which opened the way to a resurgence of culturally progressive, absentee and assimilated elements. What the conservatives accomplished by their rigid opposition to the Bureau of Indian Affairs was to isolate the

Prairie Band community from the full benefit of many technical, financial and social services available through the Bureau. Particularly, by rejecting the Indian Reorganization Act, they effectively denied the progressives access to many services which the progressives wanted, although the conservatives did not. Consequently they encouraged an alliance between the progressives and the Agency, and provided the more acculturated group with a ready-made set of issues around which its leadership could rally followers.

Having successfully warded off the efforts of their superintendent to promote adoption of the IRA, increasingly the conservative leadership insulated itself from meaningful contacts with Bureau officials. Through the years, they became more and more secretive about their activities and plans, arbitrary in their decisions, autocratic and imperious in their behavior, and threatening in their posture towards all who gave evidence of opposing them. Then the conservative council appointed itself as a special claims committee (with life tenure) charged with the responsibility of handling the disposition of their land judgment cases against the government. In short order they forgot that there was a distinction between the appointed claims committee and the elected business committee, and ceased holding elections for the latter offices. This departure from the democratic process is evidence of how badly the conservatives misconstrued their position – which was not as secure as it seemed to them then – and it shows also that they were quite out of touch with the realities of their legal and administrative obligations to the Bureau of Indian Affairs. By abrogating their responsibilities to the many members of the Prairie Band community, by antagonizing the local, area and Washington offices of the Bureau of Indian Affairs, and, finally, by not devising and accepting some kind of constitu-

tional instrument, the conservatives built into the dike surrounding them a serious structural flaw.

In the years immediately following World War II, when
most of the membership had returned to the area, it seemed
that the pot of gold promised in 1932 was soon to be made
available. With the passage of the Indian Claims Commission Act a formal avenue for land claims litigation had been
opened up, and the first Potawatomi cases were going well.
Moreover, the reservation population was swelling with returned veterans and war-workers, not all of whom were so
committed to the conservative cause as they had been in
earlier years. Thus the numbers of progressives increased,
and they began organizing and demanding a hand in community affairs. The conservatives continued to ignore them,
and the progressives struck at the weakness in the conservative position. Protesting the autocratic, arbitrary and un-
representative nature of Prairie Band government, leaning
heavily on Agency and Area Office support, the progressives
finally managed, after repeated failures, to secure the adoption of a constitution, which was approved by the Bureau of
Indian Affairs.

The membership provisions of the constitution adopted
in 1961 are of special interest. The earlier IRA constitutions
prepared by the Bureau for the Prairie Band had restricted
membership in the band (actually, the community) to persons of one-fourth or more Prairie Band descent, and had
restricted voting rights and the right of office to residents
of the reservation proper. The provisions of the 1961 constitution, quite to the contrary, granted membership to all
persons who had received Dawes Act allotments and their
descendants regardless of their degree of 'blood', and specifically excluding residence on the reservation as a qualifi-
cation for voting or office holding. The constitution drawn
for the Prairie Band in 1961 thus placed final and nearly

irrevocable power into the hands of the absentee, assimilated or progressive elements of the membership.[15] It gave jural status to a membership corporation, and therefore reorganized the structure of the Prairie Potawatomi community. It effectively put the conservatives out of power. Or at least it would have if the conservatives had been willing to accept the rules set by the new constitution, which they were not. Instead, they began a set of legal moves through state and federal courts which have not yet ended, but which have allowed an injunction preventing the progressives from distributing claims case monies. In this way the factional conflict has denied the members access to what is perhaps the one most highly valued collective goal, per capita payments from the tribe's estate.

We should mention that there are now slightly more than 2,100 enrolled Prairie Potawatomi, no more than 300 of whom may be counted as culturally conservative. Up through the 1940s the Bureau of Indian Affairs never counted more than about 700 Prairie Potawatomi. The great surge came after the settlement of the first claims cases, and as a consequence of the very permissive membership provisions of the 1961 constitution. This does not represent a natural increase from the population base as counted in the 1930s and 1940s, but rather the addition of off-reservation absentee individuals and their descendants, persons many of whom had long since severed their connections with the community. The mechanism which defeated the conservatives should now be clear. Moreover, the arithmetic of the difference between five million claims case dollars divided by 2,100 members, as against five million divided by 300 or so conservatives, is only a partial measure of the latter's sense of loss. More prominent in the attentions of the conservatives was (and is) their loss of control over the community life of the reservation population and the decline of their influence. In passing we should mention that a primary concern of the Bureau of Indian Affairs in recent years has been to see that the conservatives do not arbitrarily exclude persons from the benefits of the judgment cases who would otherwise be entitled to them, and that another concern has remained the development of some form of stable, constitutional government to administer corporate affairs and to act as an administrative buffer between the Bureau and the membership.

III

That this has been a description of a factional development, that the current dispute within the Potawatomi corporation constitutes a case of overt, unresolved conflict within a social system, there is little doubt. I have tried to show how several modes of conflict resolutions have been attempted and failed: the effort of a single sub-group to exert dominance and drive opponents out of the system is one such mode. Appeals to outside authorities have at best brought only temporary relief, while appeals to the courts have only prolonged the conflict and offer no hope of permanent solution. Other attempted modes of resolution include threats of violence, sorcery – which seems to have been especially pronounced in the mid and late 1930s[16] – avoidance, public shaming, boycotting and various other informal interpersonal control devices. It is notable that arbitration and compromise have never been seriously considered by any of the parties to the conflict, for factionalism is a phenomenon of extremes.

I would emphasize that while out-migration was a favored means of settling conflicts arising out of differences in acculturation of the 1930s, when the social system involved was primarily that of a community, with the increased importance of the reservation as a fixed point of reference for maintaining the status of Potawatomi and with the imposition of a membership corporation structure in 1961, outmigration no longer could resolve such differences. The reason for this is that place of residence is no longer a criterion for membership in the corporation or for participation in corporate affairs. For example, none of the current members of the elected Business Committee are residents of the reservation.

This is not to imply that the value of membership in the Potawatomi corporation for the absentees can be measured only in cash benefits. This is not true, although access to corporate assets is an important consideration. Perhaps equally important is the fact that in terms of ethnic status, the Potawatomi (unlike other Americans except those of Negro descent, but like all other Indians) never quite become fully assimilated. While Polish immigrants become Polish-Americans, and then, in a few generations, Americans, persons of some Potawatomi descent, no matter how small the blood-quantum, never add the hyphen. They remain Potawatomi. In part this has been the consequence of the inflated prestige attached to the status of Indian in American culture, in part the consequence of the many tangible benefits which are made available to persons of Indian descent. But the status of Indian is generally fixed in terms of enrollment in a specific tribal membership corporation, wherein membership is defined as an ascribed status, that is, in terms of descent. This fixed point of structural reference, a locus on which to hinge one's identity as Potawatomi, is what the progressives offered and the conservatives denied the absentee assimilated descendants of the Dawes Act allottees. The unique feature of the membership corporations, such as that now controlling Prairie Potawatomi affairs, is that, with the status of member fixed in terms of descent, the membership is under no further obligations and has no responsibilities. Hence the Potawatomi corporation harbors within its membership an extreme range of variation in values and cultural orientations, and it is within the structure of this corporation that factional conflicts must be worked out. It should be clear, then, that the conflict has followed the traditional lines of strain within first the community and later the corporation.

Two further matters require discussion. The first is the question of limitations in the structural effects of and the personal responses to this conflict. The second is the importance of ambiguity as an antecedent to factionalism. In previous discussions of factionalism, much emphasis has been placed upon the lack of regulation and the disorganization resultant from unresolved conflicts of this nature. Such thinking seems to presume the spread of the conflict from one to many levels, and the increasing demoralization of the persons involved. I believe that this may be because most existing studies of factional disputes have been conducted in fairly compact, culturally homogeneous geographic communities. So far as I can see, something quite different is happening in the Potawatomi case. The effects of the conflict are largely compartmentalized and do not seem to have spread much beyond the political sphere. This is possible in the Potawatomi case because of the considerable dispersal of the population, the differences in occupation, interest, life-style and values which characterize the participants, and the favored techniques of avoidance and boycotting. Opponents are not forced through co-residence to treat with one another. Moreover, the participants – at least the active leaders – seem to relish the scheming, maneuvering, researching and other behavior associated with sustaining opposition and maintaining alliances. We have little evidence that this conflict itself has contributed much to the demoralization of persons or groups. The Prairie Band members still exhibit the considerable zest for living that earlier observers have commented on. Finally, there have been efforts to extend the range of the conflict, for example into the religious system. During the past two years several conservative leaders have repeatedly attempted to intrude features of the political dispute into collective religious observances. In all instances they were effectively opposed by equally conservative religious leaders who argued that the ritual setting was no place for politics.

Thus Potawatomi factionalism, although obviously persistent, does not seem to be pervasive in the sense offered by Siegel and Beals. It has not spread across many structural levels so as to interfere with many group activities, or so as to prevent cooperative effort. Prairie Band members simply avoid extensions by exercising caution in selecting persons with whom to cooperate, so that the result is a segmentation of group activities. Perhaps what all this adds up to is that the Potawatomi are not now and for many years have not been a homogeneous cultural group, that they have adapted to the persistent presence of the factional conflict, so that they are today a conflict-oriented as well as a stress-adapted ideological community.

Finally, I am concerned with the relationship between ambiguity and the origins and persistence of the factional conflict. Following David French's definition,[17] I mean by ambiguity a relative lack of clarity, or definition or cognitive structuring with regard to appropriate normative behaviors. In the Potawatomi case there are many areas of social life not characterized by clearly stated, shared understandings. I will discuss just one, a matter that has been critical in the development of the conflict. In the Prairie Band case there is a striking lack of clarity as well as a lack of consensus surrounding the definition of member in the Potawatomi tribe, or reservation community or, more broadly, the reference group. This ambiguity lies behind those specific disputes over such issues as 'Who shall be a member?', 'Who may vote?' or, 'Who will share in the corporate estate?'

Nowhere within the local community, much less in the corporate membership at large, is there anything approaching consensus on the criteria for membership in the group. Although it is a matter continually discussed and argued, there is no consensus within either the progressive or the reservation groupings, or sub-factions thereof. I have met very few members – and those usually uncommitted and indifferent – who express commitment to a firm, unwavering set of definitional criteria, one unqualified by matters of friendship, the loyalty of henchmen, or kinship. There are many definitions, at least a dozen, in vogue, and these consist of permutations and combinations of a limited number of component principles. Some of these criteria for membership status are current fixed residence on the reservation proper, current full-ownership of an intact original allotment, bilateral descent from an original allottee or patrilineal descent from one, patrilineal descent from a member of the old Bluffs Band or bilateral descent from one, mastery of the Potawatomi language, the status of full-blood or knowledge of and participation in nativistic customs and rituals, and so on and on.

It is obvious that, if applied, these several membership definitions would yield radically different kinds of groupings, varying widely in organization, and ranging in size from something like seventeen valid members to an estimated three thousand. Because there are numerous individual Potawatomi who have some passing commitment to one or another of these definitions, it is worth noting that my practice of contrasting on-reservation culturally conservative elements with absentee, progressive elements over-simplifies the actual situation. In reality, at any one time there are only temporary alliances of several sub-groups of conservatives opposed to similar alliances of sub-groups of progressives, but these lines shift and change with the relative fortunes and success of one or another set of leaders, and with other changes in the community or corporate situation.

We might well ask after the source as well as the importance of this ambiguity concerning definition of membership. It came to be significant, I think, because tribal membership was not a serious issue to the village-dwelling, hunting and horticultural Potawatomi of the early historic period, where birth, for example, placed a woman as a Bear clan member, and birth, adoption or migration identified men as residents of local communities. I think that the boundaries around clans, families, and villages were firmly drawn, but that band or tribal membership was simply an unquestioned by-product of these fundamental identifications. Hence there was no ready-made, traditional solution to the problems which arose with changes in the culturally conditioned behaviors and beliefs of the membership changes and heterogeneity arising from contacts with French, English and Americans. Thus drastic cultural changes have combined with ambiguity in the definition of membership to set the stage for later intra-group conflicts. The possibility of conflict over social boundaries was intensified, moreover, by the fact that although they accept and adapt to culture change, all concerned have insisted on the importance of insuring the structural continuity of the group. Therefore, this ambiguity over the issue of membership is significant because it encapsulates 130 years of Potawatomi social history. But it is important also because it has been central to many features of the dispute in the last thirty years. It illustrates, as does other evidence, that the Potawatomi problem is not anomia, in the sociological sense of an *absence* of norms to which persons feel strongly committed. Rather it is a problem of *too many* norms, which they are unwilling to give up in the interest of peace and compromise.

Notes

The research assistance of Robert Bee, Faye Clifton, Gary Gossen and Barry Isaac is gratefully acknowledged. The research reported on herein has been supported by grants from the Wenner Gren Foundation and from the Faculty Research Fund of the University of Kansas, while current support obtains from National Science Foundation Grant No. GS-400. This article is an expanded and revised version of a paper delivered at the meetings of the American Anthropological Association, San Francisco, 1963.

1. Bernard J. Siegel and Alan R. Beals offer a general theory of factionalism in their 'Conflict and Factionalist Dispute', *Journal of the Royal Anthropological Institute*, XC, Part 1 (1960), 107–17; and they go on to identify several sub-types of factional disputes in their 'Pervasive Factionalism', *American Anthropologist*, LXII, 2 (June 1960), 394–417. David French clarifies some problems of defining factionalism and describes certain important attributes of this variety of conflict in 'Ambiguity and Irrelevancy in Factional Conflict', in Muzafer Sherif, ed., *Intergroup Relations and Leadership* (New York, 1962).

2. I accept French's emphasis on the importance of persistent lack of regulation as a defining criterion, which differs somewhat from that offered by Siegel and Beals (*cf.* 'Pervasive Factionalism', 394).

3. I am indebted to Faye Clifton for insisting on this point: because most studies of factional conflicts are limited to cases of culture-contact, it is quite possible that factors internal to a single community, or a single social system, may also result in factional disputes.

4. Fuller descriptions and analyses of Potawatomi social organization and demography will be found in James A. Clifton and Barry Isaac, 'The Kansas Prairie Potawatomi: On the Nature of a Contemporary Indian Community', *Transactions of the Kansas Academy of Science*, LXVII, 1 (January 1964), 1–24. Ruth Landes discusses many of the elements of conservative Prairie Band culture in her 'Potawatomi Medicine', *Transactions of the Kansas Academy of Science*, LXVI, 4 (December 1963), 553–99.

5. The name of this band is misleading, for it was composed predominantly of Potawatomi from the Chicago area, with an admixture of a few Chippewa and Ottawa migrants.

The American Indian Today

6. Technically, the Citizens Band did not acquire a formal structure until a few years later, after the allottees had lost their free lands and when they had acquired a new reservation in Oklahoma. The label 'Citizens Band' comes from the fact that the members of the abortive nation were offered the choice of remaining Indian or becoming citizens of the United States.

7. Not entirely out of their system, however, for some of the Citizen Indians who lost or sold their allotted land returned to live on the Prairie Band reservation where, because of their 'poor-white' habits, they were thorns in the sides of several Indian agents.

8. We must say 'conservative elements', for in the years after 1867 a substantial number of dissident Prairie Potawatomi responded positively to the attractions of American culture. In 1887 the Prairie Band was not of one mind concerning the allotment issue.

9. Although aimed at recovering and describing the aboriginal Potawatomi culture, Alanson Skinner's 'The Mascoutens or Prairie Potawatomi Indians', *Bulletin of the Public Museum of the City of Milwaukee*, VI (1924–5), offers a fair if piece-meal description of some aspects of community life in the early 1920s. But Ruth Landes' 'Potawatomi Medicine' and her lengthy unpublished manuscript 'Potawatomi Culture' present a far more comprehensive and systematic account of the culture of the mid 1930s.

10. It is highly probable that one *latent* function of the IRA governments, or membership corporation mode of organization, for reservation Indian communities has been to promote the continuity of Indian social systems and to increase their level of tolerance for internal cultural differentiation.

11. By the late 1930s the category of non-Prairie Band members of the community had grown confused in the thinking of the conservative leaders. At first this category seems to have included primarily the returned Citizen Indians, other Indians and the whites who received Dawes Act allotments. Later it was expanded to include many absentees and most assimilated Potawatomi, whatever their ancestry, and on occasion has included individuals of unquestionable pedigree who were opposed to particular leaders.

12. The conservatives were poor in transportation facilities and might have had difficulty getting to this place.

13. But the conservatives were there in force, although outside the hall, peering in its doors and windows.

14. It should be noted that by 1939 the conservatives were masters of the art of interpreting and using the scanty provisions of the Bald-

win Constitution, when and if it were to their advantage, but they later disavowed this constitution, claiming that it was invalid – this on the occasion where the Baldwin Constitution was used to unseat them.

15. Under the 1961 constitution the only recourse the total membership has against an irresponsible elected business committee member is via a recall petition signed by 30 per cent of the eligible voters. Yet since 1961 only about 10 per cent of those eligible have ever voted in elections, and it requires only about 4 per cent of the total eligible to elect a committeeman. In practice, therefore, a small minority elects the committee, and the membership has no control over their corporate affairs. This is very nearly the same situation as when the conservatives were in power.

16. See Landes, 'Potawatomi Medicine' (note 4).

17. See French, 'Ambiguity' (note 1).

ANN FISCHER

HISTORY AND CURRENT STATUS
OF THE HOUMA INDIANS

As Elizabeth C. Rosenthal points out, if we are to understand Indian people, we must learn to take them as they
are. Anyone who has come to know some Indian people
and then related his experiences to experts is familiar
with comments such as these:

'Oh, yes, that's an interesting group. Too small to be
significant, of course.'

'Those weren't real Indians. Most of the folks you met
live here in the city.'

'Next field trip I take, come along, and I'll introduce
you to some *real* Indians.'

'Where did you find those guys? People that conservative aren't typical. Most Indians know much more about
the rest of the world.'

'No, no. Any Indians as politically active as your
friends are unusual. Most Indians are relatively isolated.
That's how they've stayed Indian.'

'Them? Why, we're not even sure they *are* Indians.'

The experts and the Indians remind one rather forcibly of the blind men and the elephant. Lest reviewers
criticize us for including an essay on the Houma on the
grounds that Houma are not typical Indians, permit us,
as editors, to say, 'We know. That's why we like this
paper. We wanted to include a discussion of at least
one group of "so-called Indians".' – SGL & NOL

BREWTON BERRY, in *Almost White*, reports that there are
some 200 groups of 'racial orphans' in the United States.[1]
Among these, those who have some claim to Indian ancestry

are known as *so-called Indians*. This term is apt for a people of tenuous racial status and mixed ancestry. When racial identification is necessary, they emphasize their Indian blood.

So-called Indians stand in contrast to Mulatto groups, since the latter consider themselves to be midway between white and Negro. On the other hand, Indian groups living in Louisiana have consistently fought against identification with Negroes, hoping by their resistance to avoid the disadvantages of the southern caste system. As a result of this resistance, whites, Indians and Negroes agree that the Indian groups are generally more deprived than Negroes.

The Houma, a group of so-called Indians of Louisiana, live in scattered settlements isolated from the Negro settlements of the same area. The scattered settlement pattern is partially the result of migration, undertaken to escape the problems created by lack of racial identity, since the racial status of these people varies from parish to parish.

Negro settlements are easily distinguishable from those of the Houma. Negroes work in and usually live surrounded by the cane fields in identical unpainted houses in rows perpendicular to the road. Indians live in houses, often run-down, along the levees in the typical line villages of the bayou country. In many parts of this region white and Indian houses may be mixed in the line villages, due to the movement of the whites down the line. Negro and Indian housing, on the other hand, is never mixed in the situations which I have observed. Many Indians know no Negroes, and when they compare themselves to any other group it is usually to the white French.

There is much evidence that the Houma think of themselves as Indians. In many homes there are collections of items about US Indians from old newspapers. Houma search through papers for news of Indians, and on reading about the Chicago Conference for Indians being organized in 1961, one group collected money and sent representatives to the conference on the basis of these newspaper reports. Church gatherings provide occasional contacts with the recognized Choctaws on the reservation at Philadelphia, Mississippi. The Choctaw apparently acknowledge the affinity of the Houma with their own group.

The whites of the region know virtually nothing of the Houma. The local derogatory term for the Indians – Sabines – is heard in the community, but many whites would be unable to identify a member of the group, and most have never met one of them. The Houma feel that they have a reputation for sexual immorality in the surrounding white community. They reject this judgment of the whites, pointing out, probably accurately, that the same sexual patterns are common in white and Indian groups. Generally, the Houma feel that the whites resent any visible Indian economic successes. Aside from the matter of sexual conduct, whites, in my experience, complain little about Indian character traits, though they assume that their poverty is due largely to lack of industry and education. Some whites who have lived in the area throughout their lives will say that the Indians were charmingly innocent and friendly before they learned from experience that exploitation often followed the apparent kindliness of strangers.

The Houma have only a few surnames. Some of these, such as Billiot, belong almost exclusively to Indians. Others, such as Naquin, are also found among descendants of the Acadians who occupy territory slightly upstream from the Houma. These characteristic family names enable the surrounding whites to identify them; they could not do so by physical features alone. Indians look like the white population of this area in part because single male hunters and trappers of many nationalities and races have repeatedly come into the area. Some of these have established both long-term and more transient affectional ties with women of all three local groups, Indian, Negro and white. Therefore, identity within the framework of the rigid caste system of the South is not only a problem for the Houma, but for much of the surrounding population.

There is a great variation in physical type among the Indians as well as among other local French-speaking people. Hair varies from almost kinky to straight; its color varies from reddish blonde to black; eyes may be blue although they are usually brown; skin color varies from brown to very white. F. G. Speck, an anthropologist who visited the Houma in 1938, reported on their physical character to the Bureau of Indian Affairs as follows: 'In my judgment, as based upon comparisons with Indians of the southeastern tribes over a number of years, I should rate the Houma as a people possessing Indian blood and cultural characters to a degree about equal to that of the Creek, Choctaw, Catawbe, and Seminoles.'[2] A special investigator from the Bureau of Indian Affairs pronounced the Houma to be too mixed to be considered Indian by the Bureau.[3] However, aid was given to the Chitimacha, who are simply a localized group of the people who now call themselves the Houma Indians.

In the summer of 1960 I lived among the Houma, studying their herbal medicines and collecting genealogies. Since then I have been in fairly constant contact with groups living along Bayous Terrebonne and Pointe au Chênes, and, to a lesser extent, with a group on Île de Jean Charles. The Houma live in other places as well, along many bayous which divide like the fingers on a hand to flow into the Gulf of Mexico at the southern end of Louisiana. From the Mississippi west to Morgan City their shrimp boats and muskrat traps are found throughout the swamps and brackish bays separating the Gulf from dry land.

Approximately 2,000 people identify themselves primarily with the Houma. The small groups are widely separated by swampland, but genealogical relationships and names unite them psychologically.

HISTORY

There is only fragmentary documentation of the history of the Houma. They evidently originally lived to the east of the Mississippi, and moved by way of New Orleans, steadily southwestward from the time of French and Spanish settlement of Louisiana. Many accounts report that they are extinct. Ruth Underhill says, in a report to the Bureau of Indian Affairs, and I agree, that 'It is the opinion of the writer that Houma has become a generic name for a number of Muskogian remnants which mixed and concentrated in southern Louisiana.'[4] Evidence from the language indicates that the Houma dialect belonged to the Muskogian family.[5] A few numbers can be recalled by some present-day informants, who also recognize a linguistic connection with the Choctaw. Today, the Indians are French-speaking.

Some accounts mention West Feliciana Parish and others Ascension Parish as sites from which the Houma moved south to the delta near New Orleans in 1706. From a possible settlement on Lake Pontchartrain they drifted south along the bayous through LaFourche and Terrebonne Parishes. Presumably they got along well enough with the early white settlers, and since they presented no problems, they did not benefit by treaties such as those made with the more warlike groups to the west. Swanton visited them in 1907 and reported that the Houma were being pushed back steadily by the French settlers.[6] Swanton's material, however, is very sketchy, since he stayed only a few days among the Indians. Swanton based his remarks on his experience

with the same group of Houma which I studied. His contention that the Houma were being steadily pushed back seems
questionable. At that time (1907) they were located exactly
where they are today. At present they are being infiltrated.
It is literally impossible for them to be pushed back, for, as
the Indians say, 'One more step and we will be in the Gulf.'
They have been pushed back economically and socially
rather than physically.

Present-day Indians are still bitter about Swanton's chief
informant, Bob Verret. Indians say Verret misrepresented
himself as their chief, and did harm to the people. The Indians report that he was half Negro and a rogue who kept
more than one wife. There is some feeling that he was partially responsible for the present-day segregation of the
Houma. Verret is described by those who knew him as non-
negroid in appearance. It is said that he left descendants
along one bayou, causing a sub-class to develop within the
Indian group.

The history of the economic exploitation of the Houma,
which results partially from the rich natural resources of
their environment, is so clouded by rumor and passage of
time that fact and fancy have been woven into a tale in
which truth and fiction are inseparable. For our purposes
the tale is most appropriately told from the Indian point
of view.

Rosalie Courteaux is remembered as the first Indian to
have trouble with the white French. She was the Indian wife
of Jacques Billiot. Records indicate that Billiot was a half-
breed Negro and Indian.[7] Houma tradition pronounces him
French, the son of Jean Pierre Billiot and Marie Enerise.
Marie is said to have been Spanish, and a one-time recipient
of a Spanish land grant. Among the Houma little trust is put
in recorded certificates designating race. Local opinion has
it that official registrars changed certificates at will, if there

was some white advantage to be gained by doing so, or if registrars were particularly zealous in maintaining what they considered to be racial purity.

The Lirettes, the reported antagonists of Rosalie Courteaux, were her neighbors 'up front' on Bayou Terrebonne. 'Up front' is located on the high levee ground along the bayou, while the low-lying, often swampy, ground to the east of the levee is called 'back behind'. 'Back behind' is relatively unsafe in hurricane weather as the sea may rush in on the great tides which follow the high winds and engulf the land.

According to tradition, the Lirettes considered Rosalie to be an unsuitable neighbor. They burned her house and chased her 'back behind'. Presumably this episode occurred early in the latter half of the nineteenth century. It resulted in a trial. The Indians concede that Rosalie was perhaps an undesirable character with a penchant for drinking. Rumor has it that she received a land-grant for some of the 'back behind' land, perhaps as a result of the trial. There are some tales that land patents were issued in the name of Rosalie Houma, and this Indian woman made additional land purchases. Recently, patents issued in the name of Rosalie's father-in-law, Jean Pierre Billiot, have been discovered in US land patent files.

All of the existing Houma consider themselves to be descendants of Jean Pierre Billiot and Marie Enerise, but those of the Bayou Terrebonne and Pointe au Chênes area trace their ancestry in terms of the four sons of Rosalie and Jacques Billiot. A photograph of these sons – Alexander, Bartolme, Jean and Celestin – as old men indicates that physically they were completely white in appearance.

PROBLEMS OF THE HOUMA

In addition to the problems created by local prejudices against them, the Houma have been the victims of a long series of ecological and economic changes in their homeland. Beneath their homes lies one of the richest natural gas and petroleum fields in the United States. The development of this field has changed the face of the land, altered the economy and brought in outsiders. Exploitation of the wildlife resources of the area on which they live, the age-old complaint of Indians against whites, goes on apace.

The oil on the land has led to increasing agitation among the Indians to reclaim the land they feel is rightfully theirs. Various legal procedures, formerly unintelligible to them, have lost the Houma their land titles. The tax sale was the legal device which allowed companies and politicians to acquire swamp lands when they became valuable. Although the land is immensely valuable, it is my opinion, after five years of trying sporadically to get legal help to untangle the problem, that it would cost more than the land is worth to resolve the matter. Ruth Underhill came to the conclusion that the land was irrevocably lost over twenty-five years ago. At that time she reported that many lawyers had looked over the matter and had given up in despair.[8] The Indian interpretation of this has inevitably been that these lawyers were bought off by competing white title holders. My presence in the area had tended to spread hope among the Houma for recovering their land. Even though I have often indicated the practical impossibility of this task, my willingness to listen to the accounts of the land problems and to investigate them has resulted in renewed hope.

Even before the development of the oil field, land was a problem for the Houma. The land on which the Indians now trap was once public land. Public lands in Louisiana in other places were originally established on land which the Indians claimed and to which the whites disputed their titles. Doubtless the land of the Houma was such a case.[9] From the courthouse records Ruth Underhill concluded that the swampland was purchased by private individuals from the levee district of Atchafalaya in 1895.[10] In 1924 the owners noted the high price of furs and decided to charge for trapping permits. The land was suddenly offered for sale or lease in the local papers. The illiterate Indians were faced with incoming trapping companies who bought up or leased these tracts and negotiated with the Indians for the rights to trap muskrat on the land. Indians had to work for the companies, starve, or trap illicitly in the more inaccessible regions. Annually Indians were required to sign leases indicating that they had no claim to these lands. The fur companies owned the local stores to which the Indians sold furs and from which they received credit. The credit system led to further losses of other lands to which the Indians had sounder claims.

Over the years the trapping and land companies, with legal advice and technical maneuvering, have acquired titles to a considerable acreage. One method used has been to put up fences on Indian lands as an indication of ownership. Where these fences have gone unprotested fairly solid claims have been established by the companies.

While most of my summary is based on the Indian view of the matter, legal efforts have disclosed elements of truth in the Indians' stories of exploitation. The truth of all their claims is difficult to ascertain, however.

Trapping companies have meant lowered returns on furs for the individual trapper. And, since the Second World War, other things have worked to depress the trapping industry. In an attempt to raise nutria on a farm at McIlhenny Island, these animals were accidentally released into the swamps. Nutria now thrive in the swamps and fill the traps in place of the desired muskrats. There is no important market for nutria in the United States, although with assistance it is possible that one could be developed. Nutria can be sold only as dog food at present; it is not profitable for the trapper to collect it.

Rice was formerly raised as a crop in the area. Some of the older Indians can remember this period. Diversion of fresh water from the region has made this impossible.

Oil from the off-shore oil fields has polluted some of the oyster beds. Damages can be and have been collected in some cases, since oyster beds are considered to be privately owned. But the Indians, who work on but usually do not own the oyster beds, have not benefited from these reimbursements.

Sportsmen find ready access to Indian fishing and hunting grounds by means of roads built to develop the oil fields. In spite of legal protection against fishing for profit, many sportsmen fill large deep freezes with their catches, depleting the quantity available to those who are dependent on these resources for a livelihood. Indians, many of whom cannot swim, are afraid of the waters of the open Gulf. They confine their shrimping to the bays which are also most accessible to sportsmen. The white French work in the more distant shrimping grounds and have managed to maintain a higher productivity.

The economic difficulties encountered by the Houma have been aggravated by their lack of education. The history of Indian education in Terrebonne Parish is a history of bitterness and hate. From the beginning, Indians have been denied entrance to white schools in Terrebonne Parish on the basis that an Indian is equivalent to a Negro. Ruth Underhill wrote in 1938, 'the question [of their status] has been decided by the courts. They are Negroes.' The case on which this decision was based, according to Underhill, was 'that of N. L. Billout [*sic*], a so-called Indian [who] sued Terrebonne Parish for permission to send his children to the white school. This case was heard in 1918, and the plaintiff had to admit that one of his grandfathers was a slave.'

From the beginning, Indians would not attend Negro schools and were denied access to white schools. Until about 1937, Indians had no schools at all. At that time church groups began to take an interest in them. Missionaries offered education, and as a result many formerly Catholic Indians became Baptists or Methodists. But today much of the adult population is actually illiterate, and most of the remainder is functionally so. Most Indians over forty years of age sign documents with an 'X'. Their inability to read what they are signing adds to their already well-founded suspicions that they are being duped.

Eventually, schools were built exclusively for the Indians in Terrebonne Parish by LaFourche Parish, which adjoins Terrebonne. This deviousness enabled the local Terrebonne Parish government to avoid recognizing the Indians as a distinct group, somewhat in the manner in which the US Government avoids recognizing Red China. Bayou Pointe au Chênes divides Terrebonne from LaFourche, and Indians live on both sides of this bayou. In LaFourche, an Indian is considered to be white, and may attend the white schools. Until 1964 LaFourche Parish operated two schools for Indians, one on Bayou Pointe au Chênes and one on Bayou Terrebonne, in return for certain considerations from Terrebonne Parish. In 1964 one of these was closed. These schools were elementary schools; until about 1957, after a child graduated from the eighth grade, no further schooling was available to him unless he chose to drive thirty miles into LaFourche to attend high school or left Terrebonne Parish for more distant New Orleans private or public schools. Very few Indians managed this difficult arrangement, and few were able to finish high school.

A few years after the Supreme Court decision directed schools to integrate with all deliberate speed, Terrebonne Parish established a high school exclusively for the Indians. Beginning in 1957, a year of high school was added each year until in 1961 Indians in Terrebonne Parish were able to graduate from high school.

During the first year of operation the high school enrolled about fourteen students. This number increased over time to around thirty in 1963. At first the Houma from Pointe au Chênes, Terrebonne Bayou and Île de Jean Charles disliked the idea of the Indian high school, feeling that it was one more step in the direction of continued segregation. Up to the present, very few of these Indians have attended this school, preferring to go to LaFourche to the white high school, to join the armed forces for a high-school education, or to go away to live with relatives and get their diplomas in areas where they are accepted as whites. The Indians who have attended the Indian high school are mostly from Grande Caillou or Bayou Dularge, both too distant from La-Fourche for daily commuting.

Difficulties in getting an education and economic pressure combine to encourage children to drop out of school early. They provide additional economic assistance for parents as soon as they are physically able. Indian girls usually manage to finish elementary school and, if they are able students or if their parents are ambitious for them, they attempt to continue for a few years in high school. Boys generally begin dropping out of school at about the third grade. They attend less regularly during the shrimping season when they are needed to work with their fathers.

In the close school community students and teachers are all too aware of each other's weaknesses; discipline is at times difficult to maintain. Teachers are expected to act in all kinds of capacities, including that of janitor. They tend to neglect these extra duties, and the schools often appear untidy. Discipline is alternately tough and negligent. Classes usually do not last the full period allotted to them, and sometimes school lets out up to an hour and a half early.

Needless to say, no Indian school is accredited by the Southern Regional Educational Association. Parents and teachers seldom meet and have little respect for each other. Complaints on both sides may be well founded.

The Houma as a group are distinguished by law in only one sense: Indians may marry on either side of the Negro-white caste line with no objections from authorities. In the last generation or two, marriages to Negroes have meant that the Indian partner lives among the Negroes and the children of the union identify themselves as Negro. One woman interviewed in Charity Hospital, New Orleans, was the child of an Indian mother. Her mother, after bearing her, married a Negro. The Indian child grew up with Negro siblings and now identifies herself as a Negro. She is very loath to discuss any matters relating to her Indian relatives. Most marriages with whites have occurred between Houma girls and white boys from the vicinity. If the children of mixed marriages have surnames which do not identify them as Indian, and if they move into the town of Houma, the children pass into the white school system unnoticed, or at least unchallenged.

Marriages occur when Houma boys meet white girls from other parts of the country during their tours of duty in the Armed Forces. None of these partners live in the Indian communities. It can be said that the people who remain in the community for life marry within it. Out-marriage usually means departure. The exceptions to this are two marriages between Indian men and white women who came to the

Houma as missionaries. These married pairs resided in Indian communities for some time, but one pair has now left, and the second has reached the point where the son must be sent away to school. It seems possible that this pair also will leave in the not too distant future.

There are only a few routes of escape from the community, and these mostly present themselves during adolescence. For the girls, the chief method of escape involves going away to school, meeting white boys and marrying them. For boys, going into the Armed Services seems to be the easiest way to learn a trade other than that of their fathers, and they leave the community by this means.

The traditional occupations of fishing, hunting and trapping are territorial in nature; the territory must be maintained and exploited or it will fall to other hands. The territorial nature of the occupations of the Houma has forced them to remain in a region which deprives them of other opportunities, and in which a century of prejudice works to their disadvantage.

Identification with Indian-ness follows the cycle indicated above. During adolescence, when there is the best opportunity to escape from their deprived condition, a number of patterns of activity are evident. Parents with adolescent children become concerned with the problem only in cases where there has been some outside contact through missionaries or jobs on boats or oil rigs which carry the men to the outside world. Where the parents have followed traditional patterns of life, the extra impetus needed to overcome the difficulties is not present. Parents who have had a glimpse of the economic contrast between themselves and the rest of the world often become militantly interested in obtaining equal rights for their children. Once the crisis is past, and the children have either succeeded or failed in escaping the cycle of poverty and deprivation, the parents' interest in working for

Indian rights disappears, and they return to their life within the in-grown Indian community.

Another factor in escape seems to be the birth order of children in the household. Younger sons may more easily leave home than elder sons. Elder sons have at times contributed to the education of their younger brothers. Men do not like to go alone shrimping or fishing. Accidents occur, and if the men are alone they may drown. After the father has initiated one son as his helper, he is much more willing to allow the others to leave home.

The individual nature of the effort made to solve various problems among the Houma is in part responsible for the failure to find a solution for the social problems of the whole group. The oil on the land, like the pot of gold at the end of the rainbow, glitters in the eyes of many people and distorts their vision completely. For if a Houma profits from the lease of land to the oil companies, his neighbors will often suspect him of profiting at their expense. Proof of title depends largely on having birth, death and legitimate marriage records of one's ancestors. Many Indians, if they married legally, married in churches where records have been destroyed by fire or other loss. Whole volumes of land records are reported missing from State record offices. If an individual succeeds in substantiating his own claims to property it seems unfair to others who do not have the proper documents. Yet, if all are to benefit, profits will be smaller for the individuals concerned. Under such circumstances, suspicions directed at neighbors lead Indians to refuse to sign papers drawn up to help them by lawyers because they distrust the motives of their neighbors who are working with the lawyers. This is a force that pulls the Houma apart psychologically and adds to their problems of identity.

Many lawyers and 'lease hounds' hold signatures of Indians whom they presumably represent. Some Indians sign these papers easily, and readily sign up with more than one representative. Others will not sign with any of them. Eventually, this kind of behavior becomes unprofitable for the legal representatives, since they must fight even for their rights to represent certain of the people who have signed up to be represented by them. Lawyers' visions of profits fade into nothingness in the confusion.

In spite of the fact that Swanton reported that Bob Verret was the chief of the Houma, it seems unlikely that the Houma have ever had a very strong central authority among them which might act as a rallying point for action to overcome their social condition. A missionary residing among the Houma when I first visited them reported that their last chief had died just a year or so before my arrival. The missionary was concerned lest they choose a man he considered immoral as the chief's successor. If there was indeed a former chief in 1958, the Indians have followed no other's lead since that time. The scattered residences of the Houma make it unlikely that the influence of the presumed former chief could have extended very far beyond Île de Jean Charles where he lived. This lack of central authority may be the historical result of the diverse nature of the tribal origins of the group.

The Houma at Pointe au Chênes and Île de Jean Charles may have had more cohesiveness up to about twelve years ago when the first road was built into their territory. Before that time all contact with the outside world was by boat. The people are reported to have been more friendly toward outsiders prior to this time. Pointe au Chênes now has running water and a number of telephones as well as some modern fabricated houses. Île de Jean Charles has electricity, but no other modern conveniences. The development of the standard of living at Pointe au Chênes in the last five years during which I have visited there has been startling. The road has made the important difference, but it is not the only difference. What might be called a model Indian family lived at Pointe au Chênes. The father spent time in France during the Second World War, and sent his daughter to college to become a school teacher when he returned. He built a house with modern accoutrements, and as his children married they followed his example. This family served as a model for other young people who learned something about how modern standards of living might be obtained by going into debt.

Throughout the history of the Houma there have always been some individuals who have been actively working for their own social betterment, seeking help from the outside when completely frustrated by the local white community. One man wrote repeatedly to the Indian Bureau just prior to World War II. He and a few other Indians still cherish letters from the Bureau and from anthropologists sent to investigate the situation. Speck evidently visited the Houma under this stimulus. He attempted to revitalize local crafts and for a time succeeded in getting a few craftsmen to produce baskets. He is still remembered by those who had contact with him.

One Houma man is particularly active in seeking outside contacts. He has dreams similar to those found in other North American groups. One of his dreams involved a huge flag waving over the shore line with an Indian Chief's head in the position where the field of stars should be.

When I came to the Houma, the middle-aged people were most interested in soliciting my help for them. Once they were convinced that I was not an investigator sent to arrest illegal medical practitioners, they quickly told me about their problems. I wanted to learn about the local remedies, but the Houma were interested only in gaining help with their land claims. For every ounce of knowledge I painfully acquired about herbal medicines, I received pounds of volunteered information on land frauds. After they had made many appeals to my sense of justice, I agreed to contact the Association for American Indian Affairs, naïvely stating that this was as far as I intended to go. This small effort resulted in finding legal help for the Houma in New Orleans. John P. Nelson was the attorney, and he too fell under the spell of the Indians and has never completely given up their cause, although the hopelessness of the legal task gradually dampens all enthusiasm. These efforts gained the confidence of many Indians, while at the same time they increased the suspicions of others. Old interests in the Indian case were revived; leasehounds re-entered the area, thinking legal action could be expected momentarily, and new lists of signatures were acquired by all of those waiting to reap the rewards of years of sporadic effort.

In New Orleans a committee was formed under the auspices of the Association for American Indian Affairs. The committee generally agreed that the school problems could be solved, but the Indians, on their part, while complaining about their educational lot, gave no indication that they were willing to face the discomforts certain to attend an attempt to integrate the schools. So long as this was so, it appeared that there was very little the committee could do without financial help for work on the land problem. After a year of meetings, with no foreseeable way to obtain financial aid, the committee subsided into inactivity.

A year later the efforts to help the Houma suddenly jogged to new life by the appearance at Pointe au Chênes mission of a new and enthusiastic missionary, who was unfamiliar with the difficulties in the case. Like other outsiders who had come before him, he could not believe that there would be any objection to the Indian children attending the white schools. He felt, as had others, that the Indians were simply imagining that such deep prejudices against them existed. Buoyed up by his confidence and enthusiasm five children went with him to register for the white high school. The Registrar, seeing nothing out of the way in their appearance, began the registration process. When asked what school they attended last year, the Indians gave the name of the Indian school. At this point the Registrar telephoned the Superintendent of Schools, following which he informed the Indians that they would not be able to register.

Previous to this the Indians did not feel actively rejected by the whites and had been able to maintain their self-respect. The rebuff they received in response to their attempt to register set them apart as inferiors in their own eyes. They were a group in a way that had not seemed possible previously. All were eager to retaliate, although some felt the slight much less than did others. Letters from my Houma friends told of this event, and requested that I come to Pointe au Chênes to meet the new missionary and hear the story. Indian informants felt certain that if the opportunity were offered, Indians would be willing to attempt to integrate the white schools.

In New Orleans John Nelson agreed to take the school case without fee if the court costs could be met from some source. These costs were more than adequately subscribed by an appeal to personal friends for contributions. More than fifty Indian children signed as plaintiffs through their parents on Bayou Terrebonne, Bayou Pointe au Chênes and Île de Jean Charles. About ten months later, after numerous delays arranged by the opposition, the case was heard by a Federal judge. Indians developed a new pride in themselves which they expressed to me as the case progressed.

That year the judge delayed his decision until after school started in the fall. After school had already been in session for two weeks, Indians in the eleventh and twelfth grades were legally admitted to the white high school. None of the plaintiffs were in either of these grades. Indian children living many miles from the area where the suit originated were surprised to learn that they had received this new privilege.

The judge made his decision at night. The following morning teachers in the Indian high school announced to eleventh and twelfth grade children that they would be able to choose which high school they would attend. They were asked which they would choose publicly, and unanimously they chose to remain in the Indian school. Rumors spread among the children that outsiders were trying to force them into the white schools.

Mr Nelson waited until the week-end after the decision was handed down to visit the Houma. Learning that children on Grande Caillou were eligible to enter school, he visited a leader there. This leader urged the most intelligent of the school children to reconsider and to help Indians take this important step. Two of the children went through a personal struggle, deciding first one way on the advice of the leader then another when their friends urged them to remain with their own group. Finally, it seemed unwise for the leader to attempt to urge them further. He decided instead to prepare the way for a large shift to the white schools in the following year.

In October the judge lowered the entrance requirement for entrance into the white schools to the tenth grade. But it was too late. An Indian boy among the plaintiffs who would have been in the tenth grade had attempted to register at the white school at the beginning of school. When rejected, he became quite angry and decided to quit school entirely and go to work instead with his father on a shrimp boat. All in all, the first year of integrated schools was singularly unintegrated.

Word of the entire history of the effort to enter the white

schools quickly spread up and down Grande Caillou and Bayou Dularge through Indians from the areas where the integration effort had originated. One of them visited these regions for the first time and informed the people of what had been done, urging them to cooperate. By fall in 1964, Indians along all bayous were eager to join in the desegregation movement. The judge moved the requirement for entering the white schools down to the seventh grade level, the Civil Rights Bill had been passed by Congress, and the legal opposition to Indian entrance into the schools began to disappear. The Terrebonne School Board closed the Indian elementary school on Bayou Terrebonne, and the twenty-four children attending that school were admitted to the white elementary schools nearest their homes. Most of the Indian students eligible elected to enter the white schools. In all, in the fall of 1964, some sixty Indian children were admitted to six previously all-white schools.

During the year when the school problems seemed certain to be resolved, Indian minds returned to the question of the oil land. A strange messiah appeared upon the scene, and Indians were learning about him by messengers from relatives living to the East along Bayou LaFourche at Golden Meadow. Radio and television, as well as limousines bearing loud speakers, assaulted Indian ears with messages of new land-grant evidence discovered in Washington. Already loyal Indian supporters of this messiah, who was introduced into the group in a manner unknown to me, had developed a following for him among their close friends and relatives.

My friends along Bayou Terrebonne sought me out again to interpret the motives and intentions of this man and to resolve for them their natural suspicions of strangers with papers to be signed. Katherine Wright, a lawyer associated with Nelson's firm, accompanied me and two Houma friends to an Indian store in Golden Meadow. There a large crowd of Indians had gathered in response to the invitation to 'Come by car, come by plane, come by helicopter, but come to Golden Meadow on Saturday to sign for your share of Rosalie Courteaux's land.' The man we confronted there did not know that Mrs Wright was a lawyer, and his initial suspicions of our motives gradually disappeared. Eventually he showed us copies of patents he had obtained in Washington. Mrs Wright felt that Indians were being misled into believing that their problems were going to be solved simply and easily by taking the case into court immediately. This stranger, with his green Cadillac, his plastic deerslayer's jacket, and his Navajo string tie was a leasehound in a new guise. He had his own view of the rainbow's pot which could more than match that of the Indians for irrationality, but he has done a remarkable job of getting Indians to come to him and accept him as their representative. The sad part of it is that the long-time funding needed to carry on a difficult five-year legal investigation with the decided risk that all will be lost in the end is not available to him or to anyone else connected with the case.

CONCLUSION

A group which has been so frustrated and deprived as the Houma, in which internal organization is lacking, must usually get help from the outside. The Indians recognize this and have never ceased their efforts to reach possible outside sources of aid. Only when the goals of the Houma are in some accord with the goals of these outsiders is it possible for Houma to succeed. Insofar as the Houma appeal is of interest to me as an anthropologist or as representative of a people deprived of a right I believe in, that of equal educational opportunity, I will acquiesce in being of service to them. Insofar as Mr Nelson sees them as an interesting legal case, or as a group deprived of equal opportunity before the law, he will help them. Insofar as the leasehound sees in them an opportunity to get rich he will help them. But none of us behaves as a Houma himself would in support of his own cause. Even the Houma themselves do not behave in a manner in accord with some group ideal, for Houma group cohesiveness is based on ramifying kinship ties rather than on central group ties. Kin ties are often unsuitable for acting in relationship to the non-kin institutions of the larger society. Kin ties are of varying strength, in part depending upon the genealogical distance from the individuals with whom you are concerned in interaction. Group ties are of a single strength for all members of the group from the point of view of any one member.

To succeed in any venture, people so deprived need more help than a few sympathetic individuals representing the outside world can give them. For funds, I had to appeal to a group of friends who feel as I feel about the values of education. There had to be a movement in the outside world and the passage of the Civil Rights Bill or our meager efforts would have come up against a much larger opposition in the immediate and prejudiced white community. The leasehound would need powerful friends with financial resources sufficient to overcome the resistance among the land companies and other contesting title holders to succeed in winning the land. This power is not at present in evidence, and an individual here and there chipping away at the work which the problem requires will probably have little effect. The pot of gold at the end of the rainbow remains there, however, and it is certain that it will never go unsought. Eventually, the external conditions necessary to the solution to this problem, too, may be found, by which time perhaps there will be 3,000 or more descendants of Rosalie Courteaux to share in the pot.

Notes

The collection of the material on which this paper is based was made possible by a grant from the National Institute of Health.

1. Brewton Berry, *Almost White* (New York, 1963), 16.

2. Frank G. Speck, Letter to Dr Willard Beatty, 1 October 1938.

3. Bureau of Indian Affairs, File 33902 (1931).

4. Ruth Underhill, 'Report on a Visit to Indian Groups in Louisiana, 15–25 October' (Typescript), Bureau of Indian Affairs, Washington, D. C., 1938.

5. ibid., 2.

6. J. R. Swanton, 'The Indians of the Southeastern United States', *Bureau of American Ethnology Bulletin 137* (Washington, D. C., 1946).

7. Underhill, op. cit.

8. ibid.

9. Joyce Purser, 'The Administration of Indian Affairs in Louisiana, 1803–1820', *Journal of the Louisiana Historical Association*, V (1964), 401–21, 407.

10. Underhill, op. cit., 6.

DEWARD E. WALKER, JR

SOME LIMITATIONS OF
THE RENASCENCE CONCEPT
IN ACCULTURATION:
THE NEZ PERCE CASE

As we explained in the introductory essays, many of these studies were written in response to a questionnaire which asked, essentially, 'Would you say that there is a renascence going on among the Indian people you know best? If not, how would you characterize what's going on?'

When we wrote to our contributors to explain the difference between the magazine issue and this book, and to offer them guide-lines for revision and rewriting, we asked, among other things, that they remove most references to the renascence idea, which, we felt, had served its purpose in stimulating debate.

In the case of this essay, though, the idea of 'renascence' provides such a handy peg on which to hang his survey of the Nez Perce situation that we urged Mr Walker, in rewriting, to retain it. – SGL & NOL

VARIOUS anthropologists – Fred Voget in 1956 and Nancy Lurie in 1964, for instance – have suggested that a contemporary American Indian renascence is now in progress. They think that it is most evident in the development of stronger tribal governments and pan-Indian political organizations. They suggest that it is based upon renewed desires among American Indians for economic self-development and increased ethnic distinctiveness.

Limitations of the Renascence Concept

In general, 'renascence' is used to describe changes which serve to increase the cultural distinctiveness of a particular people. Conversely, 'cultural decline' refers to changes which reduce this distinctiveness. The course of recent Nez Perce history indicates that it is very difficult indeed to describe culture as 'renascent' or as 'declining'. This is seen particularly well when one considers long-term changes in Nez Perce population, religion, economy and political organization. For example, while certain areas have experienced renascences after periods of decline, others have shown only persistent decline. These and similar conclusions to be drawn indicate that some caution is required in applying the concept 're-nascence' to contemporary American Indian culture change.

POPULATION

The present Nez Perce population resurgence accords well with their contemporary political renascence. It is a reversal of a long downward trend which began perhaps as early as the late eighteenth century when the Nez Perces experienced their first smallpox epidemic.[1] From this point until about 1900, Nez Perce population was in constant decline. It dropped from an estimated aboriginal figure of approximately 5,009 to a 1900 figure of about 1,500. In 1905 the agent wrote that

with weak constitutions, a great susceptibility to tuberculosis, and a life of idleness yielding the usual fruits, the tribe is decreasing, and unless a change should occur in their manner of living, it will be only a few generations before the tribe is extinct. (Annual Report, 1905, 217)

Apparently measles, tuberculosis, smallpox, infantile mortality and other factors contributing to the reduction had reached their maximum impact by 1900, for the population fell to 1,500 and then stopped declining. It remained at this level until about 1935, when an upward trend appeared, continuing into the present so that the 1964 population was approximately 2,200. Numerous factors have been responsible for this resurgence, but perhaps most important are improvements in medical care and sanitation. Improvements in infant care and the post-1900 establishment on the reservation of a government tuberculosis sanitorium with permanent medical personnel, would seem to have been particularly important in reversing the downward trend.

*   *   *

The Nez Perces (local pronunication as in *fez* and *nurses*) are located in north-central Idaho and presently number about 2,300. They are part of the Sahaptian linguistic grouping, including such tribes as the Umatilla, Palus, Tenino, Klikitat, Yakima, Wanapum and Kittitas. They are bounded on the south by Shoshonean speaking groups and on the north and east by Salish speaking groups.

*   *   *

During the nineteenth century, important changes also had taken place in the structure, distribution and racial composition of the population. Some of these changes were rather closely related to changes in the political, religious and economic spheres and, therefore, deserve further comment. Aboriginally the Nez Perce population was distributed over a relatively large territory in villages probably averaging about fifty individuals.[2] Such village groupings were territorially based and part of larger band groupings situated along principal water courses. This distributional pattern was changed drastically by Euro-American influence. Few villages were displaced as a result of the first treaty of 1855, but the treaty of 1863 involved substantial population dislocation and was an important factor precipitating the war of 1877.[3] The 1863 treaty was prompted by the gold strikes within the boundaries established by the 1855 treaty. It produced a rapid concentration of Nez Perces around missionary stations and government agencies. The permanent villages which developed in such places were larger than any of the aboriginal villages and quickly developed serious internal disputes. Because of the relatively simple social structure of aboriginal Nez Perce culture, there were no native leaders with sufficient authority to manage these new groupings. Missionary and government agents attempted to remedy this problem by placing the tribe in the charge of a single head chief and a number of sub-chiefs. However, this step accomplished little other than to provide a rubber stamp, indigenous authority to certify in the name of all the Nez Perces the various treaties and agreements put forward by the government. Further, the system produced serious factionalism in the tribe, with a substantial minority opposing the head chief system. This was a non-Christian faction which was deprived of its lands with the approval of the newly introduced head chief and sub-chiefs; it is the same faction which was to resist the government militarily in the war of 1877.

The present on-reservation population contains a slight majority of males, a situation which may be related to recent changes in marriage patterns that have served to alter the racial composition of the population.[4] Although there was some early intermarriage between Caucasians and Nez Perces, it does not seem to have become important until after 1900 when the reservation was opened to homesteaders. Since that time, however, the rate of intermarriage has shown a constant increase, accelerating somewhat during and after World War II. In fact, outmarriage has increased to the point that the population under twenty is now predominantly non-Nez Perce. A search of genealogies has revealed, not surprisingly, that Nez Perce females in increasing numbers tend to marry out of the society, often moving off the reservation and, in effect, abandoning most tribal ties. This practice goes far toward explaining the present predominance of males on the reservation. Not unexpectedly, the growing off-reservation section of the population plays an important part in contemporary tribal politics, and in so doing reflects a long-standing pattern: those Nez Perces who are on the tribal rolls but who live off the reservation constitute an opposition to the reservation political establishment. After the war of 1877, those individuals in the dissident non-Christian faction who were not willing to become Christians were forced to reside on other reservations, particularly on the Colville reservation in nearby Nespelem, Washington. Their descendants, plus the so-called half-breeds who traditionally also have been excluded from the reservation establishment, constitute a large part of the present minority faction opposing continuation of the tribe as a corporate entity.

It would seem, therefore, that there has been a demonstrable, quantitative decrease and resurgence of the Nez Perce population. The recent increase clearly contributes to an increased distinctiveness which can be regarded as renascent. The other changes, however, do not fit so well under decline or renascence. For example, is one to regard a concentration in larger villages as contributing to a renascence or to a decline? Certainly the growing tendencies to marry non-Nez Perces and non-Indians and to move off the reservation clearly cannot be regarded as contributing to a renascence. In 1900 more than ninety per cent of the population resided on the reservation, whereas in 1964, only two thirds resided on the reservation.[5]

RELIGION

Aboriginal Nez Perce religion was organized around a system of tutelary spirits which individuals, primarily young men, obtained by fasting and isolation. Possession of tutelary spirits was widespread in the culture and essential for any other than a mediocre life. The principal religious specialists were shamans, some of whom were grouped into an influential shamanist society. Important religious ceremonies were an annual mid-winter tutelary spirit dance, a first fruits ceremony held in the spring, and a number of less important ceremonies held at various times during the year.[6]

Nez Perce religion was one of the first aspects of the culture affected by the western expansion of greater Euro-American culture. Between 1820 and 1836, according to Leslie Spier,[7] there developed in the Plateau region a religion blending Christian and native elements which he calls the 'Christianized Prophet Dance'. Apparently the Nez Perces were greatly affected by this movement.[8] The new religious offices, dogma and ritual developed at this time were to serve an important bridging function in the Nez Perce adaptation to Euro-American culture. For example, this movement probably was responsible for the 1832 Nez Perce-Flathead delegation to St Louis in search of missionaries and the eager reception given to the first missionaries who appeared in Nez Perce territory in 1836.

The first missionaries in the area failed to distinguish between the aboriginal and more recent syncretistic or 'blended' religious systems, classifying both as 'heathen'. In time many Nez Perces were to concur in this judgment and agree to ban most of the old culture. Forbidden were not only most of the cultural patterns that obviously conflicted with Euro-American norms, such as polygamy, but also overtly Indian behavior. For example, missionaries banned not only the most aboriginal ceremonialism, religious as well as non-religious, but hair styles, clothing styles and many former economic and subsistence patterns. For a time the missionaries even controlled the agency, and this period (1870–79) was a particularly formative one in the course of Nez Perce acculturation. During this time a native preacher elite was trained, and the churches, with all their offices, ceremony and missionary support, became new foci of social organization. In the case of the dominant Presbyterians, the churches with their native preachers and elders tended to substitute for the older village, band and headman complex. A smaller Catholic community was developed, but was relatively unimportant. It had little influence on tribal political affairs, which remained under Presbyterian control. Nevertheless, despite the absence of a native priestly elite, the Catholic sector developed relatively self-sufficient, theocratic communities quite similar to those found among the Presbyterian Nez Perces. This essentially religious transformation of the residential and leadership patterns was complete by 1895, with very few pagans remaining in the society, some of the last having been exiled to other reservations. This was the period in Nez Perce history of highest church membership and participation.

After this time attendance statistics show a steady decline until the late 1930s, when they level out. There is no indication as yet of any resurgence.[9] Whereas Nez Perce church participation in 1900 was much higher than that of the surrounding Euro-American community, it now seems equal to or perhaps even below that of surrounding Euro-Americans. Because many churches were constructed at the height of Nez Perce Christianity, the present congregations are relatively small and comprise little more than caretaker forces. Only during important religious holidays will participation approach that of the earlier period. The most obvious results of this decline in church attendance have been a development of a large body of unchurched individuals on the reservation and closure of two smaller churches in the more remote eastern edge of the reservation where, because of population redistribution, few Nez Perces live any longer. Although various programs of proselytization have been undertaken since World War II by the Church of Jesus Christ of Latter-day Saints, the Jehovah's Witnesses, the Pilgrim Holiness Church and other fundamentalist groups, they have not been successful. Despite its lack of success, the Assembly of God Church has had an indirect effect: two independent, Indian-oriented Pentecostal sects have developed since 1950. However, these remain small-scale operations and in no way have reversed the overall decline in church participation.

To what extent, then, do decline and renascence apply to the religious changes seen in the course of Nez Perce acculturation? This question cannot be answered by referring solely to the contemporary situation, since it is clear that during the latter half of the nineteenth century Christianity served as a means of reasserting the ethnic distinctiveness of the Nez Perces. Although this process involved great changes in the older religion, settlement patterns and leadership, it is clear that the development of Nez Perce Christianity afforded the Nez Perces a vehicle for reconstituting a radically changed culture. The churches, interestingly, have remained exclusively Indian despite attempts on the part of Euro-American Presbyterian leaders to force an integration of Indian and non-Indian churches in the area. When confronted with the very emotional Nez Perce resistance to church integration, one can hardly avoid the conclusion that these churches continue to serve as a means of preserving a distinct identity.[10]

The American Indian Today

The Nez Perce economy in aboriginal times was based in a hunter-gatherer approach to the available resources: roots, game and fish. A small economic surplus seems to have been realized in this relatively rich environment. A half-dozen or more distinct roots were dug, dried and stored for use in the seasonally permanent winter villages along the rivers. Although salmon was the most important fish taken, others such as sturgeon, steelhead and even eels were also important. Fish were dried and stored in substantial quantities as part of the winter stores. The Nez Perce area also enjoyed rather abundant game resources, principally deer and elk.

The first interruption of this pattern came with the adoption of the horse shortly after 1700. The Nez Perces' rapid acquisition of horses and cultural patterns associated with the horse resulted in an increasing exploitation of the buffalo to the east in Montana, and this practice had reached substantial proportions by the time of white contact. Additional economic effects of the horse complex were seen in the increased exploitation of more inaccessible game, fish and root digging areas. Vast herds of horses soon were developed and served to augment economic differences both within and between the various bands. Not only did incipient economic class-distinctions appear, but certain favorably situated bands were able to become extremely prosperous participants in the Plains horse complex. A few less favorably situated bands remained less prosperous and more isolated, continuing many of the older economic patterns of the days before horses.

The horse complex was one of the principal obstacles in the way of missionaries and government agents who attempted to make farmers of the Nez Perces and settle them permanently on farms and in villages. Most Nez Perces preferred to retain their freedom of movement and strongly resisted attempts to immobilize them by reducing their vast herds. Ultimately several methods were used successfully to reduce the herds; according to some older informants, the most successful was official non-recognition of the persistent rustling by non-Indians of Indian horses and cattle. By 1900 the huge herds no longer existed, and the Nez Perces were reduced to dependency on horticulture and income from allotments rented to the non-Indian farmers who had homesteaded approximately 500,000 'surplus' acres of the 756,900 acres remaining in Nez Perce hands after the treaty of 1863.[11]

Despite several reports to the contrary by agency personnel, few Nez Perces ever lived on their allotted farmlands. They remained instead in their valley homes and rented their holdings to non-Indian farmers in the area. Even had many Nez Perces wished to become farmers, it would have been impossible, because the original allotments had been split into tiny fractions by repeated inheritance divisions. An even more serious matter is the continuing sale of the original allotments. Although there have been several periods when the agency discouraged the sale of allotments to surrounding Euro-American farmers, the gradual reduction of Nez Perce owned lands seems to have been continuous. By 1940, a large number of the original allotments had been sold, and in 1964 the total land remaining in individual Nez Perce hands was only 57,062 acres.[12] This gradual loss of the only remaining source of cash income has influenced Nez Perce economic patterns in several important ways. First, more and more Nez Perces have been forced to seek employment in the surrounding Euro-American economy. The many lumber mills in the area have provided some with permanent employment, but few Nez Perces are willing to remain permanently at such jobs, preferring instead the temporary farm work available during the planting and harvest seasons. Many also have lost their homes as a result of inheritance sales and either have moved away or congregated in the principal village on the western edge of the reservation, close to the agency and the Lewiston-Clarkston urban area nine miles to the west. Here many have become, in one way or another, economically dependent, relying partially or totally on subsistence provided by welfare from the tribe, the BIA, the county, the state or some combination of these agencies.

Gradual impoverishment and loss of economic independence have been topics of long-standing debate among many Nez Perces. From the time of the first Euro-American encroachments they have watched their various resources disappear, but collective action against this trend did not appear until the 1920s, when the tribe adopted a five-year plan of economic self-development. Although it failed to create Nez Perce farmers, it did serve to teach the Nez Perces to take the initiative from the agency in solving tribal problems. This early attempt recently has been supplemented by extensive economic developmental planning by the present leaders, most of whom came to power after 1948. The adoption of a strong constitution in that year and subsequent successful appeals before the Indian Claims Commission resulted in the tribe's receiving several million dollars. There has been much talk of using these funds for economic self-development, and some few projects actually have been initiated, but the funds are rapidly being used up in economical non-productive enterprises such as repeated per capita payments and sanitation projects. These limited efforts probably are not enough to reverse the trend toward economic dependence. Despite occasional optimistic predictions, few knowledgeable individuals in the area hold out much hope for a reassertion of Nez Perce economic independence.

Limitations of the Renascence Concept

To what extent, then, do 'decline' and 'renascence' apply to economic changes in the course of recent Nez Perce history? It would seem that the efforts of present leaders to reassert Nez Perce economic independence are too limited and too late. If the Nez Perces still retained the bulk of their aboriginal territory, as do some tribes, or even if they had substantial mineral or timber resources which could be developed, the picture might be different. In private, even tribal leaders are pessimistic about contemporary plans for economic development and encourage those who have jobs in the surrounding economy to retain them.

POLITICAL ORGANIZATION

As I have implied, aboriginal Nez Perce political organization was relatively simple, with weakly developed leadership. It was a political system grounded in the village and village council, and in the band and band council; each was led by a headman who held his position because of the force of his personality and his demonstrated administrative skills. Rarely were leaders able to coerce their followers; instead, the latter had to be persuaded to cooperate. There was little in the nature of supra-band, permanent political machinery. Cooperation between different bands was limited to traditional alliances for defense and aggression, or for exploitation of the buffalo to the east. Leadership of such multi-band undertakings was elective, and lasted only as long as was required by the particular undertaking. Despite some claims to the contrary, there was no single head chief of all the Nez Perces at the time of contact, and this proved particularly trying for the early missionaries and government agents whose customary mode of operation required centralization of political power. A uniform reaction of early missionaries and government agents was that the Nez Perces had no government, that they existed in a state of anarchy. As a result these outsiders undertook what they considered the task of formulating an effective indigenous government.

In 1842 they appointed a head chief with twelve sub-chiefs, each of whom had five police assistants. This system functioned in conjuction with the older village and band headman system.[13] Needless to say, a great deal of conflict ensued, because few of the egalitarian Nez Perces were willing to accept the idea of permanent tribal leadership supported by external authorities. These external authorities disregarded the Nez Perce reluctance to accept the new system, and quickly came to regard their appointees as the only legitimate Nez Perce authorities. They rewarded them economically and provided them with means of enforcing their orders, all of which acted to reduce the importance of the older headmen. In addition to these new secular leaders, Presbyterian missionaries trained a number of native preachers who became influential in the reorganized society. In fact, they emerged as the *de facto* leaders of the society in their positions as heads of the new church-village complexes which had replaced the older village and band groupings. When the treaties expired in 1880, the government-appointed chiefs were no longer a force in tribal affairs,[14] and the only remaining competitors for the preacher elite were the agency police who received small salaries and continued to exert some authority. This competition, however, does not seem to have been serious, and the preachers retained control of the field, working closely with the agency personnel, whose interests normally coincided with those of the few missionaries who remained as advisors.

The importance of these preachers as leaders in the reorganized society was particularly clear at the time of allotment, when they were formed into a committee to assist in the division of the lands. Of the nine members chosen, there were three Presbyterian preachers, four Presbyterian elders, one ex-Presbyterian elder who out of a disagreement had established his own schismatic Methodist church, and one Presbyterian layman. Of the two alternates, one was a Presbyterian elder, the other a Catholic. The Presbyterian domination of this first executive committee was more than an expression of numerical superiority. It was an expression of a strong tradition. Presbyterians had control of the agency practically from its inception, since even the early government-supported chiefs had been predominantly Presbyterian.

Between the completion of allotment in 1895 and 1923, this committee remained relatively inactive, but its importance as a prototype became evident in the latter year. By this time a number of Nez Perces were interested in formulating a permanent representative body; this was achieved in conjunction with the development of the first five-year plan. This plan for economic self-development called for the formation of a Home and Farm Association consisting of all Nez Perces within the tribal boundaries. The importance of the earlier committee is seen in the governing board of this association, which consisted of nine men, most of whom were Presbyterians. Riley has referred to the tribal adoption of a code of laws in 1880 as the first Nez Perce constitution, but this seems unwarranted. The adoption of the first formal constitution took place in 1927, following the 1923 re-emergence of the nine-man committee. The constitution was accepted by the BIA in October of 1927; this legitimized the first permanent executive committee. Activities of this committee centered around land leases, loan applications, land claims, timber sales, grazing permits and other affairs such as marriage laws and sanitation.[15]

The powers of this executive committee were limited by its lack of control over tribal funds and by the requirement that the BIA approve all its actions. Such limitations convinced most Nez Perces that they were still very much under the control of the BIA, and that more independence was necessary if the tribe were to act successfully in its own behalf. However, when in 1934 the Nez Perces were presented with the opportunity to achieve this end, through adoption of the Wheeler-Howard Act, they rejected it. Among the complex reasons for this rejection were fear of losing government services, fear of becoming subject to taxation, a cultural resistance to leadership by a powerful few, and, particularly, a fear on the part of the Christian Nez Perces that the aboriginal religion again would become legal and threaten their theocracy.

Further attempts were made in 1940 and 1945 to formulate constitutions which permitted a stronger executive committee, but these too were rejected by the general council. After World War II the BIA began withdrawing certain services in accord with its developing 'termination policy', and that faction favoring a strong tribal government began to receive more support within the tribe. It became increasingly evident to those Nez Perces who formerly had opposed a strong executive committee that the absence of effective tribal government would no longer deter the BIA in its determination to terminate federal supervision as soon as possible. Gradually, the ineffectual tribal executive committee based on the 1927 constitution began to assume more and more responsibility. The crisis created as the committee exceeded its constitutional authority, coupled with the renewed political interests of the returning veterans and war workers, produced sufficient positive sentiment by 1948 to ratify a constitution permitting a strong executive committee. In addition, many Nez Perces had come to realize that in order to implement claims effectively before the new Indian Claims Commission they would have to have a much more effective governing body than had existed ever before. Opponents of strong tribal government, however, continued to fulminate against the new system. Since 1949, this dissident faction has made several unsuccessful attempts to reduce the power of the strong executive committee, and such efforts continue into the present.

Despite this opposition, the strengthened executive committee has been successful in implementing claims against the government. These have brought large financial awards to the tribe and therefore increased strength and prestige for the executive committee; but the use of the money for community centers, horse-breeding programs and several other tribal enterprises rather than for continuous per capita payments has produced renewed opposition. In fact, during the last half-dozen years the principal issue separating the two factions has become whether the funds will be used collectively or disbursed individually. The opposition faction contains the majority of the off-reservation Nez Perces under the leadership of a small on-reservation nucleus. Whether resident on other reservations or in metropolitan areas, members of this faction stand to gain little from use of funds for development of the reservation. On the other hand, members of the faction supporting the present executive committee and its programs of tribal development tend to be drawn from the reservation population. This political division is expressive of an even more basic division in the society, that between those whose future is not bound up with the insulated, protective reservation system, and the present majority of Nez Perces who for various reasons cling to the reservation.

One often encounters the opposition faction's charges that the people support the executive committee only because of the economic power its members wield over the lives of the reservation Nez Perces. Further, members of the opposition state that the members of this committee really could not succeed in a non-reservation environment and are engaged in long-term planning as a means to insure the continuation of their well-paid jobs on the reservation. It is clear that were tribal assets divided equally among individuals, the principal *raison d'être* of the executive committee would disappear.

Such accusations by the opposition make more understandable the great efforts exerted by members of the on-reservation faction to restrict voting privileges to individuals resident on or immediately adjacent to the reservation. They may shed light even on the strong resistance to lowering the blood quanta requirements for tribal membership to less than one-quarter Nez Perce heredity. Were the present one-quarter requirement removed, the opposition faction would be strengthened greatly. Most believe that practically all off-reservation Nez Perces (those living beyond the 1855 treaty boundaries) favor individualization of tribal assets and strongly oppose the executive committee and its supporting reservation faction. Further, that section of the population with low Nez Perce heredity tends to be comprised of individuals who have moved away, married non-Indians and taken little interest in tribal affairs, being interested only in receiving their 'share' of the claims settlements and sale of tribal property.

In view of these developments, then, to what extent do 'decline' and 'renascence' apply to political changes in recent Nez Perce history? As in the cases of population, economy and religion, the answer is not a simple one. There are 'declines' and 'renascences' throughout the period since first contact with Euro-Americans. The pattern begins with the government-appointed chiefs. It seems clear enough that the institution of the head chief and sub-chiefs resulted in a net loss of Nez Perce cultural distinctiveness. However, it is not clear how one should regard the replacement of this chief system with the executive committee system. Did this change promote or reduce Nez Perce cultural distinctiveness? No clear judgment can be made, but the gradual strengthening of the executive committee in the last few decades fits neatly under the heading 'renascent'. Through strengthening this committee the Nez Perces have been able to reassert a degree of political distinctiveness probably not realized since 1855, when they first came under government control. Despite this political renascence, however, it is clear that not all Nez Perces support such a development, some preferring instead to do away with most tribal enterprises and distribute all tribal assets individually.

CONCLUSIONS

Three principal conclusions concerning the renascence concept may be drawn from this brief overview of Nez Perce history. First, 'renascence' as the term is used in this paper has not been a uniform characteristic of all aspects of Nez Perce culture at any single time. Instead, certain aspects of the culture, such as religion in the late nineteenth century, clearly were undergoing a renascence, while others were in decline. More recently, while church participation has been declining, with a consequent loss of religious distinctiveness, there has been a concomitant resurgence of political distinctiveness. In fact, with the possible exception of population, the only apparent renascence in the culture at the present time is in political organization. Only here are there developments which clearly are promoting Nez Perce ethnic distinctiveness, since the differentiating effect of the population increase is being offset by increasing tendencies to move off the reservation and to intermarry with non-Nez Perces and non-Indians. Present attempts to develop tribal economic enterprises seem too limited and too late to reverse the overriding trend toward economic assimilation. This does not, of course, mean that such a resurgence could not take place, but there is nothing on the national, state or local levels that would cause one to think it even remotely possible.

Second, there is no consistent relationship evident between cultural decline and renascence in recent Nez Perce history. While certain aspects of Nez Perce culture have undergone renascences after periods of decline, there are others that have been in a steady decline since the time of contact. The distinctiveness of the economy has been persistently reduced, and, despite a few feeble efforts at present to reverse this trend, Nez Perces are participating in the surrounding Euro-American economy in ever larger numbers. Language, although I have not discussed it in this essay, has shown a similar steady decline. There remains only one known mono-lingual Nez Perce. The majority of the population under twenty-five years of age uses English constantly, and despite a recent attempt on the part of a few Nez Perces to revive the language, few have shown any sustained interest. In fact, there is a general feeling that the language is a handicap, and recent attempts to establish a school for adult education in English are more likely to succeed than attempts to halt the declining use of Nez Perce among the young.

These aspects of culture have persistently declined. In religion and political organization, the situation is different. Although the aboriginal religion was abandoned almost completely, Christianity in the latter half of the nineteenth century served to augment ethnic distinctiveness for a time. But it, too, has been in decline since 1900. On the other hand, despite the earlier decline of the aboriginal and transitional political institutions, recent political reorganization has served to strengthen ethnic distinctiveness. It is probably significant that in both religion and politics, as well as in the population, which has recently increased, renascence was largely generated by the actions of Euro-Americans. For example, the renascence in religion could not have occurred had not particularly effective missionaries been present, and changes in BIA policy obviously have had much to do with the Nez Perce political renascence. It seems unlikely that the Nez Perces would have developed their strong political system had there not been a threat of termination and had not new economic opportunities been presented by federal establishment of the Indian Claims Commission.

Finally, it is clear that the several Nez Perce renascences have been accompanied invariably by factional dispute, and by no means have been uniformly supported by all members of the culture. This is evident in the religious renascence of the late nineteenth century, when a substantial non-Christian faction was forced off the reservation by the dominant Christian faction. Members of this exiled faction were associated with paganism and uniformly rejected the Christianity so fully accepted by their opponents. Similar strong disagreement has accompanied the more recent political renascence, and persists into the present: an out-of-power, off-reservation faction opposes a predominantly on-reservation faction. Principal issues are the amount of power exercised by the executive committee and the disposition of the recent claims settlement monies. Perhaps it is inevitable that intense sentiments develop for and against all radical changes which result in a marked shift in the direction of an established historical trend. The complexities involved in the study of culture change among North American Indians in terms of the twin concepts of cultural renascence and decline are apparent for the Nez Perces and suggest a need for much more systematic application than is found in the present literature.

Notes

1. Clifford Drury, *Spalding and Smith on the Nez Perce Mission* (Glendale, 1958), 136–7.

2. ibid., 134.

3. Deward Walker, 'Schismatic Factionalism and the Development of Nez Perce Pentecostalism', unpublished Ph.D. dissertation (Oregon, 1964).

4. ibid., 112–16.

5. Deward Walker, *A Survey of Nez Perce Religion* (New York: Board of National Missions, United Presbyterian Church, 1964), 36–8.

6. The interested reader may find a more detailed treatment of aboriginal Nez Perce religion, politics, and acculturation in my recently published *Conflict and Schism in Nez Perce Acculturation* (Pullman, Washington State University Press).

7. Leslie Spier, *The Prophet Dance of the Northwest and Its Derivatives: The Source of the Ghost Dance* (Menasha, Wisconsin, 1935).

8. Deward Walker, 'Schismatic Factionalism', 42–50.

9. ibid., 98, 119.

10. Deward Walker, 'Recommendations Regarding Certain Problems Concerning Nez Perce Presbyterianism' (unpublished paper, 1964, available on request).

11. Deward Walker, *A Survey*, 25.

12. ibid., 26.

13. Francis Haines, *The Nez Perces* (Norman, Oklahoma, 1955), 87–9.

14. Kate C. McBeth, *The Nez Perces Since Lewis and Clark* (New York, 1908), 115.

15. Robert James Riley, 'The Nez Perce Struggle for Self-Government: A History of Nez Perce Governing Bodies, 1842–1960', unpublished Ph.D. dissertation (Idaho, 1961), 58, 45–6, 66.

ROSALIE AND MURRAY WAX

INDIAN EDUCATION FOR
WHAT?

MANY western reformers have viewed formal education as a benevolent instrument of social change and social uplift – the principal and ideal technique for developing the under-developed, or in the language of A. L. Kroeber and Gordon Hewes, a technique whereby people may enter the civilized Ecumene.[1] To reformers of scholarly mind, education has embodied many virtues, being peaceable, gradual and in-tegral with their own occupations and interests – therefore vastly to be preferred to such other modalities of entry into the Ecumene as the violent military explosions of external proletarians or 'barbarians'. Being themselves educators, social scientists have often found this view congenial. On the other hand, when functioning as scientists trying to discover why education fails to move some peoples into full status within the Ecumene, they have tumbled upon the fact that education does not look the same from the bottom as from the top. When, for example, Antiochus Epiphanes attempted to draw the Jews into the civilized world of his day, he found that the Maccabees did not share his defini-tion of development. To the people who are to be uplifted, education as a concrete institution – a school system – bears quite a different aspect than it does when viewed abstractly from the peaks of Ecumenical leadership and scholarship. Especially when children are the primary educational tar-gets, the school is much more than a nebulous locus where knowledge is transmitted; it is the arena of an intense social drama. The social, political and economic cleavages and conflicts characteristic of the cross-cultural situation are reflected into the school and transform the classroom into something quite different from what the reformer conceived of it as being.

In like manner, many of those who are involved in Indian affairs think of education as something *good for* Indians: helping to transform them into persons who are more acceptable within our national society, better qualified for employment, less prone to become charges upon social welfare agencies, and less prone to the proletarian criminality of public drunkenness and disorder, rowdiness and thievery. We would surmise that this ideology is widely prevalent in the federal schools for Indians, in the BIA generally, as well as in the national Indian interest organizations. By referring to it as an ideology, we do not intend criticism but analysis. Teachers, generally, tend to believe and to preach that education and lower-middle-class morality are the keys to a future of economic opportunity and social success. Nevertheless, for minority ethnic groups the struggle may be more devious. It is worth reminding ourselves of some of the vicissitudes of the Japanese-Americans, who were as energetically oriented toward education and achievement as it is possible to be and who were the stereotypical embodiment of the protestant virtues of thrift, diligence and industry. Yet on the west coast of the US, it was precisely these characteristics that were singled out by their competitors and enemies as justifying discriminatory and repressive action. 'They work so hard you can't compete with them' was a complaint frequently voiced by white farmers.

The contrast with Indian affairs may fruitfully be pushed even farther. During World War II, the Japanese-Americans were confined to relocation centers, institutions which have been compared to concentration camps but which perhaps are better compared with the Indian reservations of a half-century ago. (The comparison is evident even from the recruitment of administrative personnel: many had been members of the Indian Service and some were to become high officials in that service after the war.) Within some of the relocation centers, the Japanese-Americans did not adopt the passive posture so often bemoaned by whites observing Indians within their reservations, but instead organized themselves to influence the conduct of the administration. The irony is that the administrators, who had been selected by circumstances to regulate the lives of these able and energetic people, thought of and justified their task as being the educational one of inducting them into Americanism and democracy; the further irony is that they perceived the inmates' attempts at organization and self-government as dangerous threats, as was perhaps inevitable given the heavy and dictatorial responsibility from the federal government.[2]

We do not mention this in order to condemn the role of particular federal bureaucratic organizations in dealing with ethnic minorities such as Indians and Japanese-Americans, but rather to remind our audience of the accidents that affect the destiny of any such minority. Among the most significant of these accidents has been access to the ballot and sufficient local concentration to affect the election of congressmen – and school boards. Here settlement patterns have favored the ethnic Jewish and Catholic enclaves of our metropolitan areas and have worked against the rurally dispersed Japanese and Indians. Federal policies of dispersal in the urban relocating of both the latter groups have likewise limited their ability to become effective political blocs.

The foregoing prologue may serve to remind us that it is possible to overemphasize the role of education as compared to political and military power in determining either the relationship between a particular ethnic culture and the civilized Ecumene, or between a particular ethnic society and the national society. We may also be reminded that education cannot be regarded as an abstract and individual activity but must be seen as a concrete social system, itself shaped by political and social forces.

Turning now more specifically to the Oglala Community High School of the Pine Ridge Reservation and to the problem of dropping out (the focus of our most recent study), we find once again that the view of the Sioux diverges very widely from the rational views of the national leaders of Indian affairs. Moreover, the motivations or forces that direct some of the young people into the high school are rarely those that would be approved by scholastic reformers.

Many officials of the BIA tend to see high school drop-out in terms of opposing social forces: the administrators and teachers try to attract the young people into a scholastic environment in order to prepare them for entrance into the greater national society; meanwhile, the conservative Indian elders try to pull the young people back into the empty and unprogressive reservation culture. This perspective is very like that of most other American educators who believe that the rate of high school drop-out in disprivileged areas can be reduced only by drawing the young folk from their present environments and subjecting them to the stimulating and broadening influences of general American education. Once broadened and motivated, it is expected that these young people will obtain a respectable and well-paid employment and eventually play a modest role in support of the more civilized levels of our national society. On the other hand, if the pull of the old environment is too strong, they will return to their odd jobs, pool halls, relief rolls and the numbers game.

Our investigation of the Oglala Community High School

indicates that this widely held – and superficially reasonable – conceptualization of the social dynamics involved in high school drop-out is, for Pine Ridge, at least, oversimple and inaccurate.

It is true that the Pine Ridge administrators urge the Indian parents to send their children to the high school and that they try to keep enrolled students in the classrooms. On the other hand, very few of the Country Indian adolescents go to school because of the scholastic or academic advantages it offers. (By Country Indians we mean the children of the more conservative folks who live out on the reservation and send their children to the country day schools.) Most of those who enroll do so because their friends of day school years are enrolling, for to be separated from their friends is, as one of them put it, 'torture'. Young men have an additional reason – their passionate desire to play basketball and participate in sports. Indeed, a number of boys stated that the only thing that kept them from dropping out was their enjoyment of basketball. Young women are particularly attracted to the high school by its promise of novel and exciting social experiences (boys, dances, movies) and by the proximity of the agency town of Pine Ridge and of the taverns and juke-boxes of White Clay – an off-reservation hamlet that serves as the local Babylon. While many of these young people will tell an interviewer that they go to school 'to learn' and will add that their elders have instructed them that if they don't finish high school 'they will have a hard time and won't get a job', very few express interest in any scholastic achievement except 'learning to talk English'. This interest in learning to talk English may be related to the fact that many day school graduates, though they may have some facility in reading and writing English, have not yet learned to speak it with any fluency. Among these young people are some who have tried to get jobs in towns near the reservation and who have, apparently, themselves discovered the extent of their handicap.

While most of the high school teachers try to arouse the intellectual interest of their students, their success is meager. Forty-two per cent of the young people who entered high school from the district we studied intensively dropped out in the ninth and tenth grades. (Twenty-two per cent of the young people from this district left school after completing the eighth grade.) The more conscientious teachers point out correctly that many of the day school graduates are not prepared to undertake high-school work at the ninth grade level. On the other hand, our investigations indicate that relatively few students drop out of high school as a direct result of poor academic performance. Instead, long before they can appreciate how handicapped they are, more than half of the boys are propelled out of school by a head-on collision with the authorities. Many of the Country Indian youths seem to define the school authorities as enemies or outsiders and react toward them with the impulsive and un-calculating recklessness which, for them, is proper masculine behavior. They steal oranges or candy from the mess hall, play hookey, steal a Bureau car and ride about the country with pals until the gas gives out, go to White Clay and get drunk, or break an '$85.00 government-property mirror'. For these offenses they are either expelled or restricted to the dormitories – that is, forbidden to attend movies or athletic events, or to go to town. Many of these youths seem unable to endure sitting in class all day and in the dormitories all night and they are likely to say, as one put it, 'To hell with this noise,' and go home. Significantly, many of these young men told us, 'I just quit school, but I never did *want* to quit.'

In contrast to the boys, most of the girls do not *openly* defy the authorities. Instead, they drop out of high school because they are unable to tolerate their social disadvan-

tages. These girls seem to perceive relatively early in their
school careers that the children of the Bureau employees and
other moderately well-off 'Mixedbloods'[3] have far better
clothes and are 'away ahead of them' in matters of teenage
sophistication, scholastic achievement, fluency in English
language and general knowledge of how to beat the system.
They feel poor, dowdy and dumb, or as they put it, 'embarrassed ... out of place ... like freaks'. Should they
attempt to play an active role in extra-curricular activities
(clubs, committees and dances) they are likely to meet strong
and sometimes even violent opposition from the experienced
and knowledgeable young folk who have been attending the
Oglala Community day and boarding schools since they were
five and six years old. If they are shy, over age and come
from poor families of little influence, they will either drop
out or turn much of their energy into the world of hookey
playing, 'running around and raising Cain'. There are a few
students who seem to use the school only as a place to eat
and occasionally sleep. Just as many of the young people
enrolled in school to be with their friends, many now drop
out with their friends. 'My friend said: "If you're not going
to be around then I'm the only one who'll get punished, so
if you're going I might as well go too ..." I felt kinda sorry
for him, because if he'd stay'd in there he'd of been a good
basketball player.'

Before proceeding we would like to emphasize that the
above remarks are not intended to single out either the
Bureau of Indian Affairs or the Pine Ridge Country Indians
for criticism. The practices and policies of most high schools
attended by underprivileged urban children are probably
more like those of OCHS than they are unlike. Similarly,
many of the adolescents who drop out of these urban schools
are probably more like the young Sioux – in passion, energy,
loyalty to peers, attitudes toward the authorities and poor

elementary school preparation – than they are unlike. If there is something unhealthy in this situation, it is a widespread sickness.

To return to the topic of social dynamics. Our observations suggest that the Country Indian is not so much pulled out of high school by his conservative elders as he is ejected or rejected by the authorities and by a high-school social system that favors the more advantaged and more cautious students.

An additional question is raised by the fact that a small number of Country Indians somehow seem able to run this gauntlet and obtain a high-school diploma. A few even go to college – more this last year than ever before. How did they manage to do it?

We obtained life histories from a number of these young men and women and found that the majority had been given a great deal of social, psychological and financial support by their extended kin group. Apparently some Country Indian families have become convinced that their corporate well-being and prestige within the local community depend on getting at least some of their children through high school (and college, if possible) and thus into the better paying tribal and Bureau jobs. Young Sioux who have this formidable body of elders blocking their retreat do not find it easy to leave school. As some folk put it: 'All the force of his parents is behind him.' Or as one such graduate of the Oglala Community High School told us, 'Everyone in my family are proud to see others and myself graduate. My parents are pushing me upward every day for a higher education. ... I don't go to school because the government says so. I go to school to want to learn.' In some cases, this parental and kin pressure is so strong that it puts outright dullards through college. While they are in school, these 'successful' pupils do not necessarily withdraw from the boisterous and forbidden recreations of the peer groups. But they do, we suspect, tend to 'shape up' to the extent that they evaluate risks and stay out of the more rash and fore-doomed adventures. As one of them put it: 'We *do* like [as] white people.' Besides, should they get into serious trouble, their kin will raise a fuss with the school authorities sufficient to keep them in school. In addition to this intense familial support, four young people mention the aid and encourage-ment given them by a particular Indian high-school teacher. Another major force keeping young men in school until graduation is proficiency in sports and especially in basketball. The few young women who graduate often hope that their diploma will lead to an off-reservation secretarial or nursing school and the opportunity to get a good husband.

Another smaller but still significant number of young In-dians graduate from high school *because* they are alienated from their kin and from the reservation peer groups. These are usually orphans or children who have been grossly neg-lected by their parents, and have managed to attach them-selves to a particular teacher or to a group of boarding school peers. It is noteworthy that those of these young people to whom we talked did not seem to take much pride in their individualistic achievements. When asked how they got through school they launched into bitter and repetitive de-nunciations of their folks who (they said) had neglected them to drink and run around and had not helped them through school in any way. In a white student who is expected to take pride in lonely individualist accomplishment, such be-havior would appear odd and childish. But these alienated and educated young Sioux might be lamenting the fact that their accomplishment signified little because it was truly individualistic. That their parents and relatives had not helped them through school seemed to be a cause for shame.

Whether the young Sioux drop out or remain in high school, they seem to do this largely in their own way and according to their own or their elders' definition of the situation. In this respect they resemble many tribal or peripheral peoples who, when exposed to Ecumenical knowledge and theories of education, select what appeals to them and formulate it in their own terms. In brief, the Sioux, in their own small way, are using education very much as did the Jews, the Cherokee, the Northmen and, in our own day, the tribal peoples of Africa. While we participants in western civilization tend to define education and the motive for attending school in terms of individualistic success, it may be useful to remember that most other peoples have defined and still define education in quite different terms: the religious search for divine truth, the political and nationalistic strivings to develop an indigenous elite, the identification with a revolutionary or nationalistic movement. The student seeking the kingdom of God or the socialist or nationalist utopia will – like the young Sioux 'with all his family behind him' – remain in school despite repeated individualistic failures. (Conversely, the student who accepts the ideology of individual success, and then, like the Country Sioux, is subjected to repeated failures and humiliations, will not remain in school very long.) However, for the Sioux to start their own educational movement, reservation culture and reservation politics would have to have a much different cast. The rise of pan-Indian nationalism may be predisposing toward this kind of development; it is too early to tell.

Notes

Delivered at the 1964 Annual Meeting of the American Anthropological Association. In part, this paper reports research sponsored by Emory University and supported by the US Office of Education under its cooperative Research Program. The monograph report of the first phase of this research (see note 3) may be borrowed from depository libraries of federal publications (Office of Education CRP 1361) or may be purchased from the Business Manager, Society for the Study of Social Problems, P.O. Box 190, Kalamazoo, Michigan 49005.

1. Gordon W. Hewes, 'The Ecumene as a Civilizational Multiplier System', *The Kroeber Anthropological Society Papers*, No. 25 (Berkeley, California, 1961), 73–110. A. L. Kroeber, 'The Ancient Oikoumene as a Historic Culture Aggregate', *The Nature of Culture* (Chicago, 1952), 379–95.

2. Rosalie H. Wax, 'The Destruction of a Democratic Impulse', *Human Organization*, XII, 1 (Spring 1953), 11–21. See also Mrs Wax's unpublished Ph.D. dissertation, 'The Development of Authoritarianism' (University of Chicago, 1950).

3. Murray L. Wax, Rosalie H. Wax and Robert Dumont, Jr, *Formal Education in an American Indian Community*, Monograph # 1 of the Society for the Study of Social Problems (Kalamazoo, Michigan 49005, 1964).

Additional Bibliography

A. D. Fisher, 'Education and Social Progress', *Alberta Journal of Educational Research*, XII, 4 (December 1966), 257–68.

C. W. Hobart and C. S. Brant, 'Eskimo Education, Danish and Canadian: A Comparison', *Canadian Review of Sociology and Anthropology*, III, 2 (May 1966), 47–66.

A. Richard King, *The School at Mopass: A Problem of Identity* (Holt, Rinehart and Winston, New York, 1967).

Murray L. Wax and Rosalie H. Wax, 'The Enemies of the People', in Howard S. Becker and others, eds., *Institutions and the Person* (Aldine, Chicago, 1968), 101–18.

Harry F. Wolcott, *A Kwakiutl Village and Its School* (Holt, Rinehart and Winston, New York, 1967).

HENRY F. DOBYNS

THERAPEUTIC EXPERIENCE OF RESPONSIBLE DEMOCRACY

INDIAN affairs in the United States are rather more signifi-cant than the small proportion of surviving natives in the national population would indicate. This significance comes primarily from the powerful position of the country in inter-national affairs. It derives secondarily from the extensive study of tribal peoples and government carried out in this country, for these peoples constitute a great natural labora-tory for experimentation in inter-group relations, and prin-ciples applicable to parallel situations overseas can be discovered.[1] From this national laboratory have come social science generalizations about relationships between indige-nous and non-indigenous peoples anywhere in the world. One set of human relations principles of this sort, for ex-ample, was enunciated by former commissioner of Indian Affairs John Collier.[2]

Enough events have transpired within our natural social laboratory to allow us to judge the validity of our social scientists' generalizations. Yet, for all the attention that has been devoted to tribal peoples in the US, one of the most significant developments of the past several years seems to have escaped published notice or recognition as an index of the scientific validity of the generalizations about group behavior advanced by Collier.

The general sequence of events in tribal administration in the United States is well known and documented. When he became Commissioner of Indian Affairs in 1933, Collier triggered a process of change in the social structure of administration of tribal peoples. Collier based his program on the basic principle that 'The experience of responsible democracy is, of all experiences, the most therapeutic, the most disciplinary, the most dynamogenic and the most productive of efficiency.'[3] The other basic ingredient of Collier's administrative philosophy may be summed up as a generalized faith that tribal societies possessed what Leighton (1949) calls 'morale'.[4] Some such notion is a necessary base for Collier's somewhat mystical belief that tribal societies either existed or could be created and given all democratic freedoms.[5] This view defines the state as the responsibility for fostering cultural autonomy of its various ethnic components.[6]

To evaluate what the Collier program has produced in the years since 1933, one must have in mind the situation that existed when he brought his faith to bear on practical administration. The administration of tribal peoples in the US aimed at the destruction of native culture, the breaking up of native social organizations and the individualization of native land holdings for approximately eighty years prior to 1933.[7] Key beliefs behind this program were that tribal land ownership was too different from Anglo-Saxon individual ownership to be tolerated, and tribal religions too barbarous to be allowed to flourish.[8] A linear social structure of tribal administration implemented such dominant group beliefs and goals in a period of domestic imperialism. Diagram I symbolizes this linearity. This was quite similar to tribal administrations in Africa, India, Australia and Canada where other native peoples were restricted geographically to segregated *reserved* areas by English-speaking conquerors. This system evidently arose out of British governmental habits and attitudes toward non-English-speaking peoples. The US government developed, in addition, a specific administrative apparatus for dealing with natives.

Known usually as the Bureau of Indian Affairs, this agency originated in the War Department and was incorporated into the Department of the Interior somewhat over a century ago. After final military defeat of the various tribes and withdrawal by the army from active participation in native administration, the BIA long enjoyed a near-monopoly on governmental control and direction of tribal societies, especially on Southwestern reserves. Yet these reservations remained largely unallotted, and native religions

Diagram 1. The Social Structure of Indian Affairs to 1933

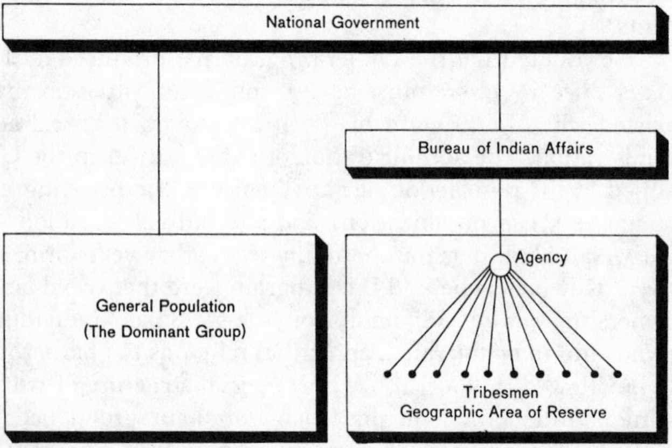

survived, since the administrative effort 'bogged down in its own complexities'.[9]

During this period, relations between the dominant and subordinate societies tended to move in straight lines from BIA administrators to tribesmen, or vice versa (see Diagram I). Thus sharply restricted contacts between tribesmen and individual members of the dominant society occurred in the reserve areas, particularly where the reserve areas were relatively isolated. Since BIA personnel was a highly selected and atypical sample of the general population of the nation, tribesmen inevitably acquired a distorted impression of the dominant society and its culture. It seems to be difficult for groups in such contact to be truly representative of their respective societies.[10] The welfare of tribesmen depended largely upon the actions of BIA personnel, and administrative behavior often appeared capricious and unpredictable to tribesmen of cultural traditions very different from those of the administrators. This was perhaps most often true in the cases of Southwestern tribesmen, who had relatively less formal education than Indians elsewhere in the nation as time went on. The structure generated considerable psychological stress among the tribal population.[11] Frequently, the stress became intolerable, and tribesmen responded with behavioral patterns of apathy, hatred, hostility and at times destructive action similar to what one finds in subordinated ethnic groups the world over. Indians oftentimes directed such emotions and actions at other members of the subordinated group, and seldom could individual tribesmen take integrated, efficient action toward overcoming the sources of their stress.

Then, as Collier reported, 'We tried to extend to the tribes a self-governing self-determination without any limit beyond the need to advance by stages to the goal.'[12] In essence, he provided every possible encouragement to the foundation of formal constitutional self-government within the external forms of US democracy. This interposed a tribal government composed of elected representatives between the individual tribesman and the full force of the administrative apparatus. Wherever tribal governments were organized, tribesmen now had slightly more chance to take efficient and integrated action toward overcoming the sources of at least some stresses induced by their subordinate socio-economic and political status. Therein lay, perhaps, the therapeutic value of tribal self-government in its opening phase – in reducing existing causes of serious psychological stress.

Not everything which has happened on reservations since 1933 has been due, of course, to John Collier. Partly by administrative intention within the BIA and largely by accident, the monopolistic hold of the BIA on national interaction with tribal peoples broke up rapidly during the 1930s and 1940s at the same time that the experiment in tribal self-determination was initiated. Since the Southwestern Indians were perhaps most heavily subjected to the BIA monolith, the change has possibly been greatest among them.

Indians are now accustomed to dealing with many federal agencies and some state agencies on an individual and a tribal basis. This shift began on a large scale with the inauguration of an Indian Division of the Civilian Conservation Corps.[13] It continued with proliferation of governmental contacts with such agencies as the Production Marketing Administration, the Office of Price Administration, Selective Service and the public schools educating tribal children under provision of the Johnson–O'Malley Act.[14] It reached the point of division of direct administrative responsibility in the fall of 1955 when the US Public Health Service took over entire responsibility for Indian health from the BIA.[15]

All this complication of relationships between Indians and the government made the administrative organization far more complex than ever before. It afforded emergent tribal governments considerable room in which to maneuver and decrease causes of psychological stress among their constituents. But it altered slightly the essentially linear nature of the relationships between tribesmen in subordinate power positions and non-Indians in dominant roles (see Diagram II).

All these changes occurred during what might be termed Phase I of the development of tribal self-determination in the United States. This phase ended formally with promulgation of the 'withdrawal' or termination policy of the

Diagram II. The Changing Social Structure of Indian Affairs, 1933–46

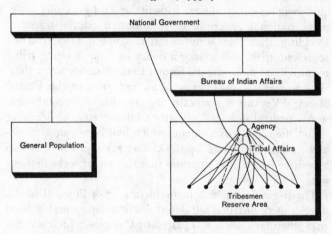

BIA and Congress, as announced by Assistant Commissioner John Provinse before the National Conference of Social Work at San Francisco on 14 April 1947.[16] Implementation of this policy began in 1950 under Commissioner Dillon S. Myer,[17] and intensified in 1953 when Congress voted to permit states to assume legal jurisdiction on reservation lands.[18]

Since then Phase II has developed, not clearly at first, but recently with greater clarity of form. Yet the numerous evaluations of the 'Collier program' which have appeared in print have hardly distinguished this new phase, nor have its indices been recognized.[19]

To be sure, Collier himself pointed out that since his resignation as Commissioner, tribes have faced increasingly hostile administrators in the BIA and legislators in the Congress during the drive begun in 1950 and continued through most of the Eisenhower administration to withdraw federal services, terminate land trusteeship, subject reserve areas and their residents to state jurisdiction and generally to remove national government from Indian administration.[20] Deciding that this administration ignored elected tribal representatives, and stating a policy of subordinating tribal to individual interests, the former Commissioner wrote that: 'The immediate prospect is bleak and grim in the United States.'[21] Yet this was only the negative side of the total situation – neutral or overtly hostile administrators toughening up on the tribal governments which had been sympathetically nursed into being by the Collier régime. There is also a positive part of the situation that this paper seeks to point out.

The beginning of this favorable aspect of Phase II of the development of tribal self-determination dates roughly from 1946 when legislation was passed by Congress which set off a new direction of growth. Not all tribes have yet entered this new phase, of course, just as there was considerable time lag between passage of the Indian Reorganization Act (48 Stat. 984) in 1934 and the actual beginnings of formal self-governments on the reserves. In general, the social structure of tribal administration and the culture change it achieved was markedly altered through the introduction of new features at intergroup interactions which can be traced in large part to the Indian Claims Commission Act of 1946 (60 Stat. 1049). That act itself produced notable changes in the economies of several tribes which won judgments.[22] The additional dimension considered in this paper is that of legal counsel hired on a year-round basis, paid by the tribal government. One Northwest Coast tribe decided good representation was important enough to hire an attorney fresh out of law school. The tribe was willing to suffer some losses while he learned the specialty of Indian law, because the tribe had in mind the long-term goal of obtaining capable, sympathetic counsel.

Attorneys are actually only one type of non-Indian specialist now employed by various tribes. The outside consultant takes many professional forms today.[23] The attorney is, however, the specialist most frequently employed by tribes on a permanent basis, and he occupies such a critical sociopolitical position in intergroup relations that only this key example of the general class of consultants is here considered.

Few tribal governments retained general counsel as such prior to 1946. When tribes hired lawyers, they usually did so for a limited period to handle a specific case of an emergency nature. The Klamath reservation Indians, for example, retained an attorney in an allotment-period struggle with the superintendent over election of Indian judges and policemen.[24] Most tribes have retained general counsel since 1946, the sharpest break with the past having come perhaps among Southwestern tribes. The impetus for this change clearly came from the Indian Claims Commission Act, a general enabling act empowering any tribe feeling it had a valid claim against the US to bring suit for recovery before a special Commission established by the Act. To file such suits tribes necessarily had to hire attorneys. As a result, many tribes have recovered damages from the United States. This paper is not concerned with these direct benefits but with indirect and unforeseen advantages obtained through a significant change in the social structure of Indian affairs.

Many of the attorneys hired to present claims cases had had no previous experience with Indian legal matters. A high proportion were apparently of higher caliber than had been involved in Indian law before, although there have been a few notorious exceptions.[25] Once tribes made their initial contact with attorneys, many of the latter discovered that their clients stood in need of legal services of a type provided by general counsel on an annual retainer basis, and undertook to represent tribes in matters other than claims. Many attorneys found that their personal value systems impelled them to champion the subordinate ethnic groups against their own dominant group.

As their experience with individual attorneys broadened, several tribes that first hired general counsel incidental to a claims case switched horses in midstream. Indian tribal officials appeared to be quite capable of jettisoning the type of attorney who sought employment in hopes of financial profit alone, and finding one who held genuine sympathy for tribal aspirations. The utility of tribally employed general counsel has been such that once a tribe has enjoyed the services of a lawyer in this role, it usually continues to employ one.

The ways in which a general counsel aids his tribal employers are numberless. When full-blood and mixed-blood Utes of the Uintah and Ouray Reservation, Utah, fell out over the division of a Court of Claims award made in 1950, the tribal attorney helped a special tribal legislative committee work out a plan to partition the tribe and its assets.[26] (This award stemmed from a special enabling act passed in 1938 and not from the later Indian Claims Commission Act.)[27]

In this emergent pattern of social interaction involving tribal peoples in the United States, the tribal attorney constitutes a 'third force' in reserve area administration. He forms the third point on an interaction triangle (see Diagram III), remaining physically outside the reserve except when conducting business there. He may actually spend only a few hours attending monthly business meetings of the governing body of the reserve to which he drives or flies, so his personal contacts are limited to top tribal officers.

Diagram III. The Emerging Social Structure of Indian Affairs after 1946

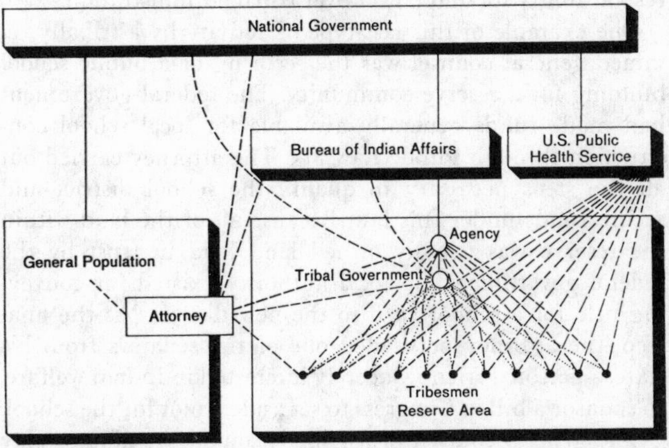

On the other hand, the effects of what he does reach every member of the tribe. He brings to this job, moreover, all his professional, political and social associations with members of the dominant society. Since his client is the tribe, he is paid to work for its interests regardless of the wishes of BIA administrators or any other member of the dominant group. The tribal government with counsel can, therefore, at any time short circuit through him the old 'direct wire' to the

BIA and seek to achieve its goals through the attorney and a triangular interaction pattern.

Being outside the old chain of command, the attorney can and does operate at any level of that hierarchy at any time. The angle of the triangle of interaction varies constantly up and down: the attorney intervenes for his tribal client with the reserve superintendent, Area Office of the BIA, its Washington headquarters, with administrative superiors of the BIA in the Department of the Interior, and if necessary directly with the Congress, which has ultimate responsibility for and power over tribal administration.

One example of this last type of activity by a tribally retained general counsel was the securing of a public school building for a reserve community. The federal government had made funds generally available for local school construction through Public Law 815. The attorney carried out all the steps necessary to qualify the school district and secure funds under this law. Because all of the land within the reserve was tribally owned land held in trust by the federal government, no local authority existed for conveying title for a school yard to the new district. As the final step, the attorney persuaded one of the senators from his state, a personal friend sincerely interested in Indian welfare, to sponsor a bill in Congress to set aside a plot for the school.

The general counsel of a tribe is sometimes able to play off one part of the dominant society's governmental apparatus against another for the benefit of his Indian clients. Officials of one Southwestern reserve applied for permission to begin growing cotton, a very profitable cash crop, as part of their economic development program. The local Department of Agriculture official with powers of approval informed them that no reservation land could be planted to cotton under the price support program because the tribe had not previously grown this crop and the county's permitted acreage was already allotted to non-Indian farmers who had grown it previously. The tribe's general counsel contacted a senator from the state with a record of friendship to Indians. Then he was able to telephone the Department of Agriculture official to say: 'Senator X thought the tribe could obtain an allotment for thirty-five acres of cotton.' The allotment was approved.

In the event interaction in this triangular pattern is not effective in gaining ends sought by his tribal client, the attorney provides a bridge from the tribe to the general population by which political action can be initiated. This may be thought of as a quadrilateral interaction, an initial stimulus moving horizontally from the tribe to its attorney and his political associates and the populace at large. Then it moves vertically to the national government in the form of protest campaigns, petitions and/or actual voting. One of the striking examples of this type of interaction pattern was the efficient mobilization of public opinion behind the tribal (and attorney) position opposing the attempt of former Commissioner of Indian Affairs Dillon S. Myer to propose administrative regulations governing attorney contracts.[28]

Having reached Washington, the impulses of this interaction pattern spread horizontally through the various departments, particularly that of Interior and specifically the Bureau of Indian Affairs, and then descend vertically through the chain of bureaucratic command to the tribe again (see Diagram III). In the example cited, the tribes successfully resisted the proposed regulations, which were disapproved by the then Secretary of the Interior.

The tribally retained general counsel also provides his clients with a direct window looking into state government, an increasingly significant area of tribal concern. In 1954, for example, one tribal attorney persuaded the long-resistant

Arizona State Welfare administration to approve its first
grant of general aid to a reservation resident (*Arizona Daily
Star*, 22 December 1954). Although legally entitled to such
state aid, no reservation Indian had received it until an
elderly woman on the San Carlos Apache jurisdiction was
granted assistance through the work of tribal attorneys, 'just
doing a job for our client'. Another tribal attorney in this
state advised his reservation clients to proceed with their
economic development program involving drilling deep irri-
gation wells, despite state legislation prohibiting further
well-drilling in critical areas. When the state Attorney General threatened to prosecute Indians, the tribal attorney – a
former county chairman of the political party to which the
state official belonged – pointed out that the state lacked
jurisdiction on the reserve and that there were plenty of
non-Indian violators of the ground water code with whom
the Attorney General could well concern himself. No Indian drillers were prosecuted.

It must be pointed out that the phrase 'responsible democracy' in the title of this paper applies not merely to the experience of Indian tribesmen, but equally to that of their
attorneys. The examples of attorney achievement cited in
this discussion have all been drawn from the relatively open
democratic society in the United States. Not all societies
are equally open nor do attorneys occupy an equally powerful position in all. In agrarian societies dominated by land
owners, the lawyer who attempts to represent subordinate
group members may expose himself to serious attack. Certain Peruvian Indians engaged in a territorial dispute with
a powerful landlord charged, for example, that the latter
had deprived them of the right to legal defense by the simple
expedient of charging each of four attorneys the Indians
hired with complicity in their alleged misdeeds.[29] In another
case, an attorney who undertook to represent Indian laborers

on the estate of a Peruvian senator found himself imprisoned for obstructing the administration of justice.[30] The lessons drawn from the US intergroup relations laboratory may be applied only where conditions are truly parallel.

The implications of this largely new social structure of intergroup interaction for cultural change among US tribal peoples are considerable. A much wider sample of the culture of the dominant society becomes available to the tribesmen for borrowing, either directly from the tribal attorney or as a result of his efforts. A much larger proportion of what was previously interpreted as capricious and unpredictable behavior by members of the dominant group is made comprehensible by the explanations of tribal attorneys, thereby reducing psychological stress in the interactions between tribes and the larger society. Broader acquaintance with the culture of the dominant groups results in acceptance of more alternatives: hiring specialists other than lawyers is one index of this change. Their attorneys train tribal officials in many practical techniques of social action in the politico-legal-business circles of the United States, even down to the level of the off-color joke. Indian leaders previously have not had such training, least of all in the Southwest. This is not to claim that other important social mechanisms of Indian integration are not operative. The service of 25,000 Indians in World War II led to the increasing participation of veterans in wider US society. Rising Indian literacy has permitted increased Indian voting, recently taken into account by members of Congress.[31] The role of the tribal attorney is especially important, however, in its direct effects on Indian leaders as well as in obtaining benefits for the general tribal population.

The new social structure of tribal administration has important practical implications for administration of subordinate subcultural groups wherever they occur. This new interaction pattern which places tribal general counsel in a key two-way interpretative role between subordinate and dominant groups has been rapidly adopted by tribal governments not so much for the hidden benefits stressed in this paper, but because of the visible and tangible benefits to tribesmen it yields. For example, a national highway passes through the village where most of the tribesmen reside on one reservation. When this tribe recovered lands long controlled by the Santa Fé railroad, business concerns operated by non-Indians paid twenty-five dollars per year for the use of the land they occupied. The tribal attorney upped this income from a few hundred dollars to $5,000 a year. Later he negotiated the first timber cutting contract this tribe had drawn for thirty years. More recently he has negotiated mining leases for this tribal client which provide assured income from advance royalties and an advantageous contract for power-generating rights.[32]

On a different reserve with irrigated farm lands, BIA officials for many years told tribesmen who held trust allotments that they could lease their lands for only one dollar per acre annually. Leases ran indefinitely at the pleasure of the non-Indian lessee. Where tribal lands were leased along the reservation boundary, BIA officials saw that non-Indians operating adjacent farms were leased contiguous Indian acreage. The non-Indian farmers then drilled wells on their own lands near the boundary fence and pumped water to irrigate both plots. Improvement provisions written into BIA-drawn leases were not enforced. After the Indians on this reservation retained general counsel, he suggested that he be allowed to intervene in this situation. He put the leases up for competitive bidding and his clients received as much as $45 per acre per year for leases limited to five years. He enforced, furthermore, existing improvement provisions that permanent improvements were to be made on the leased lands and left there at the end of the lease period. At one time he was simultaneously prosecuting two leaseholders for contract violations in matters of fencing, land leveling, and drilling wells on the reserve land instead of just across the fence. In addition, if cotton were grown on these leased Indian lands, the leaseholders paid a royalty on each bale produced over a stated minimum.

Another attorney negotiated a settlement of $2,800,000 with the US Corps of Engineers for the loss of Indian property rights for which the Corps originally offered exactly nothing.

Some of the psychological benefits Indians have derived through retaining general counsel have been obtained directly as a result of the creation of a more advantageous economic position. In an Arizona town adjacent to a reserve, theaters, until 1952, segregated Indian patrons in their seating. Then the town government renegotiated its lease on a section of reserve lands used as the local airport. The tribal attorney, guiding negotiations, brought discrimination under discussion. Discriminatory seating of Indian theater customers ended.

This sort of increase in the tribal share of the benefits of the national socio-political structure apparently does result in the kind of therapy John Collier had in mind in encouraging tribal self-government. Self-government in itself may be therapeutic, but *successful* self-government of the type resulting from retention of tribal legal counsel is certainly dynamic in its results in tribal societies. This success in increasing the tribal share of benefits objectively reduces the degree of subordination of the tribesmen. This appears as the true therapy: bringing subordinate groups into a more egalitarian socio-economic position within the national polity,[33] in part by destroying 'artificially' created barriers to self-development[34] and permitting that Indian participation in planning and shaping its own future which is essential for successful cultural change.[35]

Since the total store of benefits in any society is fixed at any point in time, it might appear that by gaining an increased share, tribal groups subtract from the portion of the dominant group. This does not, however, seem to be the case, simply because total benefits are increasing concurrently. The economic cost of geographically segregated tribal populations in the United States has been relatively high. Indeed, it constitutes a drain on the national economy, as is readily discerned in the annually mounting appropriations to the Bureau of Indian Affairs during a period in which it has tried to 'work itself out of a job'. On the other hand, as tribal government becomes more successful, tribal economies become less of an economic drain. While the San Carlos Apaches, for example, have developed their tribal program with the aid of general counsel (and other outside help), they have integrated more and more into the economy and society of the Southwest and the nation. They have developed business and employment opportunities on their reservation for many Apaches who would previously have had to leave to compete with non-Indians for the jobs available elsewhere until their tribal herds and other tribal business enterprises were organized.[36] The motel and restaurant operated by the Navajo Tribe at Window Rock and Shiprock (*New York Times*, 3 May 1964) create Indian employment and additional capital in the same way as tribally leased oil, gas and uranium ore deposits. When the Mescalero Apaches borrowed money from the BIA to purchase a $2,000,000 ski facility at Sierra Blanca in Lincoln National Forest, they entered upon a large scale campaign for profits from the tourist trade. They saw employment for individual Indians as only a long-range possibility dependent upon training suitable candidates (*New York*

Times, 3 November 1963). In effect, as each tribal community increases its integration into national socio-political patterns, a new 'point in time' is reached at which the total store of benefits available to the society as a whole has increased.

A corollary proposition is that the possibility of nativistic movements, separatist movements or revolt is lessened as psychological stress in the tribal population decreases. Significantly the clearest example of a nativistic movement among US tribal peoples today seems to be a faction known as 'Traditional Hopi Chiefs'. Indulging in histrionics such as sending ultimata to the President forbidding drafting of Hopi youths on religious grounds, or threatening to secede, this movement exists in a group united by little more than speaking a common language. The formal self-governing apparatus above the native village level constitutes merely another faction, so the experience of successful self-determination remains elusive for lack of ability to make decisions.

A specific characteristic of the present situation in tribal administration in the US is that a dominant group imposes a government-of-law upon subordinate groups. In a statute-stifled society such as this one, attorneys inevitably assume a central role in determining the distribution of financial, social and political benefits within the total social structure. For this reason subordinate peoples must be *specifically* free to employ their own competent legal counsel if they are to maximize their share of socio-political benefits and avoid severe psychological stress.

It is doubtful whether John Collier foresaw that this particular aspect of tribal self-government would assume the importance it has. Nor is there any reason to expect any social scientist to predict correctly in such detail all the consequences of an action program. It is as a social scientist that Collier is viewed in this paper, aside from his role as one of the great moralists and preachers of our time[37] who can laud tribal non-linear conceptions of time as 'society-building, action-sustaining, wisdom-giving' and even 'world-shaping'.[38] In his more sober writing Collier has consistently employed the same indices of success of his program of tribal administration. These are in the main the biological index of Indian birth rate relative to death rate, and the economic index of rate of loan repayment. Collier claimed that the Indian death rate fell fifty-five per cent in less than ten years, and that of over $10,300,000 loaned in a decade only $69,000 was delinquent.[39]

These statements[40] Collier still repeats, and others follow his lead.[41] Actually, the loan repayment index does not show such 'good' Indian behavior, a 'serious delinquency' situation having come about early in the last decade.[42]

In other words, Collier's evaluation of his own program appears frozen to indices he envisioned at the time of its formulation, and he now feels that relations between Indian and government and whites in general have become productive.[43] Collier attributes these improved relations to an about face in Indian policy made by the Eisenhower administration in 1958, when it returned to New Deal policies.[44] He seems not to have appreciated the extent to which tribal self-government in the United States has advanced beyond the Phase I type operations and activities he originally predicted so that additional indices should be used to evaluate the accuracy of his predictions as to the therapeutic effects of responsible democracy upon tribal peoples. As already indicated, other social scientists specifically evaluating the Collier program appear to have analyzed it largely on Collier's own terms. Spicer has, however, stressed the need for Indian economic interdependence with other peoples in the Southwest as a precondition for self-determination in modern industrial society.[45] He pointed out that such interdependence as has developed has emerged on the basis of wage labor by Indian individuals, yet recognized that the individual may abandon tribal life – and the fact that many do so constitutes one major factor stabilizing several tribal societies.[46] Wage labor can be, in other words, the economic basis for only the most minimally rewarding sort of tribal self-government in the highly capitalized modern society.

The impact of tribal attorneys upon tribal self-government suggests the following list of additional appropriate indices for evaluation:

1. Realized dollar income of tribal governments and tribesmen from land leases for farming, mining, logging, etc., and tribal business enterprises, relative to resource potential.

2. Overt discrimination by adjacent non-Indian population toward any reservation population.

3. Level of psychological stress in the tribal population, as measured by nativistic movements (negatively), conscious cultural pluralism (positively) or smaller scale phenomena.

In conclusion, it appears that in terms of such indices as these, Collier's prediction of the dynamic quality of tribal self-determination was essentially correct. The employment of non-Indian specialists, particularly attorneys, by tribal governments, is one sign that tribal peoples are truly developing that 'more true self-government and less dependence on a government bureau for protection' which Embree pointed out is a necessary condition 'if they are not to become exploited all over again *as Indians*'.[47] The examples of attorney action on behalf of tribal clients cited in this paper have indeed increased tribal lease income, diminished overt racial discrimination against Indians, and apparently reduced psychological stresses among reservation inhabitants.

Notes

1. John F. Embree, 'The Indian Bureau and Self-Government', *Human Organization*, VIII (Winter 1949), 11.

2. John Collier, *Indians of the Americas* (New York, 1947); also Laura Thompson, 'US Indian Reorganization Viewed as an Experiment in Social Action Research', *Estudios Anthropologicos publicados en Homenaje al Doctor Manuel Gamio* (Mexico City, 1956; Universidad Nacional Autonoma de Mexico, Sociedad Mexicana de Antropologia).

3. John Embree, 'The Indian Bureau', 226.

4. Alexander H. Leighton, *Human Relations in a Changing World* (New York, 1949).

5. John Collier, *Indians*, 261–2.

6. Laura Thompson, 'US Indian Reorganization'.

7. John Collier, 'La permanencia del descubrimiento social', *America Indigena*, XV, 3 (Julio 1955), 179; also 'The Permanence of Social Discovery', *Estudios Antropologicos publicados en Homenaje al Doctor Manuel Gamio* (Mexico, 1956), 325.

8. Edward H. Spicer, 'Worlds Apart – Cultural Differences in the Modern Southwest', *Arizona Quarterly*, XIII, 3 (Fall 1957), 219.

9. ibid.

10. Ralph Linton, *Acculturation in Seven American Indian Tribes* (New York, 1940), 496.

11. Leighton, *Human Relations*, 76–7.

12. John Collier, *Indians of the Americas*, 263.

13. Henry F. Dobyns, 'Blunders with *Bolsas*', *Human Organization*, X, 3 (Fall 1951), 25.

14. Henry F. Dobyns, 'Experiment in Conservation: Erosion Control and Forage Production on the Papago Indian Reservations in Arizona', *Human Problems in Technological Change*, ed. E. H. Spicer (New York, 1952).

15. William Zimmerman, Jr, 'The Role of the Bureau of Indian Affairs since 1933', *The Annals of the American Academy of Political and Social Science* (May 1957), 37.

16. 'Juvenile Delinquency Among the Indians', Report of the Committee on the Judiciary made by its Subcommittee to Investigate Juvenile Delinquency; 84th Congress, 2nd Session, Report No. 1483, 236, 239.

17. 'Letter to General Eisenhower', *The Nation*, CLXXVI (10 January

1953), 29: also John Collier, 'Social Discovery', and William Zimmerman, Jr, 'The Role of the Bureau of Indian Affairs', 35.

18. John Collier, 'Back to Dishonor?', 579; also Collier, 'Indian Takeaway, Betrayal of a Trust', *The Nation*, CLXXIX (2 October 1954), 290.

19. William H. Kelly, ed., *Indian Affairs and the Indian Reorganization Act, The Twenty Year Record* (Tucson, 1954); see also John Provinse and others, 'The American Indian in Transition', *American Anthropologist*, LVI, 3 (June 1954), 388, 392; Laura Thompson, 'US Indian Reorganization', William Zimmerman, Jr, 'The Role of the Bureau of Indian Affairs'; Theodore H. Haas, 'The Legal Aspects of Indian Affairs from 1887 to 1957', *The Annals*, CCCXI (May 1957), 12–22; Edward P. Dozier, George E. Simpson, and J. Milton Yinger, 'The Integration of Americans of Indian Descent', *The Annals*, CCCXI (May 1957), 158–65.

20. John Collier, 'Back to Dishonor?', 579; also, 'Collier 'Indian Takeaway, Betrayal of a Trust', *The Nation*, CLXXIX (2 October 1954), 290.

21. John Collier, 'La permanencia del descubrimiento social', 183; also, 'The Permanence of Social Discovery', 327.

22. Nancy O. Lurie, 'The Indian Claims Commission Act', *The Annals*, CCCXI (May 1957), 68–9.

23. Anthropologists constitute one type of non-Indian specialist employed by a number of tribes. Several score anthropologists are or have been employed by tribes as expert witnesses before the Indian Claims Commission (see note 22, 60 ff). Dr Tom T. Sasaki has acted as consultant on resettlement problems to the Navajo Tribal Council, a professional role quite different from that of ethnohistorian. Sasaki and Harry W. Basehart directed a three-year study for the Jicarilla Apache Tribe (see Tom T. Sasaki and Harry W. Basehart, 'Sources of Income Among Many Farms – Rough Navajo and Jicarilla Apache: Some Comparisons and Comments', *Human Organization* XX, 4 (Winter 1961), 187–90). A team of anthropologists surveyed the Uintah and Ouray Reservation during the dispute between fullblood and mixed blood groups that led to their splitting apart and dividing tribal assets (see Robert L. Bennett, 'Building Indian Economies with Land Settlement Funds', *Human Organization*, ibid., 159–63). The San Carlos Apache Tribal Council in 1953 authorized along with the local BIA superintendent an anthropological study of the range cattle industry on that reservation which was carried out during the next three summers (see preface, Harry T. Getty, 'San Carlos Apache Cattle Industry', ibid., 181–6). The Hualapai Tribe has

a Consulting Anthropologist on matters ranging from archeology to negotiations with stage agencies (see Robert C. Euler and Henry F. Dobyns, 'Ethnic Group Land Rights in the Modern State: Three Case Studies', ibid., 203–7). Some specialists had been hired by tribes prior to 1946, of course. The White Mountain Apaches hired, for example, a forester to begin developing their now quite remunerative recreational facilities (see Newton Edwards, 'Economic Development of Indian Reserves', ibid., 197–202).

24. Theodore Stern, 'Livelihood and Tribal Government on the Klamath Indian Reservation', *Human Organization*, XX, 4 (Winter 1961), 174.

25. United States Senate, 1953, *Attorney Contracts with Indian Tribes*. 83rd Congress, 1st Session, Report No. 8, 1–15.

26. See Bennett (note 23), 161.

27. Gottfried Lang, Economic Development and Self-Determination: The Northern Ute Case', *Human Organization*, XX, 4 (Winter 1961), 164–71.

28. Theodore H. Haas, 'The Indian Reorganization Act in Historical Perspective', in Kelly, *Indian Affairs* (see note 19), 9–25; and Helen L. Peterson, 'American Indian Political Participation', *The Annals*, CCCXI (May 1957), 116–26.

29. *1957* (Lima, Peru, periodical), 13 March, 37.

30. *La Tribuna* (daily newspaper, Lima, Peru), 15 January 1961, 1.

31. Peterson, 'American Indian' (see note 28), 122–6.

32. Euler and Dobyns (see note 23), 206.

33. Allan R. Holmberg, 'Participant Intervention in the Field', *Human Organization*, XIV, 1 (Spring 1955), 23–6.

34. Thompson, 'US Indian Reorganization' (see note 2), 513.

35. Dobyns (see note 13), 31; Edward H. Spicer, *Human Problems in Technological Change* (New York, 1952), 292–3.

36. Getty (see note 23); see also his 'The San Carlos Indian Cattle Industry', *University of Arizona Anthropological Papers*, number 7 (Tucson, 1963).

37. Edward H. Spicer, 'Worlds Apart – Cultural Differences in the Modern Southwest', *Arizona Quarterly*, XIII, 3 (Autumn 1957), 197–230. 219; 223–4.

38. John Collier, *Patterns and Ceremonials of the Indians of the Southwest* (New York, 1949), 19.

39. *Indians* (see note 2), 268; 267.

40. (See note 7), 180; see also John Collier, 'Slow Recovery Since Wounded Knee', *Saturday Review*, XLVI (15 June 1963), 31–2.

41. Edward P. Dozier, George E. Simpson and J. Milton Yinger, 'The Integration of Americans of Indian Descent', *The Annals of the American Academy of Political and Social Science*, CCCI (May 1957), 158–65.

42. Haas (see notes 28 and 19), 20–21.

43. Collier, 'Slow Recovery' (see note 40), 31.

44. John Collier, 'Indians' Heritage', *Americas*, XIV (September 1962), 34–8.

45. Edward H. Spicer, *Cycles of Conquest* (Tucson, Arizona, 1962), 550.

46. ibid., 557–8.

47. Embree, 'The Indian Bureau' (see note 1), 26.

Afterword

✦

NANCY OESTREICH LURIE

AN AMERICAN INDIAN
RENASCENCE?

In 1964, when I was asked to help with the work on a special issue of the *Midcontinent American Studies Journal* to be devoted to the American Indian, I suggested that we try to investigate the contemporary scene. The idea was accepted and I gratefully availed myself of the chance to test and explore some hypotheses I had begun to form regarding the existence of a kind of socio-political movement taking place among Indian people across the country.

Certainly there had been strenuous resistance during the 1950s to the government's policy of termination and relocation. Some of the resistance was on a coordinated, inter-tribal level; this was particularly true of the efforts of the National Congress of American Indians. But by the 1960s opposition to termination-relocation was coupled with positive expressions of what Indian people wanted: broader educational programs and community development. There seemed to be both a ferment for meaningful action at the local, tribal level and a proliferation of inter-tribal organizations along regional and national lines. Means of communication among Indians improved as Indian news publications, from mimeographed tribal newsletters to inter-tribal newspapers, appeared.

In the past, Indian people had responded to undesirable policies largely as they were implemented at the tribal level. But the usual techniques were no longer practical in the 1950s, because government policy was designed to destroy Indian community life. Heretofore, even though the

Allotment Act reduced the land base for many tribes, it was possible simply to sit out an unsympathetic administration: passive resistance, negativism or factional disputation would keep the administrators busy and allow Indians to hold the line as Indians until something came along that they might want to use. Termination-relocation was designed to solve the Indians' problems by systematically denying the existence of Indian people in terms of their communities. Even non-reservation groups, such as the Wisconsin Winnebago, who had maintained a sense of tribal identity despite the fact that their residences were scattered over some ten largely rural counties, were contacted and strongly encouraged to avail themselves of the relocation program. Significantly, a high proportion of the Wisconsin Winnebago were already 'commuters' to nearby cities on a weekly or seasonal basis. The relocation program sought to send them much farther than the several hundred miles between their home communities and Milwaukee or Chicago which they took in stride as comfortable driving distances.

My own experiences from about 1961 – the American Indian Chicago Conference, involving tribes from all over the country, and my work in specific programs initiated by the Wisconsin Winnebago – struck me as evidence that Indian people seemed to be newly and strongly motivated to take positive steps in their own behalf. I was impressed that the Wisconsin Winnebago, notorious for their tribal parochialism and aloofness from other tribes, took an active part in the Chicago Conference and drew inspiration from it to carry out local programs. But I wondered whether this was really something new for the tribe or simply a natural and inevitable development. From impressionistic data available on other tribes in the region, I felt that they too were experiencing stirrings similar to those among the Wisconsin Winnebago.

An American Indian Renascence?

We must realize that inter-tribal activities were not new. Even during the nineteenth and early twentieth centuries, when the policies of the Indian Bureau were particularly repressive, inter-tribal pow-wows had begun to develop, old boarding-school chums had visited or written to each other, members of tribes which had been split into geographically separated segments through the vagaries of land sales and treaties managed to keep alive ties of kinship and friendship, and a good deal of visiting went on (generally to obtain resources traditionally shared by given tribes with others toward whom they stood in a formal host-guest relationship). These activities were relatively safe from Bureau interference. However, such links between tribes involved individuals, families, or, at most, members of religious movements which cross-cut tribal lines, but represented factions within given tribes. Cooperation between entire tribes in organized alliance for political purposes was pretty well precluded by the nature of the system. The economic interests of each tribe were tied to administration of the local reservation, and tribes had no direct control over their own resources for local efforts, let alone for broader organizational purposes.

However, it appears that a fundamental political ideology did emerge and diffuse widely in the course of casual and limited visiting between members of different tribes. It was, and to a great extent is still couched in terms of treaties. Perhaps it would be more accurate to say it is based upon the nature of a treaty relationship. The concept was enunciated by John Marshall in 1832, in *Worcester v. The State of Georgia*:

The settled doctrine of the law of nations is that a weaker power does not surrender its independence – its right to self-government, by associating with a stronger and taking its protection.

If anthropologists and others compare notes on the specific tribes with whom they are familiar, they find certain recurrent sentiments, even to phraseology: grievances can be ultimately traced to 'broken treaties' or 'bad faith on the part of the government'; everything could be made right by the president if he cared to do so, 'by a stroke of the pen'. Even the Brookings survey picked up this theme:

> The disturbing influence of outside agitators seeking personal emoluments, and the conviction in the Indian mind that justice is being denied, renders extremely difficult any cooperation between the government and its Indian wards.[1]

The outside agitators actually included sincerely motivated attorneys as well as opportunists and a type of pan-Indian nativistic leader who had a smattering of the law and a good deal of charismatic appeal in promoting the message of restoring respect for treaties, a general message with which a great many tribes could identify their local needs. One such individual is discussed in James Clifton's paper in this volume.

In viewing the socio-political activity of the 1960s, I wondered whether the 'renascence' was but a logical continuation of older trends. One would begin with the treaty ideology, show how it was diffused through the pow-pow circuit since the nineteenth century and conclude by assuming that it had acquired more sophisticated expression in phenomena such as the National Congress of American Indians. This organization was founded in the 1940s to help tribes utilize the Indian Reorganization Act effectively and influence policy developed out of the Act itself. It is worth noting that a rather militant segment of Indian opinion which cross-cuts tribes throughout the country (although we have no way of judging what proportion of Indian people share it) views the NCAI with suspicion as Bureau-oriented rather than treaty-oriented in its goals and program planning. The 1960s saw continuation of the treaty ideology in both its unreconstructed form and in various modifications. One modification was the idea that while the Indian Claims Commission Act could settle old grievances on treaty payments and close that book, the government still had a continuing responsibility to assist Indian communities to get back on their feet after decades of neglect and efforts to destroy them. The treaty intransigents want a stronger contract. They insist that treaties remain in effect, and feel that any restitution made to Indian tribes in their claims is simply overdue recognition of treaties, and not an end to the contract.

People who try to grasp what Indian people want are confused by the different interpretations of the treaty ideology. Most Indian people who identify strongly as Indian are opposed to termination, which means withdrawal of federal jurisdiction over Indian land and the automatic phasing out of the Indian Bureau, which would then be unnecessary. However, there are also a number of Indian people (we don't know how many) who would just as soon eliminate the Indian Bureau, but want their lands protected in perpetuity by the terms of existing treaties or perhaps by newly negotiated treaties. They would then deal directly with the United States through Congress. In the case of grievances, they feel their recourse should be to the UN. It is very confusing for the well-intentioned but insufficiently informed non-Indian to hear some Indians argue against termination and then to encounter other Indian people who say, 'They ought to get rid of the Bureau.' The latter may add a few unkind remarks about the National Congress of American Indians and similar organizations as 'tools of the Bureau' and 'sell-outs to the government' who are trying to get the reservations away from the Indians. Actually, these groups share a far more similar point of view than outsiders are apt to realize. Their disagreement centers in how best to achieve their goals.

All these familiar elements were present and, indeed, thrown into sharper perspective in the 1960s, but there seemed to be something more. I wondered if it was something new or simply the cumulative effect of old trends. Perhaps it was a striking out in new directions to reach and influence a larger public in regard to Indians' problems. Within the limits of my own observations, it was apparent that non-Indians were often surprised as they began to grasp what Indian people seemed to want. There was even indignation about the moral, ethical and political connotations of the Indian definition of 'rights' under the American form of government. Sympathetic people, while accepting the justice of the Indians' arguments, nevertheless often found they could not offer Indian people their whole-hearted support or assistance because they felt that sadly, but surely, the inevitable fate of Indian people would be assimilation and loss of identity.

In 1964, it was still difficult and at times even embarrassing to talk about the Indians' termination-relocation crisis. In the first place, liberal minded people had tended to equate the question of civil rights almost entirely with those specific rights of individuals denied to Negroes – the vote, decent education, housing – in short, integration. At that time there were few doubts; Negroes were only trying to share the American dream of middle-class respectability, as was their right, and for the time being were forced to bring their plight before the public by dramatic means. Termination-relocation was peddled to the public and uninformed members of Congress in the language of the Civil Rights Movement, as *desegregation* and integration. When Indian people opposed the policy of the 1950s, they were placed in the unfortunate position of appearing to oppose decent American sentiments. To make matters worse, when Indian people were asked why they did not demonstrate, join the NAACP, or march for their rights, the reply was, 'It is not the Indian way', or 'They might think we're Niggers'. Understandable liberal distaste for such 'racism' obscured the basic point that what Negroes wanted were not the things Indians wanted. If he embraces middle-class values and symbols, the individual Indian encounters few obstacles to integration. Even in areas fringing reservations and poor Indian communities where there is prejudice against Indians, the educated, regularly employed Indian person can find acceptance in the local white community in a way no educated southern or a good many northern Negroes could hope for. The basic problem, of course, is that circumstances of poverty and inadequate education have kept many Indians, like many Negroes, from rising in the system.

Beyond that lies another problem. Indian people would like improved educational and community programs designed to give the individual a free choice in using his abilities, provided that such programs are not explicitly or implicitly designed to reduce his Indianness. If he wants to leave, that is and always has been his choice. But community development for Indian people is seen as *community* development. It means raising the living standards of people who will go their separate ways once they can leave the ghetto or rural slum.

The difference in Indians' and Negroes' aspirations is shown in the few instances when Indian people have seen demonstrations, not as something peculiarly Negro, but as an appropriate means of protest for Indians. During the Kinzua Dam controversy involving Iroquois lands in New York state, a small group of Indian people tried to picket the UN. They were indulgently laughed away or ignored. More conservative Indians who sympathized with their problems but considered their position on treaties unrealistic and extremist were embarrassed and upset by their actions. While we may consider fruitless the hope that Indian communities could become 'mini-states' standing in formal treaty relations to the United States, the position of these Indians reflects adaptability to the modern world. They chose to picket the UN for recognition.

Another demonstration was the Indian 'fish-in' of 1964 held in the state of Washington, with Marlon Brando taking a well-publicized role as a white sympathizer. The 'fish-in' was perhaps inspired in name by the 'sit-ins' which were then popular in the Negro Civil Rights Movement, but its objectives were quite different. The Indians were not protesting denial of rights due all citizens, but abrogation of their special rights to fish, irrespective of game laws, which they felt were due them as Indians under given treaties. Significantly, individuals from distant tribes took part, and the fish-in was initiated with the help of the National Indian Youth Council, a new inter-tribal organization. I was interested that a group of this kind, composed of young people with better educations than most Indian people have, could rally around the treaty ideology. At the same time, they also want to keep the Indian Bureau in business, but to prod and needle it to do a better job.

I

In 1964 I could only speculate whether some kind of reconciliation might be in the making between the various Indian points of view. In order to elicit a sampling of opinion on the contemporary Indian scene in regard to my impressions that some kind of movement was taking place among Indian people, I circulated a statement and a questionnaire regarding it. I was not sure then and I am still not sure whether we are witnessing a striking but quite predictable out-growth of historic precedents or a new phase in Indian-white relations, with Indian people taking the initiative. In earlier definable phases, such as the allotment period or even the Collier era, the initiative had come, in contrast, from the government. I decided to take a definite stand by suggesting an 'Indian Renascence' in the hope of either intriguing or annoying people sufficiently so they would feel compelled to reply.

By way of a history of this study, I am going to quote my original statement and tentative analysis as they appeared in 1965. To this material I have added commentary written in 1967 to bring things up to date. A number of important things have occurred in the last two years. An Indian Commissioner who increasingly expressed Indian hopes in Indian terms, Philleo Nash, was systematically edged out of office in 1966. His replacement, Robert F. Bennett, an enrolled Oneida Indian, is, to date, far less explicit in his opinions. There are expressions of anxiety about his policy among Indian people. The 'racism' of Indian people concerning Negroes seems to be abating. In 1964 when work on this project was begun, the Black Muslims were generally considered a crackpot minority and the cry of 'Black Power' had not been raised. My hunch is that this development, which has tended to alienate some white support of the Negro movement, has indicated to Indian people that the general Civil Rights Movement may now be broadening sufficiently to include them. I have only impressionistic data to go on, but cite two instances from a number that seem to characterize the situation. A friend who attended a civil rights conference in which Indians, Negroes and other minority members participated told of the astounded Negro participant who was referred to by an Indian as a white man. The Indian person was perfectly serious. Whatever the color of the man's skin, he sounded like a white man in assuming that the goal of most Indian people was individual integration into the larger society. An elderly Indian of conservative tribal religious persuasion but long a resident of Chicago, and on previous occasions given to disparaging remarks and joking about Negroes, was asked about 'Black Power'. His reply: 'Now they're getting smart. They're proud of who they are.'

Finally, public awareness that Indian people have special problems worthy of respectful consideration seems to be increasing. Whether this understanding is deep enough or widespread enough to influence government policy is an open question. As I write, an Omnibus Bill, designed to deal with a multitude of Indian problems, is under consideration in Washington. Indian people have already dubbed it the 'Ominous Bill'; many see in it tendencies toward termination procedures on the one hand, and increased Bureau power at the expense of Indian self-determination as communities on the other.[2]

For legislators pondering the future of American Indian people and for the general public interested in learning about the contemporary Indian scene, I believe that the results of the study begun in 1964 are still important and timely. The statement and questionnaire were sent to some eighty people familiar with Indian affairs, including anthropologists, government personnel, church workers and individual Indians. In some cases, a given person filled several of the above roles. The letters were sent out on 20 July 1964, with the request that replies be made by 25 September 1964. Thirty-one people replied. Of these, nineteen filled out the questionnaire; a number of those who did also volunteered to write papers. Five wrote separate extended commentaries, seven people wrote to express interest in the project; three preferred to write papers and therein set forth views evoked by the questionnaire, while four felt that their own data were not sufficiently recent or complete to permit comment. At the time the letters were mailed, many anthropologists were preparing to attend the several scholarly conferences held in Europe during the summer of 1964 – some had already left – while others were engaged in summer field research. Even with the late September deadline and the usual flexibility regarding such deadlines, I knew that many people would be returning to teaching and administrative duties after a busy summer and might not be able to take the time to read the statement and answer the questionnaire. In view of all these circumstances, the fact that better than twenty-five per cent return was obtained far exceeded my hopes. Furthermore, at scholarly gatherings held during the fall and winter of 1964, a number of colleagues took the time to explain personally that for various reasons they hadn't been able to fill out the questionnaire but considered the project both timely and valuable and asked to be kept informed of developments. Indian friends also expressed similar views.

Following an explanation of purpose and of the mechanics of questionnaire and deadlines, the statement read:

When I was invited to put together a special issue [of the *Midcontinent American Studies Journal*] I at first thought of something similar to the May 1957 *Annals* of the American Academy of Political and Social Sciences, bringing it up to date. You may recall that the issue bore the title, 'American Indians and American Life', and dealt with then current facts on health, population, education, welfare, legal questions and the like. However on further thought, it seemed that at least a decade ought to elapse between such assessments. I believe that a topic of special and timely interest is what I have tentatively designated a renascence among American Indian people. I am not irrevocably committed to this term if you do not happen to care for it and would like to suggest another. But I do believe that there is a real and discernible social movement on the part of Indian people at the present time, whatever it may be called. While the characteristics of the movement are certainly not new, what is new is the gathering momentum throughout the country to make a body of Indian opinion explicit and widely known. I would date the publicized and formalized expression of ideas from about 1960. Perhaps it was partly a response to the unpopular federal policies and legislation of the 1950s.

My own opinion that there is a general movement in terms of agreement upon and publicizing of Indian goals derives from several sources: the response to the American Indian Chicago Conference of 1961 and the form taken by the 'Declaration of Indian Purpose' which resulted from the Conference; the formation at the Conference of the National Indian Youth Council which brought together relatively younger Indian people who considered the 'Declaration' correct but too mildly stated and in any case requiring organization and action to achieve Indian purposes; the example of increased tribal consciousness and action for group welfare of Wisconsin tribes, particularly the Wisconsin Winnebago with whom I have worked closely over a period of twenty years and so can note marked changes since about 1960; activities of other Indian groups in the Midwest such as the formation of the Great Lakes Inter-tribal Council; and finally the consistency and increased articulateness of Indian participants in various recent conferences dealing with Indian affairs. I have the impression that what I have been observing in the Midwest is paralleled in other parts of the country. I would like to get expression of opinion on the matter from Indian people, anthropologists, and others concerned with Indian affairs in local and federal governmental vantage positions or private organizations and agencies. The following are characteristics of the movement which I discern and about which I would appreciate your opinions, pro or con, and other thoughts on the matter.

I. I use the term renascence, rebirth, rather than revitalization or nativism, because leadership is diffuse, emphasis and action vary from place to place, and the common characteristic seems to be a heightened desire for Indian identity coupled with vocalized insistence on recognition of the right of Indian groups to persist as distinctive social entities.

II. Although differing from place to place in content, two basic objectives seem to be stressed: improvement of material standards of living and general welfare of Indian groups by means of increased formal education of Indians in professions and vocations to better serve Indian communities; emphasis on Indian identity in terms of reactivating or encouraging perpetuation of tribal languages, customs, and tribal residential communities.

III. I am not sure to what extent the rising Negro militancy and articulateness of the last decade have contributed to the Indian movement. It is possible that the widespread national concern for the Negro has contributed a sense of need on the part of Indians to make their position clear to the larger society. However, the following points seem to have pertinence.

A. Many well-intentioned but uninformed whites tend to equate Negro and Indian problems in terms of poverty, discrimination, segregation, etc., and assume the goals of Indian people parallel those of the Negro people.

B. Certain not-so-well-intentioned whites sympathize with and accept Indians but not Negroes and try to deflect interest away from the Negro by arguing that we ought to consider '*First Americans first*', and would readily grant Indians the goals sought by Negroes.

C. Indian people as individuals or groups, tribal and intertribal, have generally reacted against this equating of their problems with those of the Negro. It is my impression that Indian people are sometimes more drawn to white racist demagogues in seeking a sympathetic hearing as represented in B. above than they are to educable whites represented in A. above simply because the second type of white for his own reasons distinguishes Indians from Negroes as 'superior'.

1. The reason lies in part in simple racism borrowed by Indians from certain segments of the white population.

2. In some cases Indian racism takes a distinctive form in arguing against assimilation with non-Indians and in asking for white acceptance of Indian 'segregation' as desired by Indians.

3. In some cases the arguments are cultural rather than racist, that America may have much to gain in the long run by permitting model groups such as Indian communities to pursue their own values which Indians conceive of as less materialistic, competitive, prosaic, ulcer-producing and mass-cultural-monotonous than those of the society at large. However, even such philosophical arguments devoid of racist overtones come as a shock and surprise to well-intentioned whites who in concern for minorities' welfare generally have expected that Indians' goals are those of assimilation, loss of Indian identity, and acquisition of middle-class values along with increased acquisition of middle-class creature comforts. At a recent conference on Indian affairs held at Eau Claire, Wisconsin [1964], when a number of Indian speakers voiced their views, some heretofore sympathetic if not informed whites dubbed the gathering a meeting of the 'Red Muslims'!

4. Many Indians feel that they simply do not have the same problems as the Negro or at least not in the same degree in regard to prejudice, discrimination, abrogation of civil rights and the like. They see their problems as stemming from their special historical status as Indians and that their means of bringing their problems and needs to the attention of the public should also be distinctive. By way of illustration, at the same conference noted above, an Ojibwa observed at a workshop discussion that it is good that Indian problems are being discussed and solutions sought but went on to say, 'And I hope I never see the day that Indian people feel they must throw themselves in the path of bulldozers. You could get run over!' Indian reactions were also heated and equivocal in regard to the recent Indian 'Fish-in' involving Marlon Brando.

IV. Indian distinctiveness is stressed culturally and historically: emphasis on treaties rather than judicial recourse in obtaining perceived rights of Indians; ineffable attachment to land; attitude that all other Americans are 'immigrants' and that Indians as 'First Americans' deserve special consideration; or that it isn't really special consideration but that the nation as a whole permits and at times even protects cultural pluralism of other ethnic minorities such as Jews, Amish, etc., and it is only that whites find it hard to accept the distinctive criteria of Indian ethnicity; and, the nation still 'owes' the Indians something for taking their land.

V. Stress on *tribal* identity as inseparable from Indian identity. Many Indian people dislike the anthropologists' term 'Pan-Indianism', arguing that pow-wows, the Peyote or Native American Church, etc., are cases of mutual borrowing and enrichment of different tribes' own cultures. In terms of legal and political action, they recognize a need for tribes to pull together in helping one another to achieve the different tribes' goals and to oppose by concerted action measures threatening to all tribes' distinctiveness. The National Congress of American Indians and other inter-tribal organizations which may not even be in sympathy with the NCAI have always tended to pattern action on recognition of tribal distinctiveness and cooperation between tribes as tribes rather than generalized 'Indians' although objectives may have general Indian significance.

It is my impression that the more romantic, antiquarian, mystical and less tribally oriented expressions of the movement derive from individuals of more white than Indian descent or early conditioning who have chosen in later life to be Indians, or from those groups which have maintained a social continuity with their past, sometimes imposed from the outside by racial considerations, but retain little cultural distinctiveness from their own tribal origins.

VI. The movement is recognized and viewed with distaste in whole or part by different types of Indian people. To date, my observations relate to individuals rather than tribal groups.

A. Those who have chosen the path of assimilation but proudly admit to their Indian origin, taking pride in having beaten the white man at his own competitive, economic game in terms of middle-class criteria of success, status symbols, etc. They are perturbed and distressed that they are rejected as models for other Indian people to emulate. I am uninformed about Indian people who have rejected their identity completely; they do not show up at Indian gatherings or conferences on Indian affairs. It would be interesting to know if such people are aware of what other Indian people are doing at present and what they think about it.

B. Those who are in fundamental agreement with the movement in terms of respect for continuation of Indian identity and improvement of material welfare, but who deplore the racist overtones.

C. Those like III. C.2 above who are in agreement but deplore the participation of 'recent' Indians whose romanticism they consider pseudo-ethnicity and comparable to Boy Scouts who dress up as Indians without understanding what they consider the *real* sense of being an Indian. In this same connection I have detected distaste for publicists of the movement who gain personal recognition as somehow 'un-Indian' in their seeking of ego-fulfillment.

D. Those active in the movement who resent their hard work being equated with glory-seeking or personal aggrandizement on the part of Indians otherwise sympathetic to the objectives of the movement.

Four questions were posed concerning the statement:

1. Do you agree with the foregoing statement regarding what I have called an American Indian Renascence? If you agree please indicate your reasons briefly.

2. Do you disagree in whole or in part? Please indicate your reasons briefly.

3. Do you have further comments you feel are pertinent to the issue?

4. Would you like to submit an article for inclusion in the American Indian issue of the *Midcontinent American Studies Journal*? If so, please indicate the subject briefly.

Because the responses varied in format from letters going through my entire statement point for point to simple yes-no answers on the questionnaire, a precise statistical breakdown of replies to the first three questions cannot be made. However, certain generalizations are clearly evident which, though not adequate unto themselves, suggest a framework which would lend itself to more concise testing by means of coordinated studies among different Indian groups. I shall only attempt to discuss disagreements and striking expansions on my statement.

While all but six people took immediate exception to my statement – often with heavy underlining and bristling exclamation marks – it turned out that disagreement centered in connotations attaching to the term 'renascence' or the emphasis given certain points. Everyone agreed that *something* is going on but differed in opinions as to content and significance. The outstanding corrective of my term was that 're-birth' signified something revived, whereas Indian cultures did not die out to become recently re-established, but have simply changed through time, as cultures do, and that current developments represent a logical point in a historical trend of adaptations and adjustments to changing circumstances. On this there was general agreement. However, some respondents felt that the current situation is marked by new experiments and revolutionary departures from familiar adaptations, while others felt that no more than a cumulative effect is involved, particularly the presence of more eduated and vocal Indians which makes current efforts appear more revolutionary than they really are.

I have begun to appreciate that a major consideration in what I called a renascence does not derive from within the Indian social setting alone, but consists of the increasing visibility of Indians as a distinct feature in the total social landscape of the United States. Whether vocal about themselves or not, they can no longer be ignored or disregarded by the public at large. Anthropologists and others familiar with the course of Indian affairs have long abandoned the simplistic view of acculturation as the breakdown of traditional culture followed by a period of transitional culture when old elements are gradually replaced by borrowed ones and culminating inevitably in the total assimilation of Indians into the dominant society. In recent years the facts of continuity of Indian identity – despite cultural changes and adaptations – and actual population increase are becoming more widely known to the general American public. The official policies of the 1950s, which aimed at rapid termination of reservations and dispersal of Indian people throughout the population by means of relocation in cities far distant from reservation areas, may eventually be understood as an almost frantic attempt to fulfill forcefully an entrenched social prophecy when it was becoming ever more evident that the prophecy was not fulfilling itself. Whatever other stubborn ethnic groups such as the Hutterites might do in regard to assimilation was a matter for sociologists, but Indians under the federal jurisdiction could at least be dealt with by law. There were two compelling but specious arguments to justify the policies of the 1950s: Indian administration cost the taxpayer money; analogies could be made to Negro segregation to win general approval of right minded citizens to 'free' the Indians.

In regard to the first argument, it was soon apparent that termination of such groups as Menomini and Klamath resulted in economic hardships for the Indians involved. The costs of study and administration were simply shifted to the local states. The second argument has already been shown to be untenable.

If my sample of responses is a fair indication of information on current events in the Indian world, we find that there are many different kinds of action promoted and promulgated in various ways, but the appearance of a kind of unified movement rests in the fact that when goals are made explicit, they are expressed in much the same form. It is worth noting that no one disagreed, and a majority added positive agreement, with my view that education is seen generally by Indian people as the key to opening a brighter future for them. Furthermore, there was general agreement that goals of material improvement by means of education are emphatically coupled with expressions of the importance of retaining Indian identity, whether generalized Indian or specifically tribal in content. Education in itself has been the traditional route to social betterment, and often, by definition, assimilation into the larger society. As such it has always been supported and promoted by the government, philanthropic agencies, missionaries and others dealing with American Indian people. That younger Indians particularly are taking up the cry as if they had personally discovered the benefits of education for the first time must strike 'old Indian hands' as ironical. However, when Indian people stress the importance of education they stress that it is not necessarily synonymous with assimilation but can make *Indian* life better.

It is in the matter of what constitutes Indian identity that complexity and cross-purposes occur within the movement and result in different assessments by participants and observers. The questionnaire responses and contributed papers indicated that the greatest weaknesses in my statement lay in confusing the types or levels of activity and publicizing of the movement or aggregate of movements, and in not taking regional differences into account. These levels are not mutually exclusive; given persons and groups sometimes operate on several levels, and people with different preferences for action sometimes work together. Taking all the responses together, I find that four levels are involved. Most people, however, contrasted only two levels, and none discussed all four. Thus, my delineation of four levels may distort the intent of given respondents' comments, so let me make clear that when I cite examples from each of the levels, the respondents involved may or may not agree with the data regarding the other levels or the way their data are compared to them. I feel that my synthesis is valid in terms of all the information volunteered to me. Arguments could arise among the respondents, since, as shall be shown, there were differences of opinion on given topics.

The terms used for the different levels are sometimes the same, but the content of questionnaire responses and contributed papers shows the nature of the differences perceived. Thus, the first level which I will accept as 'nationalism' for purposes of discussion was also designated as 'supra-tribal', 'generalized Indian' and 'pan-Indian'. The second level, which seems best described as 'inter-tribal' or 'pan-Indian', was also referred to as 'tribal federalism' and 'generalized Indian'. It is not sharply distinguished from the first, although differences in emphasis are apparent. The third level I shall call 'tribal', but respondents used such terms as 'local community', 'parochial' or 'reservation', while the fourth level was variously discusssed as 'country Indians', 'grass-roots Indians', 'real Indians' and 'full-bloods'.

Most respondents seem to feel that the majority of Indians are of the third and fourth types, and that while the fourth type includes the greatest numbers and the real hard core resisters, its members are least heard from. They just go on as always, being particular kinds of Indians, borrowing selectively and retaining their identity without feeling a need to verbalize or perhaps even introspect very much about who they are and where they are going. Such people are often quite isolated from other tribes and sometimes even quite estranged from their own more inter-tribally oriented members.

An American Indian Renascence?

At the tribal level we find a variety of forms. Usually, there is an acculturated elite. This is sometimes the power faction which determines tribal policies; in other cases, it is split into factions vying for and alternating in holding power. Or it is sometimes a faction which has little power in its own group, but identifies with inter-tribal or nationalist efforts while the tribe as a whole is parochial in orientation. The important point is that there are tribes which operate primarily in regard to their own communities and include people who are vocal and command attention and commitment to the goal of Indian identity-education in purely local terms. These tribes have little to do with other Indians on an inter-tribal or nationalist level, although they may look to other tribes as models and examples. It is the similarity of structure in leadership and interaction with country Indians on the one hand and relationships to the Indian Bureau and other outside agencies on the other that gives an appearance of a unified movement. Actually, these are largely independent replications of similar situations.

At the inter-tribal level tribes are jealous of their identity and retain distinctive traits, but interact with other tribes for particular purposes of a social, religious or political nature. Such interaction is often widespread in attendance at pow-wows and meetings of Indian rights groups far from home. The respondents agreed that many Indian people who are involved in inter-tribal activities resent the term 'pan-Indian'. As one anthropologist put it, 'They fear the entity-dissolving implications.' However, a generalized Indian identity which derives most of its external symbols of song, dance, costume and ritual from the Plains area is indeed developing and spreading, although to date tribal identity takes precedence in many cases. Three respondents noted that in the Plains and East, exclusive of the Iroquois, Cherokee and Seminole, identity is more likely to be general or pan-Indian. One person would include the Midwest, but the others felt that both the Southwest and Midwest are typified by strong tribal identifications. The curious fact is that in some groups, pan-Indian traits may be borrowed in order to symbolize identity in local tribal terms, while in other cases they may reflect commitment to a general Indian identity. One of the questionnaire respondents dwelt on the presence of organizations, often including interested and active whites, seeking to be the spokesmen for THE American Indian. This person felt that no one organization is able to do so and should not attempt to do so because of the heterogeneity of Indian cultures, types of leadership and gradations between tribal and general Indian orientation.

Finally, despite the suspicion in which even inter-tribal organizations are held because of their pan-Indian tendencies, although they frequently spell out the need to respect tribal integrity, there is a genuine voice of nationalism which admits to supra-tribal objectives. The National Indian Youth Council generally falls into this category, although individuals with such sentiments have long been found in the conventionally organized inter-tribal organizations such as the National Congress of the American Indians, the American Indian Defense League and various regional and urban inter-tribal councils and clubs. Although only the last paragraph of Section V in my statement was devoted explicitly to overtly supra-tribal expressions, several respondents criticized me for giving it more attention than it merits. On the other hand, two Indian people suggested that the term 'nationalism' was entirely acceptable in describing what they considered a new and creative force to pull Indians together as a power bloc. They do not feel that tribal identity should be abandoned, but rather that Indian people would be better off if they thought of themselves first as *Indians* and then as members of given tribes. They feel that the present primary emphasis on tribal identity results in obstructing organized inter-tribal efforts to cooperate in actions of interest to all Indians, such as opposing undesirable legislation. A number of other respondents recognized the presence of such conscious nationalism, but feared or disparaged it because it involved more noise than direction, because it lacked clear-cut objectives or because it played upon a generalized shared hostility toward the larger society rather than positive features of a shared Indian identity.

In 1967, I am inclined to feel that while there may have been some mere soreheads to be written off in 1964, the very vocal and generally younger Indian group has become both more purposeful in its objectives and responsible in its public utterances. I do not know to what extent the National Indian Youth Council is a wellspring, but, as an organization which publishes its views, it at least reflects and makes available for study what seem to be new orientations in Indian thinking, particularly in regard to civil rights. Taking the language and some of the methods of the Civil Rights Movement as promoted by Negroes, Indian people – on both the inter-tribal or pan-Indian and nationalist levels – have begun to put special Indian twists on the methods and language. As in the case of the 'fish-in', these expressions clearly indicate that Indians' goals are distinctive but properly part of a more broadly based concept of civil rights than integration of the individual into a kind of generalized American culture. Equally significant of this new trend is the publicizing and utilization of the kind of humor which has always typified Indian life but was usually unknown to non-Indian Americans. To me, this humor is more than minority humor and evinces an older tradition. It is strong on puns, word play in general, and stunning juxtapositions of seemingly unrelated concepts and contexts, reminiscent of the witty irony found in treaty journals of the nineteenth century and texts of certain kinds of narrative legends. Oratory, including the judicious use of humor, was a highly valued and highly developed art among American Indian people, as is often the case among preliterate societies. Today there is still admiration for the native speaker and for the Indian person who has a good command of English but still embodies ineffably Indian form, timing, humor and metaphor in public speaking. Even the 'quickie' humor now being made public is somehow strikingly Indian, combining old irony and new media. For example, both bumper stickers and buttons are available which read, 'Custer Died For Your Sins'[3] and 'Bring Back the Buffalo'. I was recently handed a small printed card bearing a stylized Indian head and underneath it the words, 'We Shall Over Run'. A number of jokes which probably began with the National Indian Youth Council, but have received word-of-mouth diffusion all over the country are worth recounting. They are in the form of definitions.

An Indian fink: Uncle Tomahawk
Integration: Marrying an Indian from another tribe
Assimilation: Marrying a non-Indian
Cultural deprivation: A white, middle-class, suburban child.

II

Further study is clearly indicated in order to understand what regional and other factors are at work in explaining the numerical strength, composition and interrelationships of the levels of activity if we are to attempt any predictions as to the future of the American Indians. I am reluctant to view the levels as a continuum moving from grass-roots or country Indians to Indian nationalism. I get the impression that the nationalists encountered by many of my respondents have come to know the larger society and find it wanting. They are unlike those individuals who are successfully and con-

tentedly assimilated in their work, friendships, class standing and, frequently, marriage. Some of the latter make
capital of their Indian ancestry for purely personal reasons
consistent with the American ideal of the 'poor immigrant
boy who made good' – a role traditionally exploited by politicians and 'self-made men' of the business world. Those
nationalists who still have strong ties of culture and kinship
to distinctive tribal traditions have the option of returning
to, or at times operating most effectively in, inter-tribal and
tribal efforts, and, in fact, do so. The questionnaire aside,
young people with whom I have spoken frequently express
their annoyance with the hidebound leadership of the older
members of their tribes and feel frustrated in their sincere
efforts to be helpful. But the complaints of youth vary from
tribe to tribe. In some cases a highly acculturated elite in a
position of leadership is believed to have sold out to the crass
values of the white man and middle-class mediocrity,
thereby repressing the creative and adaptive continuity of
the traditions of the people. In other cases, power resides
in people whom the young believe to be incapable of adjust-
ing to the demands of the twentieth century. Their intransi-
gence likewise threatens the continuity of Indian tradition
because, if it cannot bend to a changing world, it can only
break apart.

On all levels, but particularly in inter-tribal and supra-
tribal activities, one finds helpful whites who recognize and
usually accept as a good thing the need to respect Indian
identity in promoting socio-economic programs in behalf of
Indian people. On the tribal and country Indian level, local
whites such as social workers, teachers, missionaries and employers are more apt to expect that their concern and help
will lead Indians to identify with their own social class and
to assimilate into it. Certainly there are exceptions to this
situation, but it raises a point for further exploration. To

what extent do these whites with whom country Indians
and local tribal leaders most frequently interact serve to reinforce resistance to assimilation? These friendly whites
share much of the outlook and many of the habits of whites
who are unconcerned about their Indian neighbors or down-
right hostile toward them. At this level the local ethnic content of Indian tribal identity is likely to be most extensive,
intensive and meaningful to existence. It underlies daily
interpersonal relationships, expectations, decisions and behaviors. It is thus the most sensitive to overt and implied
threats of destructive changes. The cultural gap between
Indian and white people is also greater than it is between
more sophisticated inter-tribal and supra-tribal leaders who
can meet the white world on its own terms and encounter
whites who respect and do not threaten their often close
identification with those less able to operate beyond the
tribal community. Inter-tribal and supra-tribal leaders recognize that material changes which would improve and not
destroy community life are possible at the grass-roots and
tribal level. However, they are suspect among their own
tribesmen unless they are exceedingly skillful in keeping
their home fences mended, because they interact easily with
whites, often enjoy standards of living comparable to whites
and hob-nob with the Indians from different tribes who are
both overtly assimilationist and overtly nationalist. Such
leaders operate in the face of obstacles posed by friendly but
assimilation-oriented whites and their own people who
tend to think that all whites are assimilation-oriented and to
be avoided. Some highly vocal if not representative nationalist leaders often recognize the social insularity of grass-
roots Indians and consider it somehow necessary to Indian
identity. In the face of the current Civil Rights Movement
in regard to the Negro they often alienated potential white
sympathy by talking of Indian 'segregation' as a desirable

goal. For outsiders, it is sometimes difficult to distinguish their arguments from those of Indian leaders who seek legal safeguards to Indian lands, promote land acquisition programs and oppose termination. Land is the primary resource for effective community development. Such leaders feel it can articulate community economic life into the broader socio-economic system and still allow a healthy localism which gives vitality, meaning and distinction to a variety of communities throughout the United States, non-Indian as well as Indian.

Of the ten respondents who took explicit notice of the general civil rights question or specifically the matter of Negro militancy, all agreed that Indian and Negro problems are decidedly different and that Indian people almost universally resent equating of Negro and Indian problems. One respondent in the South noted that Negroes as well as whites are prone to make this comparison while Indians reject it. It should be noted that Indian people are frequently outspoken on a very sensitive point in the integration crisis, and they shock liberal white sympathizers with the frank opinion, 'I don't want my child to marry a white person.' The responses divided evenly as to the catalytic effect of the Negro movement on the Indian movement. Respondents speaking for Alaska and Canada felt that current Negro strivings have little or no influence in those areas, but that there is, perhaps in less well developed form, evidence of Indian movements of an inter-tribal nature found throughout the United States as well as opposition to unpopular government policies and an increase in tribal effort at self-improvement.

As noted, in 1967, this situation seems to be changing. I doubt that Indian people are any more eager to be identified with Negroes than before, but they can now see some analogies between themselves and Negroes in regard to the larger question of civil rights. In the past Indian people have pointed to analogies between Indians and Jews as people who know their old tribal identity and manage to maintain their uniqueness while sharing fully in the benefits of modern life.

One anthropologist observed that more than a racist deflection of sympathy from the Negro issue may be involved in the concern of certain whites for the 'First Americans'. Some whites have much to gain through the tourist industry in fostering the distinctiveness of local Indian communities while catering to Indian good will as a matter of good business. Since I sent out the questionnaires I have had the opportunity to see the salutary effect of new super highways on Indian-white relations in a number of Wisconsin towns where tourists once stopped at service stations and restaurants. An Indian friend observed with a smile, 'We're their only natural resource to pull the tourists off the highway.'

In reviewing the questionnaires, I was surprised that only one respondent commented on a point which I thought would be much more frequently mentioned – the ubiquity of energetic and outspoken women at all four levels. Perhaps the fact that women have weathered acculturational storms more effectively in psychological terms than men is now so much taken for granted that no one bothers to re-examine the idea. In my opinion, there is more involved than that women's roles were less shattered than those of men. Granted that families still had to be reared and households managed through all the upheavals of removal, undercutting of local leadership, loss of game and termination of warfare which affected men's roles, girls received and continue to receive the kind of education which qualifies them to meet the larger society on its own terms and deal with it. At the high school level the acquisition of clerical skills, such as typing, shorthand and book-keeping, introduced them to the managerial side of the business world, whereas boys' training in manual arts places them on the side of labor. Likewise, training for girls beyond high school frequently involves nursing and teaching, vocations rising in status recognition. Until very lately a great number of boys who sought higher education were supported and guided by missionaries who encouraged them to go into the clergy, a career carrying considerably less prestige than it did formerly. Advanced vocational training for boys comparable to training as practical nurses or stenographers for girls has also placed them in the production end of the labor market and isolated them from opportunities to learn or at least observe administrative skills and higher organizational techniques.

Finally, two respondents made a pointed suggestion in regard to the American Indian Chicago Conference coordinated by Sol Tax and similar gatherings of a local nature patterned after it which I mentioned in my statement. They observed that people such as Tax and even I may be contributing more than we realize to the stir and turmoil by providing public platforms contributing to the development of an actual movement. It is too early to attempt predictions of future effects, but I think it is worth noting that a surprisingly large number of younger Indian people who are deeply committed to the idea of Indian identity are seeking degrees in anthropology! One person felt that even this publication will have an impact and influence on Indian thinking and further action.

In retrospect, I feel that the feelings and strivings of Indian people created the American Indian Chicago Conference, rather than the other way around. Certainly, it had a profound influence on a number of tribes in offering a model for action and a good deal of moral support for what in 1961 were, as far as the general public is concerned, unpopular and incomprehensible goals. However, the Indian views were there before the conference, and I believe would have found outlets one way or another. AICC may have expedited their expression but did not bring them about initially.

The papers gathered in this volume represent a remarkably accurate reflection of the major trends revealed in responses to the questionnaire. In some cases the writers had already devoted thought to certain aspects of the situation and simply volunteered papers (or somewhat revised versions of them) which they had already prepared but had not yet published. In other instances, the questionnaire served to stimulate the actual setting forth on paper of ideas and observations which the writers had been mulling over. Thus, Shirley Witt presents us with an excellent summary of the history of Indian administration and the reactions to that administration which have resulted in nationalistic philosophies. The origin and spread of a generalized pan-Indian identity is detailed by Robert K. Thomas, who distinguishes this trend from organized and consciously-held sentiments of Indian nationalism. Carol Rachlin shows that in Central and Eastern Oklahoma, despite inter-tribal activities for social, political or religious purposes, strong tribal allegiances and distinctive practices continue.

Four of the papers show the varying interplay of tribal and inter-tribal orientations within and between tribes. The Kansas Potawatomi described by James Clifton comprise one community of a once large tribe and are an excellent example of a group which has managed to perpetuate a conservative tradition while adapting it to changing circumstances. By both 'spin off' and self-isolation, this group sees itself first as Potawatomi, yet avails itself of inter-tribal or general Indian contacts and benefits in a highly selective manner. The Eastern Cherokee discussed by Harriet Kupferer are likewise a segment of a once larger tribal entity.

Compared to the Potawatomi their culture contains many more elements borrowed from white and pan-Indian sources than native traits, and the population itself is more heterogeneous in racial terms and acculturational levels, but the orientation is primarily tribal rather than inter-tribal or nationalistic. The presence of a real schism between segments of the Nez Perce population is detailed by Deward Walker in terms of a series of operationally defined 'renascences' gradually superseded by greater and more frequent declines in distinctively Nez Perce or even general Indian identification. The result today is a factional dispute between those who have a vested interest in at least continuing a general Indian identity and those who would prefer to divide the tribal patrimony and go their separate ways as assimilated Indians. Ann Fischer's account of the Houma of Louisiana illustrates the case of people outside the federal jurisdiction who have lost almost all recollection of any distinctive tribal language or culture. The external features or symbols of their Indian identity are not derived from pan-Indian sources to any great extent. The Houma are aware of and interested in general Indian or inter-tribal activities, but their social and economic isolation precludes active participation in such endeavors as a means of obtaining assistance in working through their own problems of law suits involving land. Although their questionable racial heritage raises obstacles to assimilation into the white population, Fischer's data reveal that they would be better off than they are in economic and educational terms had they chosen to identify as Negroes.

In all of the papers there is a common thread of concern about education as this relates to attempts to improve the material side of Indian life. Rosalie and Murray Wax provide us with a most perceptive analysis of the different meanings of education as viewed 'from above' by outsiders engaged in the business of education and as viewed 'from below' by those seeking education or having it foisted upon them. Of special interest is the discussion of the selective and adaptive response to education now evident even among the 'country Indians' on the Pine Ridge Sioux Reservation as something useful and not threatening to the Indian identity. The school can become part of *Indian culture* just as the auto-mobile and manufactured clothing have become part of Indian culture along with those parts deriving from tribal sources, such as the give-away ceremony in commemoration of important events in an individual's life, and those parts relating to pan-Indian developments, such as the inter-tribal pow-wow.

That Indian people are no longer to be considered simply the special concern of the Bureau of Indian Affairs, or of interest only to themselves until they fade away, is strikingly evident in the study by Henry Dobyns. Dobyns concentrates on the articulation of Indian communities into the larger socio-economic system and their effective control over their own destinies within the larger system by means of recourse to lawyers sympathetic to their peculiar interests as Indians. Anthropologists and other professionals in the social sciences have also been engaged in the role of liaison people between tribes and the dominant society in helping to realize goals decided upon by tribes. But the involvement of the legal profession is of particular significance. It means that members of a powerful, highly articulate and notoriously realistic segment of the society at large are able to accept continuation of Indian communities as a fact of American life. Perhaps in the last accounting, the renascence is the change in the non-Indian world in regard to the Indian world rather than the reverse, as I first perceived it. The paper by Elizabeth Clark Rosenthal bears this out. Indian people are among us and becoming more visible as Indian people wherever they are – and not simply in their 'proper' historical, social or cultural setting. It behooves us to know them on their terms.

Notes

1. Lewis C. Merriam and associates, *The Problem of Indian Administration* ... (Baltimore [The Brookings Institution], 1928), 805. It is significant that despite enlightened views, the Brookings report in this passage completely missed the basic issue. While recognizing a widespread sense of grievance and pleading for justice, it failed to see that to Indian people the fundamental injustice was in being treated and considered as 'wards' on an individual basis rather than as mature people organized in viable communities desiring to manage their own affairs on lands guaranteed to them as communities in various treaties and agreements.

2. The May 1967 issue of *ABC* (Americans Before Columbus), published by the National Indian Youth Council, carries (on page 6) an extensive analysis of the pending Omnibus Bill which is fairly typical of views and protests concerning the bill expressed by many Indian groups, both tribal and inter-tribal, throughout the country.

3. I think it is worth noting that I first saw the 'Custer Died For Your Sins' button in the early spring of 1967 as it was being sold by young Indian people in Minneapolis-St Paul to raise funds to start an 'Indian Coffee-House'. Co-editor Levine had by then seen both buttons and bumper stickers in the Lawrence, Kansas, area.

ABOUT THE AUTHORS

James A. Clifton is in the Department of Anthropology, University of Kansas, where he has been directing an extensive research project on the ethnohistory and contemporary culture of the Prairie Band of Potawatomi of Kansas. He has previous research experience involving studies of cultural change and stability among the Ute Indians of Colorado and the Klamath Indians of Oregon. During 1965–7 he was in Chile for advanced study and research among the Mapuche Indians and with German and Spanish communities.

Henry F. Dobyns is Chairman of the Department of Anthropology at the University of Kentucky. Formerly Coordinator of a comparative study of cultural change at Cornell University, he has conducted research on Indians in Mexico, Peru, Ecuador and Bolivia after working as an anthropological researcher for the Hualapai and Papago Indian Tribes of Arizona. He has published several books and scholarly articles and edited items ranging from an army officer's journal of an expedition from Nuevo Leon to California to a volume of analyses of recent internal migrations in Peru. He studied at Cornell University and the University of Arizona.

Ann Fischer has the A. B. degree from the University of Kansas and a Radcliffe College Ph.D. Since 1959, she has been at Newcomb College of Tulane University, where she's currently Associate Professor of Anthropology and Co-director of the Family Survey of Metropolitan New Orleans. She has taught at the University of Hawaii, been consultant to the Peace Corps for Micronesia and to the Veterans' Administration; done research at Stanford University and Harvard, and in Truk and Ponape, Caroline Islands; a New England village; Children's Hospital, Boston; Japan and New Orleans. Her essay describes her work among the Houma. She has published extensively.

Dr Harriet Kupferer, an anthropologist, is on the faculty of the Department of Sociology and Anthropology, University of North Carolina at Greensboro. In addition to extensive research among the

Eastern Cherokee, she has studied the Santo Domingo Pueblo people (1962) and more recently has worked in Canada with Indian people at Rupert's House (1963) and Indian and Eskimo groups at Great Whale River (1964).

Stuart Levine is Chairman of the American Studies Program at the University of Kansas. His A.B. is from Harvard, the M.A. and Ph.D. from Brown. Before coming to Kansas in 1958, he was a professional concert musician and radio commentator; since then, he has taken leaves for one Fulbright professorship in Argentina and two in Costa Rica, and visiting professorships at the University of Missouri at Kansas City, Kansas State University and the University of South Dakota. He has also given a 'short course' at the University of Wisconsin and lectures at Earlham College, the University of Wisconsin–Milwaukee and other schools. He has a book and numerous articles in print, and is Editor both of the *Midcontinent American Studies Journal* and the American Studies Monograph Series.

Nancy Oestreich Lurie is Professor of Anthropology and Chairman of the Department of Anthropology at the University of Wisconsin–Milwaukee. In 1961 she was Assistant Coordinator to Sol Tax in the American Indian Chicago Conference. Her primary field work has been among the Winnebago of Nebraska and Wisconsin and the Dogrib Indians of the Sub-Arctic. Her B.A. is from Wisconsin, M.A. Chicago, and Ph.D. from Northwestern; and she held a Fulbright-Hays Lectureship at the University of Aarhus, Denmark, in 1965–6.

Carol K. Rachlin is an anthropologist whose scholarly interests began with archeology and have expanded into ethnology and applied anthropology. In 1960 Alice Marriott and Miss Rachlin founded the Southwest Research Associates, which undertakes research in a wide variety of anthropological areas from Indian land claims cases to appraisal of museum collections of Indian artifacts. She and Alice Marriott organized the Oklahoma Indian Council which since 1962 has served some 8,000 Indian people in programs ranging from reading classes for adults and children to emergency welfare assistance and counseling services. She is the author of a number of articles, and, with Alice Marriott, a book, *A Mythology of North American Indians*. She is currently Artist-in-Residence at Central State College, Edmund, Oklahoma.

A non-Indian of reservation background, *Elizabeth Clark Rosenthal*

About the Authors

was brought up on the Crow Creek Reservation in South Dakota and went to school there. Her grandfather, the Rev. Aaron B. Clark, went to the Rosebud Reservation in the 1880s as an Episcopal missionary and linguist. Her father, the Rev. David W. Clark, grew up at Rosebud, and then, as a missionary himself, lived with his wife and family at Fort Thompson, South Dakota for 25 years, at Fort Defiance, Arizona on the Navajo reservation for 15 years, and finally in the newly developing urban Indian communities in the Twin Cities and Denver until retirement a few years ago. Mrs Rosenthal has maintained close family and community ties in the Indian world throughout her life. She lives now in Lexington, Massachusetts, with her husband, Robert, and four children. Elizabeth Rosenthal is one of the founders of the United Scholarship Services Inc. for American Indian and Spanish-American students, located in Denver, Colorado, and serves as Chairman of the Board of Directors of USS, Inc. She is a national staff officer of the Executive Council of the Episcopal Church, New York, N.Y., as Consultant on Special Field Ministries, particularly American Indian Work. She is a member of the Council on Indian Affairs, a cooperating council of organizations active on the contemporary Indian scene. Her A.B. is from Mt Holyoke, the M.A. from the University of Wisconsin, and the Ph.D. from Harvard.

Robert K. Thomas did his graduate work in the field of anthropology at the University of Arizona and the University of Chicago. He has done formal field work in several American Indian communities, the Sac and Fox of Oklahoma, the Sioux of South Dakota and the Cherokees of North Carolina and Oklahoma. At the opposite end of the folk-urban continuum, he was involved in teaching and urban research of Monteith College, Wayne State University in Detroit, Michigan. More recently he has been associated with the University of Chicago and is Co-director of the Carnegie Corporation Cross-Cultural Education Project, a research project involved in studying the process of learning, literacy, and education among American Indians generally and the Oklahoma Cherokees particularly. Mr Thomas is a Cherokee Indian and has observed growth of the Pan-Indian movement from an inside view as well from the viewpoint of a social scientist.

Deward Walker is Chairman of the Department of Sociology and Anthropology at the University of Idaho, and Research Collaborator at Washington State University. He has been Editor of Northwest Anthropological *Research Notes,* has held positions for Washington

The American Indian Today

State, the George Washington University, the University of Oregon and the Board of National Missions of the United Presbyterian Church. His research areas include ethnology of the Plateau and Northwest Coast, and the Nez Perce Indians. Dr Walker is the author of several monographs and articles and is a consultant to several groups involved in Indian affairs.

Rosalie Wax is Associate Professor of Anthropology, and *Murray Wax* is Professor of Sociology at the University of Kansas. Both have Chicago Ph.D.s. They are the co-authors of *Formal Education in an American Community* (1964) and numerous articles, published jointly and individually. Rosalie Wax has done field work in the Relocation Center for Japanese-Americans and has published about that work. Their major interests are American Indians and their education, religion and magic. From 1966 to 1968 they worked among Cherokee people in northeastern Oklahoma.

Shirley Hill Witt is of Mohawk descent and a charter member of the National Indian Youth Council. She has done field work among a number of American Indian tribes and has assisted in research on claims before the Indian Claims Commission. She received her B.A. and M.A. at the University of Michigan, and is currently a Ph.D. candidate at the University of New Mexico, Albuquerque.

BIBLIOGRAPHY

CONTEMPORARY

ABC (Americans Before Columbus). Newspaper format. Comes with membership in National Indian Youth Council. $5.00 per year includes quarterly, *ABC* and other news of group. Non-Indians may only be associate members.

Catalogs of publications including maps are available from:

Bureau of Indian Affairs, which also puts out regular news releases and a newsletter, *Smoke Signals,* which will be sent on request.

Indian Division, Public Health Service, Department of Health, Education and Welfare, Washington, D.C.

Indian Office, Ottawa, Canada.

National Congress of American Indians. Washington, D.C.

Declaration of Indian Purpose. American Indian Chicago Conference. $2.00. Anthropology Department, University of Chicago.

Indian Voices. Newspaper. University of Chicago, 1126 E. 59th Street, Chicago, Illinois. $2.50 Indian – $3.50 Non-Indian.

Navajo Times. A leading tribal newspaper. Window Rock, Arizona. $4.00.

ETHNOLOGICAL

Driver, Harold. *Indians of North America.* University of Chicago Press, 1961. Reference book, organized primarily by topics such as distribution of languages, religious forms, etc.

Driver, Harold, ed. *The Americas on the Eve of Discovery.* Prentice-Hall, 1964. Selected readings on various groups and topics.

Hodge, Frederick Webb, ed. *Handbook of the North American Indian.* In two volumes. *Annual Report,* Bureau of American Ethnology, Smithsonian Institution, Washington, 1937. An old 'classic' listing tribes, place names, famous Indians and cultural attributes alphabetically.

Kroeber, Alfred L. *Cultural and Natural Areas of Native North America.* University of California Press, Berkeley, California,

Bibliography

1939. A reference book with special attention to ecological factors relative to culture areas.

Linton, Ralph, ed. *Acculturation in Seven American Indian Tribes.* Appleton-Century-Crofts, New York, 1940. Reprint by Peter Smith. An early study of the processes of acculturation.

Murdock, George Peter. *Ethnographic Bibliography of North America.* Yale University Press, Human Relations Area Files (check latest edition; it is regularly up-dated). The 'Bible'. It lists articles, books and monographs by tribe and culture area.

Oswalt, Wendell H. *This Land Was Theirs.* John Wiley and Sons, Inc., New York, 1966. Ten representative tribes from across the country. A textbook.

Owen, Robert C., Deetz, James J. F., Fischer, Anthony D., eds. *The North American Indians, A Source-book,* Macmillan, New York, 1967. Selected readings from the 'classics' on general topics and the various culture areas. Includes a valuable appendix of films available on the American Indian, although critical annotations for the films would be desirable.

Spencer, Robert F., Jennings, Jesse, D., *et al. The Native Americans.* Harper and Row, New York, 1965. Textbook. Good treatment of the modern scene.

Spicer, Edward, ed. *Perspectives in American Indian Cultural Change.* University of Chicago, 1961. Selected tribes, mainly from the western areas.

Underhill, Ruth. *Red Man's America.* University of Chicago Press, 1953. A junior level textbook, but in many ways still the best over-all introduction to the subject.

SOCIO-POLITICAL

Annals of the American Academy of Political and Social Sciences, May 1957. Entire issue devoted to then current problems of American Indians; demography, termination, Indian Claims Commission, etc.

Cohen, Felix. *Handbook of Federal Indian Law.* Washington, 1946. Preferable to the later edition.

Kappler, Charles J., ed. *Indian Affairs, Laws and Treaties.* In two volumes: I. Laws; II. Treaties, Washington, D.C., 1904. A source book reproducing all treaties to 1871, and laws to 1900.

Levine, Stuart and Lurie, Nancy Oestreich, eds. *The Indian Today* (special issue of *Midcontinent American Studies Journal*, VI, 2). An earlier and shorter version of the present study, designed to

Bibliography

brief students of other aspects of American culture – historians, sociologists, political scientists, specialists in literature, art historians, urban planners, etc. – on the current situation in the Indian world.

McNickle, D'Arcy and Fey, Harold. *Indians and Other Americans.* Harper and Row, New York, 1959. A response to the termination crisis, but with historical background, and well documented.

Royce, Charles C. and Thomas, Cyrus. 'Indian Land Cessions in the United States'. *Annual Report,* Bureau of American Ethnology, Smithsonian Institution, Washington, D.C., Vol. 18, Pt 2, 1896–7. Lists treaties and other cessions with detailed maps of land areas involved.

HISTORICAL

Brandon, William. *The American Heritage Book of Indians.* Simon and Schuster, New York, 1961. (Paperback, Dell, 1964.) Historical review of tribes and frontier.

Fritz, Henry E. *The Movement of Indian Assimilation: 1860–1890.* University of Pennsylvania Press, 1963.

Hagan, William T. *The American Indian.* University of Chicago Press, 1961. Traces the history of the conflict between Indian rights recognized in law and wider 'national interest'.

Josephy, Alvin. *Patriotic Chiefs: A Chronicle of American Indian Leadership.* Viking, 1961. A book of biographies.

Spicer, Edward H. *Cycles of Conquest: The Impact of Spain, Mexico and the United States on Indians of the Southwest, 1533–1960.* University of Arizona Press, Tucson, Arizona, 1962.

Washburn, Wilcomb. *The Indian and the White Man.* Anchor Books, Doubleday, Garden City, New York, 1964. Compendium of documents from first contact to Declaration of Indian Purpose of 1961. Includes John Marshall's famous decisions on the Cherokee and examples of Indian oratory.

INDEX

ABC (Americans Before Columbus) 327n

Arrow, Inc., 106
  See also National Congress of American Indians

Acadians, 214

Adams, Henry, 125n

Africa, 43n, 44n, 139, 266, 269

Agriculture, 51, 52, 55–6, 66, 72, 104–5, 120, 148, 161, 162, 192, 197, 213ff, 244, 245–6, 278–9, 283

Alabama, 110

Alabama-Coushattas, 110

Alaska, 56, 62, 106, 321

Allotment, 71, 73, 77, 81n, 99, 102, 113, 117, 162, 189–90, 197ff, 245, 248, 271, 275

American Anthropological Association, 209n, 267n

American Indian Capital Conference on Poverty, 116–17

American Indian Chicago Conference (AICC), 16, 22, 26–7, 39, 42–3, 45n, 112, 214, 296, 306, 323

American Indian Defense Association, 100, 316

American Indian Development, Inc., 112

American Studies, 13, 29, 44n
  See also Midcontinent American Studies Journal

Amish, 39, 309

Annals of the American Academy of Political and Social Sciences, 305

Anthropology, nature of, 83; cultural conservatism of, 14; methodology of, 83–9, 184
  See also Social scientists, preconceptions of

Apache, 54, 280, 284ff, 289n

Arapaho, 85, 161ff

Arctic Circle, 52

Arizona, 106, 114, 117, 280, 283; Window Rock, 284

Arizona Daily Star, 280

Arizona State Welfare Administration, 280

Asia, 139

Assembly of God, 243

Assimilation, *see* Discrimination, segregation, assimilation; Tribal membership

Association for American Indian Affairs, 229

Attorneys, 107, 108, 220, 226–34 esp. 229, 268–91, 298, 326
  See also Dobyns, Henry

Australia, 139, 269

Baldwin Constitution, 193, 197ff

Baptists, 163, 164, 177, 222

Baseheart, Harry W., 289n

Beals, Alan R., 185, 206, 209n

Beatty, William W., 125n
Bee, Robert, 209n
Bennett, Robert L., 289n, 303
Berry, Brewton, 159n, 212, 235n
Billiot, Jacques, 217ff;
  Jean Pierre, 217;
  Alexander, 218;
  Batolme, 218;
  Jean, 218;
  Celestin, 218
Black Hawk, 97
'Black Muslims', 143, 303
Black Power, 43, 44n, 303-4
  See also Negroes; Civil Rights
    Movement
'Blood', degrees of, *see* Tribal
  membership
Bluffs Band, *see* Prairie Band
Border states, 28
  *See also related area and state
    names*
Boston Irish, 38
Boy Scouts, 310
Brady, Mark, 181
Brando, Marlon, 115, 302, 308
Brandon, William, 79n
Brant, Joseph, 95, 97, 125n
Brookings Institution, *see* Lewis
  C. Merriam
Buffalo, 53-4, 55, 183, 318
Bureau of Indian Affairs (BIA)
  ('Indian Bureau'), 13, 18,
  23-7, 31, 33, 45n, 68, 70, 72,
  74, 80n, 96, 101, 102, 103-4,
  105, 108-9, 147, 149, 155,
  155-6, 161, 168, 169, 171, 172,
  179, 180-82, 191, 194-211,
  215, 228, 234, 246, 249-50,
  258, 260, 262, 263, 268-91,
  298-9, 304, 326
  administrative philosophy of,
    269, 295, 296-7;
  founded, 63;
  shifted to Department of the
    Interior, 68;
  put on Civil Service, 74
Burgess, N. Elaine, 158n
Burke Act, 99
Bursum, Bill, 100

Caddo, 100ff
California, 55, 109, 110, 117;
  San Francisco, 38, 115;
  Los Angeles, 169
Canada, 58, 59, 61, 69, 118, 269;
  Ontario, 59;
  Quebec, 59;
  Northwest Territories, 80n;
  Saskatchewan, 118
Capp, Al, 18
Cargo cults, 144
Carlisle (Indian school), 85, 156
Carruth, J. Wagner, 127n
Castro, Fidel, 37
Catawba, 153, 215
Catholics, 55, 163, 164, 197, 215,
  242, 249, 259
Cayuga, 64, 94
Cherokee, 12, 20, 65, 66, 97, 99,
  128, 130, 159n, 194, 266, 315,
  324
  See also Isolated Eastern Chero-
    kee
Cherokee Chamber of Commerce,
  156
*Cherokee Nation, The, v. The
  State of Georgia*, 67
Cheyenne, 131, 161ff
Chicago, University of, 112

Index

Chickasaw, 64, 99

Chippewa, 95, 103, 109, 110, 188, 209n

Chitimacha, 215

Chinese, 38

Choctaw, 64, 99, 153, 214, 215, 216

'Christianized Prophet Dance', 241, 242
  See also Prophet Dance

Church of Jesus Christ of the Latter-Day Saints, *see* Mormons

Cities, Indian experience in 13, 30, 42, 45n, 72–3, 77, 82ff, 104–6, 134, 162–3, 168, 171, 192, 200, 258–60, 296–7

Citizen's Band, 190

Civil Liberties Union, 115

Civil Rights Movement, 12, 28, 43n, 117, 230–34, 300–302, 303, 317, 318

Civilian Conservation Corps, 272

Clifton, Faye, 209n

Clifton, James A., 184–211, 288, 324;
  biography, 329

Clyde Warrior Institute for American Indian Studies, 29, 44n

Coastal regions, 52, 55
  See also related area and state names

Cochise, 97

Cohen, Felix S., 94, 125n

Collier, John, Sr, 75–7, 102, 104, 124, 126n, 127n, 268–74, 285–7, 303

Comanche, 55, 161ff

Commission on the Rights, Liberties, and Responsibilities of the American Indian, 112

Colorado, 44n;
  Denver, 117, 169

Committee of One Hundred, 100

Conflict, *see* Factional conflict

Constitution, 60

Council on Indian Affairs, 117

Courteaux, Rosalie, 217ff, 233, 234

Crazy Horse, 97

Creek, 64, 97, 99, 130;
  Creek Confederacy, 95

Creoles, 38

Crévecoeur, Hector St John de, 38

Crow, 109

Cubans, 37

'Culture', concept of, 82ff, 269;
  contact situations, 186–7;
  diversity of Indian, 11–12, 57;
  in crisis, 75;
  cultural purity, 26, 41, 52ff, 143ff, 308–10
  See also Identity; Material culture

Curtis Act of 1924, 100

Daily Oklahoman, The, 181

Dances, 41, 173, 179

Daughters of the American Revolution (DAR), 37

Dawes Allotment Act of 1887, *see* Allotment

Decision-making, characteristic Indian process of, 16–17, 32–4

Declaration of Purpose, *see* American Indian Chicago Conference

Delaware (tribe), 95, 161ff

Deloria, Vine, Jr, 118

Democratic process, 16; therapeutic effects of, 269–91

Department of Health, Education, and Welfare, 170

Department of the Interior, *see* Bureau of Indian Affairs

Discrimination, segregation, assimilation, 12, 18, 24, 25, 27–8, 29, 31–2, 33ff, 39, 41, 64, 67, 69, 71–2, 74, 76, 77–8, 93–4, 98–9, 100, 106–14, 114–15, 116, 131, 137, 157, 163–4. 169, 171–2, 204, 206–8, 213, 217–18, 214–23, 224–6, 229, 231–2, 243, 258, 263, 283, 300–302, 307–10, 312, 316–22, 324–5
    See also Civil Rights Movement; Identity; Tribal membership; Racism

Dobyns, Henry F., 38, 268–91, 326; *biography*, 329

Dogmatism, 164
    See also Religion

Dozier, Edward P., 289n, 291n

Dream Dance, *see* Drum (Dream Dance) religion

Driver, Harold, 79n

Drum (Dream Dance) religion, 193

Drury, Clifford, 256n

Dumont, Robert V., Jr, 267n

East, 55, 130, 315
    See also related area and state names, e.g. New England; New Jersey

Eastern Band of the Cherokee, *see* Isolated Eastern Cherokee; Cherokee

Eastern Keresan Pueblos, 144

Eastern Seaboard, 50
    See also related area and state names

Eastern woodlands, 52, 135
    See also individual tribal names

Economic situation, 13, 148–51, 154ff, 166–72, 181, 213ff, 244–7, 286–7, 307, 312

Education, 20ff, 33ff, 40, 71, 75, 99, 102, 116, 119, 122, 126n, 151, 166–72, 180, 221ff, 229ff, 258–66, 271, 272, 282, 300, 301, 307, 313–14, 322–3, 325–6

Edwards, Newton, 290n

Eisenhower, Dwight D., 113, 273, 286

Embree, John F., 287, 288n, 291n

Emory University, 266n

Enerise, Marie, 217

Episcopalians, 115, 157, 164

Erie, 95

Eskimo, 52

Euler, Robert C., 290n

Factional conflict, 31–2, 108, 178, 184–211, 239–40, 247–9, 255, 295, 314–16, 325;
    source of, 270–71
    See also Tribal membership; Identity; Tribal government

Family structure, 16, 25, 26, 43, 73, 77–8, 86, 105, 123, 132, 134–5, 136–7, 153, 154, 155, 162–3, 167–8, 168–9, 172–3, 174, 177, 178, 224–7, 228, 234, 239–40, 263–5, 297

Index

Feezor, Mrs Walter B., 28–9

Federal Aviation Administration, 170

Federal employees as a subculture, 170

Felton, Marguerite, 158n

Fey, Harold E., 126n

First World War, 74, 100, 192

Fischer, Ann, 63, 212–35, 325, 329

Fish and Wildlife Department, 115
  See also Fishing

Fishing, 57, 115, 221ff, 244, 302, 308, 317

Five Civilized Tribes of Oklahoma, 99

Flathead, 110

Florida, 38, 95, 110, 126n

'Folk', Indian people as, 129, 153

Foreign policy, implications for, 35, 268
  See also Africa, Australia, etc.

Foreman, Grant, 140n

Fort Berthold, 109

Fox, 65, 95, 103, 128, 133
  See also Sac-Fox

France, 51, 58, 216, 227
  See also History

Franklin, Benjamin, 97, 125n

French, 213, 214, 216, 221–34 *passim*

French, David, 185, 206, 209n, 211n

Friends Indian Committee, 116

Friends of the Indians, 100

Frontier, 35

Fur trade, 50–51, 55, 58

Gayaneshagowa, 94

Germans, 37, 164

Geronimo, 97

Getty, Harry T., 289n

Ghost Dance, 97, 132, 144

'Gift Friends', 175

Give-away, 41, 173–8

Gossen, Gary, 209n

Government administration, efforts at reform of, 69–79
  See also History; Bureau of Indian Affairs

Governors' Interstate Indian Council, 117–18

Great Basin, 55
  See also related area and state names

Great Britain, 51, 56, 58, 59, 95, 269
  See also History

Great Lakes Area, 133
  See also related area and state names, e.g. Northern Great Lakes Region

Great Lakes Inter-Tribal Council, 306

Greeks, 38

Green, Arnold W., 158n

Gulf of Mexico, 217

Gulick, John, 146, 159n

Hass, Theodore H., 289n, 290n

Hagan, William T., 80n, 126n

Haines, Francis, 256n

Hand game, 176, 177

Handlin, Oscar, 15, 38

'Harmony Ethic', 150–51, 159n

Harrison, William Henry, 95

Haskell Institute, 18, 24–6, 32, 156

Havasupai, 12

Index

Health, 50, 55, 99, 117, 122, 127n,
151, 169, 237–8, 272, 285–6

Helm, June, 80n

Hewes, Gordon, 257, 267n

Hiawatha, 97

History, 9–45 *passim;* 49–81;
before white contact, 49ff, 130;
239, 247;
in period of discovery and
early contact, 49–57, 129, 154,
245–6;
in twentieth century, 74–81, 98–
120;
US, 35, 37
*See also individual headings
for specific topics*

Holmberg, Allan R., 290n

Hoover, Herbert, 102

Hopi, 12, 135, 285

Hopkins-Dukes, Amos, 117

Horses, 53, 55, 132, 175, 176, 183,
244–5

Houma, 63, 212–35, 325

Housing, 116
See also Welfare; Economic
situation

Howard, James, 140n

Howard-Wheeler Act, *see* Indian
Reorganization Act of 1934

Hualapai, 289–90n

Humor, 19, 318

Hunting and trapping, 51–2, 53,
55, 66, 131, 208, 220, 220–21,
225ff, 224

Huron, 95

Hutterites, 312

Idaho, 106, 236–56;
Lewiston, 246

Identity, 10–11, 39–43, 71, 73, 78,
82–9, 93ff, 123, 129ff, 143,
144, 163, 187, 206ff, 212–35,
esp. 224; 287, 209, 306, 308–9,
313, 315, 324–5
See also Cultural purity; Tribal
membership

Illinois: Chicago, 39, 112, 128,
188, 189, 209n, 296, 304

Immigrants, 9–45, esp. 36ff, 204

India, 269

Indian Allotment Act of 1887,
see Allotment

Indian Claims Commission, *see*
Indian Claims Commission
Act

Indian Claims Commission Acts
of 1946 and 1966, 81n, 96,
106, 108, 121, 246, 250–51,
274, 276,

Indian Clubs, 136

'Indian grapevine', *see* 'Moccasin
telegraph'

Indian history, *see* History

Indian Renascence, *see* Inter-
tribal cooperation; 'Renascent' and 'declining' cultures;
Questionnaire on current
trends

Indian Reorganization Act of
1934, 76, 96, 102, 105, 107,
196ff, 210n, 250, 274, 298

Indian Rights Association, 100

Indian Territories, 67–8

Indian Voices, 127n, 145, 159n

Indian Welfare Department, 149,
151

Indian Youth Councils, 136, 178
See also National Indian Youth
Council

Index

Industry on reservation, 13, 73, 149, 152, 245
See also Navajo; Isolated Eastern Cherokee; Economic situation
Inland regions, 51, 52
See also related area and place names
Inter-tribal cooperation and interaction, 12, 17, 26, 32, 49, 51–2, 67–8, 93–127, 129–40, 143ff, 152, esp. 163, 179ff, 213, 268, 295, 296, 314–27
Intermarriage, see family structure
Iowa (state), 103, 133
Iowa (tribe), 123
Iroquois, 94, 97, 130, 135, 315; League of the, 64
Isaac, Barry, 209n ff
Isolated Eastern Cherokee, 143–59, 324–5;
involved in pan-Indianism, 144–5, 152;
location, 145–6;
racial makeup, 146–71;
economy, 148–9;
culture, 149–50;
social divisions, 152–8
See also Cherokee

Jackson, Andrew, 67
Japanese, 37, 258
Jefferson, Thomas, 66
Jehovah's Witnesses, 243
Jews, 37, 257, 259, 266, 309, 322; Hassidic Jews, 39
Jicarilla Apache, 118, 289n
See also Apache
John Birch Society, 18

Johnson-O'Malley Act, 272
Joseph, Chief, 97
Josephy Alvin M., Jr, 125n

Kansas, 30, 44n, 130, 187–211; Lawrence, 24, 24–5, 31, 327n; Mayetta, 41, 45n; Topeka, 25, 192, 194;
Kansas Potawatomi, see Potawatomi
Kansas, University of, 44n, 209n
Kappler, Charles J., 80n
Kaw, 161ff
Kaw Reservation, 188
Kelly, William K., 289n, 290n
Kennedy, John F., 112
Kickapoo, 18, 65, 95, 97, 198
Kinship groups, see Family Structure
Kinzua Dam, 116, 301
Kiowa, 161ff
Kiowa and Kiowa-Apache Black Leggings Societies, 175
Kiowa-Apache, 113, 161ff
See also Apache
Kiowa Gourd Dance Clan, 175
Kittitas, 238
Klamath, 110–11, 275, 290n, 312
Klikitat, 238
Korean War, 163
Krimmer Mennonite Brethren, see Mennonites
Kroeber, A. L., 257, 267n
Kupferer, Harriet, 20, 143–59, 324;
biography, 329–30

La Barre, Weston, 127n
Land ownership, concepts of, 269
Landes, Ruth, 209n, 211n

Lang, Gottfried, 290n

Language, 11–12, 70, 105, 122, 129, 132, 170, 180, 216, 254, 261, 263, 285

Latvians, 38

Lawyers, *see* Attorneys; Dobyns, Henry F.

Leadership training, 33, 44n, 70–79, 105, 111–13, 177–8, 268–91, 319

See also Dobyns, Henry F.

League of the Hodenosaunee, *see* Iroquois

Leighton, Alexander H., 269, 288n

Lesser, Alexander 124, 127n

Lincoln National Forest, 284

Lions Club, 156

Little Big Horn, 69

Little Turtle, 125n

Louisiana, 213–34, 325;

Bayou Terrebonne, 215, 230, 232;

Bayou Pointe au Chênes, 215, 223, 230;

Morgan City, 215;

New Orleans, 216, 223–3, 224, 229;

West Feliciana Parish, 216;

Ascension Parish, 216;

Lake Ponchartrain, 216;

LaFourche Parish, 216, 222, 222–3;

Terrebonne Parish, 216, 221–2;

Atchafalaya, 220;

McIlhenny Island, 220;

Île de Jean Charles, 223, 227, 230;

Houma (town), 224;

Pointe au Chênes, 227–8, 229;

Grande Caillou, 231;

Bayou Dularge, 232;

Bayou LaFourche, 232;

Golden Meadow, 232

Louisiana Purchase, 62, 64

Levine, Stuart (SGL), 9–45, 93, 143, 160, 217, 236, 327n; *biography*, 330

See also Midcontinent American Studies Journal

Lewis and Clark, 56–7

Linton, Ralph, 288n

Lirettes (family), 218

Loram, C. T., 93, 125n, 126n

Lower Mississippi Valley, 50

See also related area and state names

Lumbee, 63, 157

Lurie, Nancy O. (NOL), 42, 49–81, 80n, 81n, 93, 143, 144, 159n, 160, 212, 236, 289n, 295–327; *biography*, 330

McBeth, Kate C., 256n

McIlwraith, T. F., 93, 125n, 126n

McNickle, D'Arcy, 9, 13, 22, 101, 125n ff

Madison, James, 125n

Marriott, Alice, 175, 183n

Marshall, John, 67, 80n, 297

Massachusetts: Boston, 38

Material culture, 41, 50–51, 54, 55, 57, 66, 73, 88, 105, 124, 161, 227–8, 308

Mennonites, 37, 39, 164;

Krimmer Mennonite Brethren, 38

Menomini, 65, 103, 110, 312

Merriam, Lewis C., 74, 81, 81n, 101–2, 165, 183n, 298, 327n

Mescalero, 118

Mescalero Apaches, 284
  See also Apaches

Mesquakie, *see* Fox

Methodists, 164, 177, 222, 249

Metis: in Canada, 60;
  United States, 63

Mexicans, 42

Mexico, 50, 53–4, 65, 95

Miami, 64, 95

Michigan, 65, 103, 117

Midcontinent American Studies Journal, VI, 2 (Fall 1965), 159n 236, 295, 305ff, 310 *Most of the material in the present volume is developed out of this issue; some is reprinted without change Stuart Levine is Editor of MASJ; for VI, 2, Nancy Lurie served as Guest Editorial Consultant. . . . For a history of the project, see Afterword*

Midwest, 130, 306, 316
  See also related area and state names, e.g. Prairie and Plains region

Military service, 40, 61, 74, 104, 162, 175, 199, 223, 224, 272, 281, 284–5

Mingo, 95

Minnesota, 65, 103, 117;
  Minneapolis, 45n, 327n;
  St Paul, 327n

Minority group, Indians as a, 9–45, esp. 14ff, 36ff, 128–40, 259, 264, 308, 319–22

Misconceptions about Indian people, 10–14, 82–3, 181–2

Missionary activity:
  as result of treaties, 58–9;
  impulse toward in BIA, 26–7;
  in colonial period, 44n;
  in education, 99–100, 323;
  Spanish, 55;
  training preachers, 248;
  mentioned, 70, 187, 190, 225, 227, 239, 241

Mississippi (state): Philadelphia, 214

Mississippi River, 50, 55, 216

Missouri: Kansas City, 145;
  Platte Purchase, 188

'Moccasin telegraph', 122, 172

Mohawk, 94, 159n

Montana, 117, 126n

Mooney, James, 174

Moore, Frank, 168

Mormons, 39, 164

Mountain Ute, 108, 290n
  See also Ute

Munsee, 103, 191

Muskogian, 216

Muskrats, 221

Myer, Dillon S., 110, 273, 279

Nanticokes, 95

Nash, Philleo, 116, 303

Nation, The, 9

National Association for the Advancement of Colored People (NAACP), 301

National Conference of Social Work, 273

National Congress of American Indians (NCAI), 22–3, 97, 106, 111, 113–14, 114ff, 133, 145, 179, 295, 298, 299, 309, 316

National Indian Association, 100

National Indian Youth Council (NIYC), 13, 45n, 97, 113, 115ff, 302, 306, 316, 317–18, 327n

National Institute of Health, 235n

National Institute of Mental Health, 158n

National Science Foundation, 209n

Nationalism, *see* Inter-tribal co-operation and interaction; National Indian Youth Council

Native American Church, 31, 120, 165, 176, 193

Natural gas rights, 219ff, 284

Navajo, 13, 20, 54, 118, 135, 159n, 284, 270n

Navajo Times, The, 33

Nazarene, Church of the, 164

Nebraska, 64, 81n, 110

Nebraska Omaha (tribe), 110
See also Omaha

Negroes, 12, 13, 18, 28, 37–8, 43n, 44n, 63, 157, 163, 164, 194, 204, 213, 215, 217, 221–34, 300–301, 303–4, 307, 308, 312, 317, 320–21, 325
See also Civil Rights Movement

Nelson, John P., 229, 230, 232

Neutral, 95

Nevada, 118

New Deal, 75, 286
See also Collier, John, Sr

New England, 16, 58, 133
See also related area and state names

New Mexico, 22, 106, 118;
Gallup, 157;
Shiprock, 284;
Sierra Blanca, 284;
Lincoln National Forest, 284

New York (state), 39, 42, 65, 110, 301;
Allegany Reservation, 116;
Kinzua Dam, 116, 301

New York Times, 284

Nez Perce, 236–56, 325;
population, 237–40;
religion, 241–3;
economy, 244–7;
political organization, 247–53;
as 'renascent', 254–5
See also 'renascent' and 'declining' cultures

Nipmuck, 95

Non-Christian religions, 31, 165, 192ff, 206, 239–40, 240, 249

North, 54, 55
See also related area and state names

North Carolina, 63, 145, 154, 157;
Snow Bird, 146;
Cherokee County, 146;
Winston-Salem, 28–163;
Asheville, 145, 152;
Great Smoky Mountain National Park, 146;
Qualla Boundary, 146;
Wolfetown, 146;
Paint Town, 146;
Cherokee, 146, 152–3;
Big Cove, 146;
Birdtown, 146;
Ocunaluftee River, 146;
Tennessee River, 146

Index

North Dakota, 103, 117

Northern Great Lakes region, 50
See also related area and state names

Northern Ute, 290n
See also Ute

Northeastern University, 169

Northmen, 266

Northwest Coast, 56, 56–7, 275
See also related area and state names

Northwest Ordinance, 62

Nutria, 220–21

Ocunaluftee River, 146

Office of Economic Opportunity, 20, 21, 27, 116ff, 105, 145

Office of Price Administration, 272

Oglala Community High School (Oglala, South Dakota), 260–66

Oil rights, 219ff, 284

Ojibwa, 65, 308

Oklahoma, 13, 30, 64, 99, 128, 130ff, 156, 160–83, 324;
  Oklahoma City, 161–2 163, 164, 166, 169;
  Andarko, 162;
  Pawnee, 161;
  Fort Sill, 170;
  Lawton, 170;
  Tinker Air Force Base, 170, 170–71;
  Concho, 171, 180;
  Norman, 180

Oklahomans for Indian Opportunity, 180

Oklahoma Health and Welfare Association, 181

Oklahoma Indian Council, 180

Oklahoma Mental Health Planning Commission, 168

Oklahoma, State of, Planning and Resources Board, 173

Oklahoma, University of, 179, 180

Omaha Reservation, 81n

Omaha (tribe) in Nebraska, 110; in Oklahoma, 161ff

Oneida, 65, 94, 103, 303

Onondaga, 94, 95

'Operation Bootstrap', 114, 117

Orans, Martin, 140n

Oregon, 56

Osage, 13, 97, 161ff

Oswalt, Wendell H., 79n

Oto, 161ff

Ottawa, 95, 103, 109, 187ff, 209n

Pacifism, 40

Packard, Vance, 136

Paiute, 97

Palus, 238

Pam-to-pee, Phineas, 125n

Pan-Indianism, *see* Inter-tribal cooperation; 'Renascent' and 'declining' cultures; Questionnaire on current trends

Parrington, Vernon L., 38

'Patterson Opinion', 109

Pawnee, 161ff

Peckham, Howard H., 125n

Pembroke, 157

Pennsylvania, 38

Pentecostal sects, 243

Personality, 12
  See also Identity

Peru, 95, 280

Index

Peterson, Helen L., 290n

Peyote religion, *see* Native American Church

Pfeiffer, Jules, 136

Philip, King, 95

Pilgrim Holiness Church, 243

Pine Ridge Sioux, 109, 114, 128, 261–6, 326
  See also Sioux

Plateau area, 132–3, 241
  See also related area and state names

Platte Purchase, 188

Playboy, 136

Poland, 43n, 204

Political affiliation, 13–14
  See also Bureau of Indian Affairs

Ponca, 13, 161ff

Pontiac, 85, 125n

Popé, 95

Population, 10, 71, 82, 98–9, 104, 146–7, 161, 202, 214–15, 237–40, 312

Potawatomi, 41, 64, 95, 97, 103, 161ff, 184–211, 325

Powhatan Confederacy, 58

Pow-wows, 41, 45n, 138, 173–8, 180, 298, 326

Prairie and Plains region, 52–3, 53, 55, 67, 130–2, 175, 184–211, 315–16
  See also related area and state names

Prairie Band, 188ff

Prairie Potawatomi, 184–211;
  location, 187;
  history, 187–203;
  See also Prairie Band; Citizens Band; Factional Conflict

Presbyterians, 242, 248–9

Production Marketing Administration, 272

Professions, Indian people in, 13–14
  See also Economic situation

Prophet Dance, 144
  See also Religion; 'Christianized Prophet Dance'

Proposal for an institute for young Indian people, 35–6

'Protestant Ethic', 151

Provinse, John, 123, 127n, 273, 289n

Public Law 815, 278

Pueblo peoples, 54, 95, 100–101, 118, 129;
  'Pan-Puebloism,' 135
  See also Eastern Keresan Pueblos

Puerto Ricans, 13, 42

Puritans, 37

Purser, Joyce, 235n

Quakers, 39

Quapaw, 161ff

Questionnaire on current trends, 236, 302–27

Rabeau, Erwin S., 127n

Rachlin, Carol K., 160–83, 324;
  biography 330

Racism, 27–31, 77–8, 157–8, 171, 300–301, 303, 307–8, 321
  See also Tribal membership

Rebellion, 18

'Red Muslims', 308

Redfield, Robert, 129, 139, 140n

Reisman, David, 136

Religion, 12, 26, 31, 44n, 58, 69, 97, 130, 132, 144–5, 163–6, 189, 192, 197, 206, 222, 225, 229, 238, 241–3, 248, 249–50, 253, 254, 266, 270, 297, 315, 323;
Amish, 39, 309;
Assembly of God, 243;
Baptist, 163, 177, 222;
Black Muslims, 143, 303;
Catholics, 55, 163, 164, 197, 215, 242, 249, 259;
Christianized Prophet Dance, 241–2;
Drum (Dream Dance) religion, 193;
Episcopalians, 115, 157, 164;
Ghost Dance, 97, 132, 144;
Indian Shaker Church, 144;
Jehovah's Witnesses, 243;
Jews, 37, 257, 259, 266, 309, 322;
Hassidic Jews, 39;
Krimmer Mennonite Brethren, 38;
Mennonites, 38, 39, 164;
Methodists, 164, 177, 222, 249;
Missionary activity, *see separate heading*
Mormons, 39, 164, 243;
Native American Church, 31, 120, 165, 176;
Nazarenes, 164;
Non-Christian religions, 31, 165, 192ff, 206, 239, 240, 250;
Pentecostal sects, 243;
Pilgrim Holiness Church, 243;
Presbyterians, 242, 248, 249;
Prophet Dance, 144;
Quakers, 39

'Renascent' and 'declining' cultures, 236–56, 295–327;
defined, 236–7;
in population, 237–40;
in religion, 241–4;
in economy, 244–7;
in political organization, 247–53;
For groups other than the Nez Perce, see Inter-tribal cooperation, Population, Religion, Economic situation, Agriculture, Tribal government, Identity, Questionnaire on current trends, *and* Lurie, Nancy O.
Reservations, 72, 77, 78, 83, 85, 108ff, 131, 169, 182, 188ff, 213, 239ff, 255, 270, 273, 277, 282, 289n, 296, 301
See also History
Revolutionary War, 59, 61, 95
Rhodes, Charles J., 102
Riley, Robert James, 256n
River bottom lands, 53
See also related area and state names
Roosevelt, Franklin D., 75, 197
Roosevelt, Theodore, 66, 80n
Rosenthal, Elizabeth Clark, 82–9, 212, 326;
biography, 330–31
Rough Rock Navajo, 289
See also Navajo
Royce, Charles C., 80n
Russia, 56

Sabines, 214
Sac, 95, 97, 128, 133, 191, 198
See also Sac-Fox

Sac-Fox, 161ff, 198
    See also Sac
Sahaptian linguistic grouping, 238
St Lawrence River, 50, 52
Salish-speaking groups, 238
San Carlos Apache, *see* Apache
Santals of Chotonagpur, 140n
Saponis, 95
Sasaki, Dr Tom T., 289n
Sauk, *see* Sac
Scandinavians, 37
Schusky, Ernest L., 140n
Seaton, Fred A., 111
Second World War, 76, 101, 104, 163, 199, 220, 228, 239, 243, 250, 281
Segregation, *see* Discrimination; Tribal membership
Selective Service, 272
    See also Military service
Seminole, 65, 99, 135, 153, 215, 315
Seneca, 64, 94, 157
Shawnee, 64, 95, 161ff
Sherif, Muzafer, 209n
Shoshonean-speaking groups, 238
Siegel, Bernard J., 185, 206, 209n
Simpson, George E., 289n, 291n
Sioux, 12, 85, 103, 131, 132, 159n
    See also Pine Ridge Sioux
Skinner, Alanson, 210n
Slave, 8on
'Smoking for Horses', 175
'So-called' Indians, 213ff
Social scientists, preconceptions of, 257–8
    See also Anthropology
Society for the Study of Social Problems, 267n
Sons of Italy, 37

South, 28, 215, 321
    See also related area and state names
South Dakota, 103, 114, 118, 128, 260–66;
    Oglala, 260–66;
    Pine Ridge, 261
    Pine Ridge Reservation, 260–66;
    White Clay, 261
Southeast, 50, 54, 66
    See also related area and state names
Southern Regional Educational Association, 224
Southwest, 54, 128, 129, 134, 135, 270, 272, 275, 278, 281, 286, 290n, 316;
    See also related area and state names
Spain, 51, 53, 55, 58, 58–9, 216
    See also History
Speck, F. G., 215, 235n
Spencer, Robert F., 79n
Spicer, Edward H., 125n, 286, 288n, 290n
Spier, Leslie, 241, 256n
Sports, 260–62
State of Oklahoma Planning and Resources Board, *see* Oklahoma, state of
Stern, Theodore, 290n
Stockbridge, 103
Supreme Court, 67, 107, 119, 223
    See also Attorneys; Dobyns, Henry
Susquehannock, 95
Swanton, J. R., 202, 235n

Task Force for Information Officers, 172

Index

Task Force on Indian Affairs, 112

Tax, Sol, 16, 323

Tecumseh, 95, 97, 125n, 130

Tenino, 238

Tennessee, 145–6, 154;
Knoxville, 145–6, 153;

Tennessee River, 146

Termination, 77, 79, 80n, 81n,
273, 295, 296, 299, 312;
defined, 96

Teton, 86

Texas, 110;
Dallas, 168

Thomas, Cyrus, 80n

Thomas, Robert K., 128, 159n,
324;
biography, 331

Thompson, Laura, 288n, 290

Thoreau, Henry David, 43

Tocqueville, Alexis de, 38

Tourists, 72, 148, 284, 322

Towle, Leslie P., 181

'Traditional Hopi Chiefs', 285

'Traditional Indian', 134

Trapping, see Hunting and trapping

Treaties, 58–68, 80n, 108ff, 143–
59, 238–9;
nature of, 298–9, 302;
use of treaty funds, 108ff
See also History; Bureau of
Indian Affairs; Factional
conflict

Tribal government, 102–14ff, esp.
118–19, 122; 147–8, 177–8,
184–211, 226–8, 236, 246–53,
268–91, esp. 272ff; 285, 286

Tribal membership, 11, 84, 108,
147, 149–50, 154–6, 160–61,
204–209, 213ff, 251, 275–6,
289n
See also Identity

Turner, Eldon, 43n

Turner, Frederick Jackson, 38

Turtle Mountain Chippewa, see
Chippewa

Tuscarora, 94

Tutelos, 95

Tylor, Edward Burnett, 88, 89n

'Typical' Indians, 10–12, 21, 212ff

Udall, Stuart, 22

Umatilla, 238

Underhill, Ruth, 80n, 216, 219,
235n

Unemployment, 116
See also Welfare; Economic
situation, and related topics

United Band, 188ff

United Nations (UN), 299, 301–2

United States Corps of Engineers,
283

United States Department of
Agriculture, 278

United States Office of Education,
266n

United States Public Health Service, 272, 279, Diagram

United States Public Housing
Administration (USPHA), 114

University of Oklahoma, 179, 180

'Unto These Hills', 153

Urban society and tribal cultures,
139–40
See also Cities, Indian experience in

Utah, 110, 276;
Uintah and Ouray Reservation,
276, 289n

Ute, 108, 109, 276, 290n
  See also Mountain Ute

Verret, Bob, 217, 227
Vietnam War, 45n
Virginia, 58
Voget, Fred, 236

WNAD, 180
Walker, Deward E., Jr, 236–56,
  325;
  biography, 331–2
Wampanoag, 95
Wanapum, 238
War Department, *see* Bureau of
  Indian Affairs
War of 1812, 61
War of 1877, 239, 240
War on Poverty, *see* Office of
  Economic Opportunity
Washburn, Wilcomb, 80n, 125n
Washington (state), 115, 133;
  Clarkston, 246;
  Nespelem, 240
Washington, George, 65
Washo Drainage Project, 118
Watkins, Arthur V., 110, 126n
Wax, Murray, 34, 257–67, 325–6;
  biography, 332
Wax, Rosalie, 34, 257–67, 325–6;
  biography, 332
Wea, 95
Welfare, 14ff, 20–22, 116ff, 145,
  149, 151, 158, 166–72
  See also Economic situation;
  Education; Health; Bureau of
  Indian Affairs; *specific welfare
  agencies by title*
Wenner Gren Foundation, 209n

West, 55
  *See also related area and state
  names*
Wheeler-Howard Act (Howard-
  Wheeler Act), *see* Indian Re-
  organization Act of 1934
White Mountain Apaches, 290n
  See also Apaches
Wichita (tribe), 161ff
Winnebago, 64, 97, 103, 296, 306
Wisconsin, 38, 95, 103, 296, 306;
  Milwaukee, 296;
  Eau Claire, 308
Wisconsin Winnebago, 296, 306;
  See also Winnebago
Witt, Shirley Hill, 93–127, 324;
  biography, 332
Woehlke, William V., 101, 125n
Women, prominent role of, 322–3
Worcester v. The State of Georgia,
  67, 297
Work, Herbert, 101
Workshop of American Indian
  Affairs, 112
World War I, *see* First World
  War
World War II, *see* Second World
  War
Wounded Knee, 69, 99
Wovoka, 97
Wright, Katherine, 232
Wynadott, 95

Yakima, 133, 238
Yaryan, Rev. John J., 115
Yinger, J. Milton, 289n, 291n

Zimmerman, William R., 103,
  110, 288n, 289n

The
North American Indians

Distribution of Descendants of the Aboriginal Population of Alaska, Canada, and the United States.

This map was prepared under the direction of Sol Tax, Department of Anthropology, University of Chicago. The data for the United States were compiled by Samuel Stanley and Robert K. Thomas in 1956. In 1957 Bruce MacLachlan added the data for Canada, and Stanley for Alaska. The composite map was then made by MacLachlan and Myron Rosenberg, and finally revised and corrected by Stanley.

Note on the Fourth Edition: This fourth edition was published in preparation for the American Indian Charter Convention, June 13–20, 1961, held at the University of Chicago. It is intended to include all self-identified American Indian communities as of 1950.

This map is intended to include all self-identified American Indian communities as of 1950. After the U. S. Census of 1960 is available, the map will be revised to show also how many Indians live outside of these communities.

The map was originally begun in 1956 and revised successively in 1958 and 1959 to provide accurate information about the American Indian population and to serve as a base for study of Indian problems. How many Indians are there? Are they increasing or decreasing? Where do they live and work? What are their different legal, social, and economic situations? All of these questions require for study a base like this map.

Each revision of this map should bring corrections as to location, size, and identification of Indian groups with which readers are familiar. We gratefully acknowledge the co-operation of those individuals who have contributed their personal knowledge in the past. Nevertheless, the map is still incomplete, and we invite further comments and corrections.

SYMBOLS

1:5,000,000

" "   Actual identity of tribe doubtful.

( )   Separate distinct community but counted as part of another population unit.

•   Community, reservation, rancherio, or colony, or cluster thereof.

∷   Scattered individuals or families in the U. S.

↻   Larger reservations in the U. S.

—   Boundary of special groupings.

•   Indicates a mixed Native population e.g. 22 Eskimo and 4 Indians in a village appear on the map as (E) 26*.

AL	– Aleut	HA	– Haida
AT	– Athabaskan	TL	– Tlingit
E	– Eskimo	TS	– Tsimshian

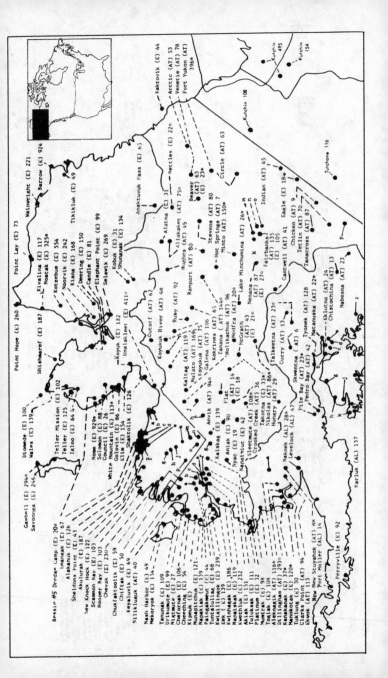

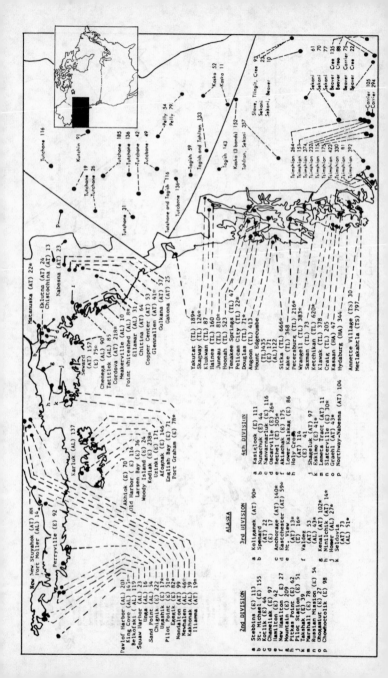

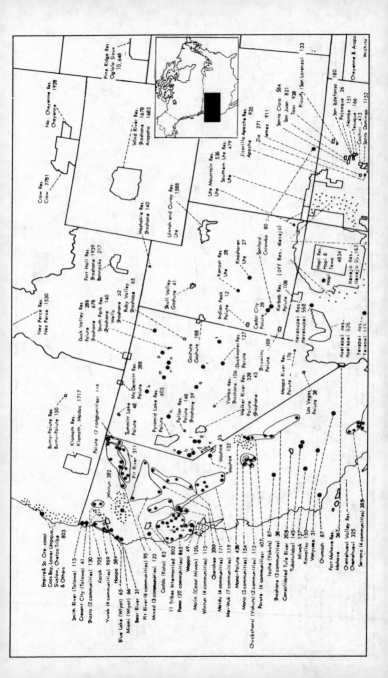

Empire& So. Ore. coast
Coos Bay, Lower Umpqua
Siuslaw, Chetco Tribe
& Others 803
Smith River (Tolowa) 113
Crescent City (Tolowa) 41
Karok 705
Shasta (2 communities) 130
Yurok (4 communities) 959
Blue Lake (Wiyot) 65
Miami (Wiyot) 66
Hoopa 58v
Bear River 31
Pit River (6 communities) 95
Mixed 122
Caddo (Kato) 83
11 Tribes Intermarried 802
Pomo (20 communities) 865
Wappo 49
Marin (Coast Miwok) 120
Wintun (4 communities) 115
Cherokee 300
Maidu (4 communities) 171
Mer-Wuk (7 communities) 119
Mono-Paiute 436
Mono (3 communities) 154
Ouitchansi (Yokuts) 112
Paiute (4 communities) 407
Iache (Yokuts) 87
Shoshone (3 communities) 39
Consolidated Tule River 205
Tubatulabal 145
Miwok 137
Kawaiisu 150
Vanyuma 31
Chumash 87
Fort Mohave
Mohave 367
Chemehuavi Valley Res. 325
Chemehuavi (4 communities) 385
Serrano (4 communities) 325

Pit River 382
Wintun 382

Klamath Res.
Klamath, Modoc 1717

Burns-Paiute Res.
Burns-Paiute 150

Paiute (2 communities) 114

Summit Lake
Paiute 48

Pyramid Lake Res.
Paiute 148

McDermitt Res.
Shoshone 603

Fallon Res.
Paiute 326
Shoshone 59

Walker River Res.
Paiute 326
Shoshone

Washoe 132
Washoe 25

Nez Perce Res.
Nez Perce 1530

Duck Valley Res.
Paiute 286
Shoshone 678
South Fork Res.
Shoshone 140
Ruby Valley
Shoshone 52

Goshute
Goshute 188

Yomba Res.
Shoshone 106
Duckwater Res.
Paiute 43

Las Vegas
Paiute 38

Moapa River Res.
Paiute 176

Shivwits
Paiute 108

Cedar City
Paiute

Indian Peak
Paiute 12

Kaibab Res.
Paiute 106

Kanosh
Paiute 28

Skull Valley
Goshute 41

Fort Hall Res.
Shoshone 1939
Bannocks 217

Washakie Res.
Shoshone 140

Uintah and Ouray Res.
Ute 1588

Ute Mountain Res.
Ute 536
Southern Ute 479

Sanford
Colorado 80

Koosharem
Ute 27

Havasupai Res.
Havasupai 568

Hualapai Res.
Hualapai 676

Yavapai Res.
Yavapai 116

Crow Res.
Crow 2781

No. Cheyenne Res.
Cheyenne 1928

Wind River Res.
Shoshone 1678
Arapaho 1683

Jicarilla Apache Res.
Apache 271

Zia 271
Jemez 911

Hopi Res.
Hopi & Tewo
Hopi 4834

Navajo Res.
Navajo Co. 167
Navajo

Pine Ridge Res.
Oglala Sioux
10,648

Santa Clara 564
San Juan 821
Picuris (San Lorenzo) 133

San Ildefonso
Nambe 151
Tesuque 166
Cochiti 413
Santo Domingo 1152

Pojoaque 26
Taos 938

Cheyenne & Arapaho
Wichita

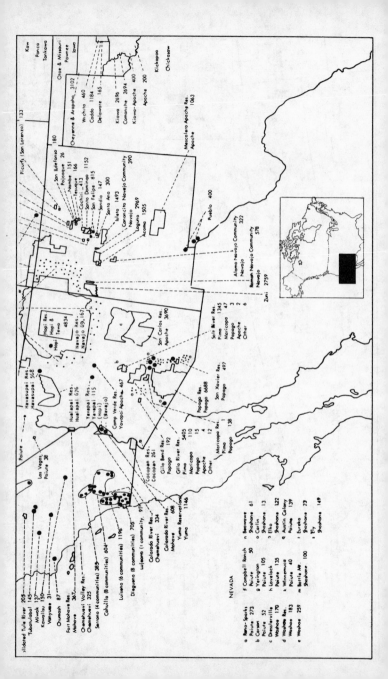

Kaw
Ponca
Tonkawa
Pawnee

Otos & Missouri
Iowa

Cheyenne & Arapaho 3102

Wichita 460
Caddo 1184
Delaware 165
Kiowa 2696
Comanche 2694
Kiowa-Apache 400
Apache 200

Kickapoo
Chickasaw

Picuris (San Lorenzo) 133

180
Oterevano (San Lorenzo) 180

San Ildefonso
San Ildefonso 26
Pojoaque 151
Nambe 166
Tesuque 413
Cochiti 1152
Santo Domingo 815
San Felipe 147
Santa Ana 300
Sandia 1493
Isleta 2969
Camancito Navajo Community 390
Navajo
Laguna 1505
Acoma

Mescalero Apache Res.
Mescalero Apache 1063

Pueblo 400

Alamo Navajo Community 322
Navajo 578
Zuni 2759
Ramah Navajo Community

Hopi Res.
Hopi & Tewa 4834
Navajo Res.
Hopi 69, 167
Navajo

Havasupai Res.
Havasupai 508

Hualapai Res.
Hualapai 676

Yavapai Res.
Yavapai (Hopi) 115

Camp Verde Res.
Yavapai-Apache 467
(Navajo)

San Carlos Res.
Apache 3690

Salt River Res.
Pima 1345
Maricopa 47
Papago 3
Apache 2
Other 6

Fort Mohave Res.
Mohave 367

Chemehuevi Valley Res.
Chemehuevi 325

San Xavier Res.
Papago 497

Serrano (4 communities) 385

Cahuilla (8 communities) 604

Papago Res.
Papago 6688

Gila Bend Res.
Papago 192

Gila River Res.
Pima 5405
Maricopa 110
Papago 15
Apache 4
Other 12

Luiseno (6 communities) 1176

Diegueno (8 communities) 705

Maricopa Res.
Pima 138
Maricopa
Papago

Cocopah Res.
Cocopah 761

Colorado River Res.
Mohave 608

Yuma Reservations
Yuma 1146

Las Vegas
Paiute 38

Paiute

Oroville 87

Vanyumi 31

Kawaiisu 150

Miwok 137

Koweelah 145

Tubatulabal 205

Mildorod Tule River 205

Paiute

NEVADA

a	Reno-Sparks Paiute 273	f	Campbell Ranch Shoshone 50	n
b	Carson Paiute 52	g	Yerington Paiute 105	o
c	Dresslerville Washoe 170	h	Lovelock Paiute 135	p
d	Washoe Res. Washoe 183	k	Winnemucca Paiute 40	q
e	Washoe 259	m	Battle Mtn. Shoshone 100	r
				s

Beowawe 61
Carlin 13
Elko 122
Austin Colony Paiute 139
Eureka Paiute 73
Ely Shoshone 23
Shoshone 149

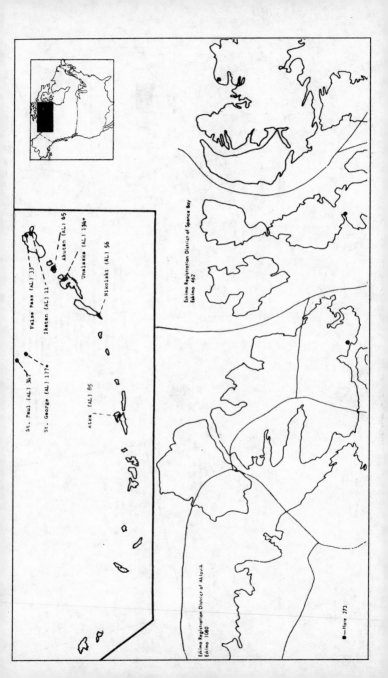

St. Paul (AL) 347

False Pass (AL) 33

St. George (AL) 177°

Ikatan (AL) 11

Akutan (AL) 85

Unalaska (AL) 134°

Nikolski (AL) 56

Atka (AL) 85

Eskimo Registration District of Spence Bay
Eskimo 462

Eskimo Registration District of Aklavik
Eskimo 1680

●—More 273

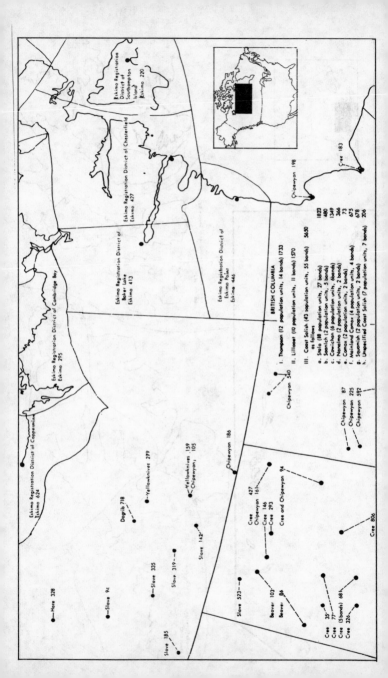

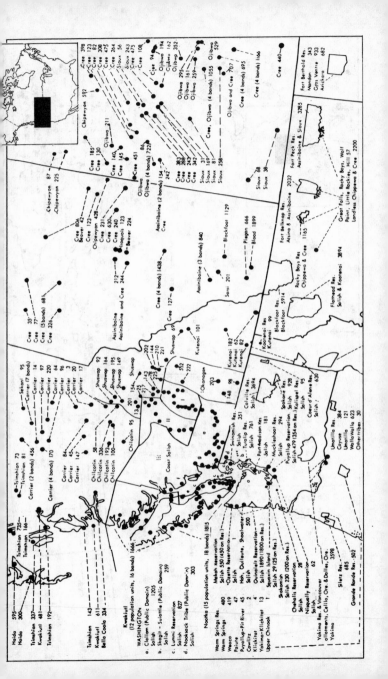

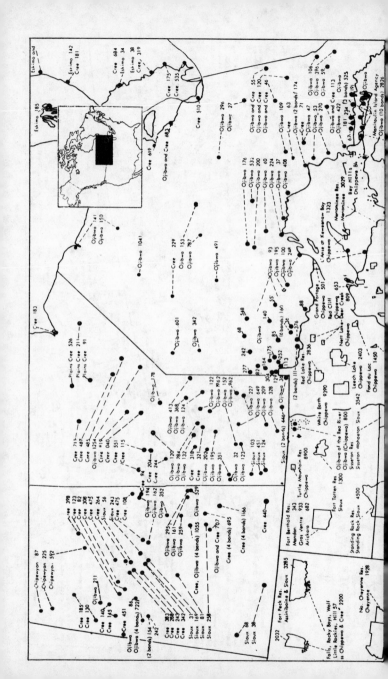

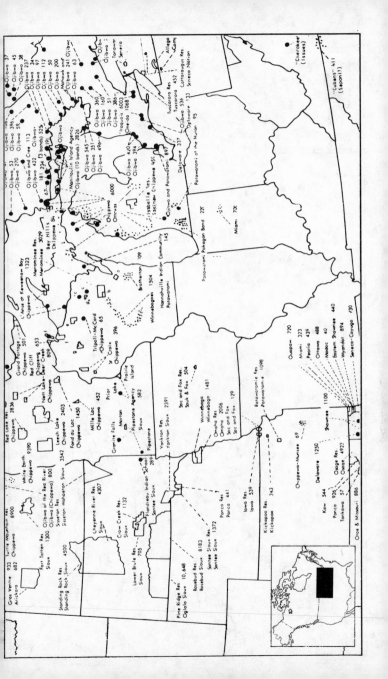

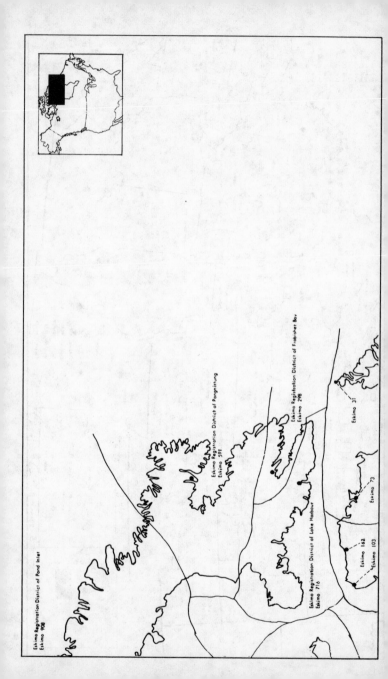

Eskimo Registration District of Pond Inlet
Eskimo 908

Eskimo Registration District of Pangnirtung
Eskimo 591

Eskimo Registration District of Frobisher Bay
Eskimo 298

Eskimo 31

Eskimo Registration District of Lake Harbour
Eskimo 716

Eskimo 73

Eskimo 162

Eskimo 103

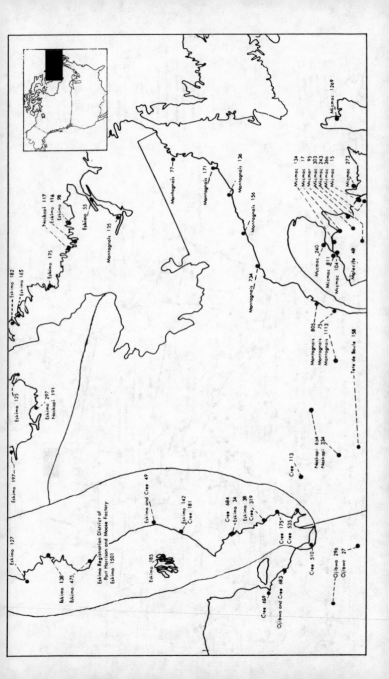

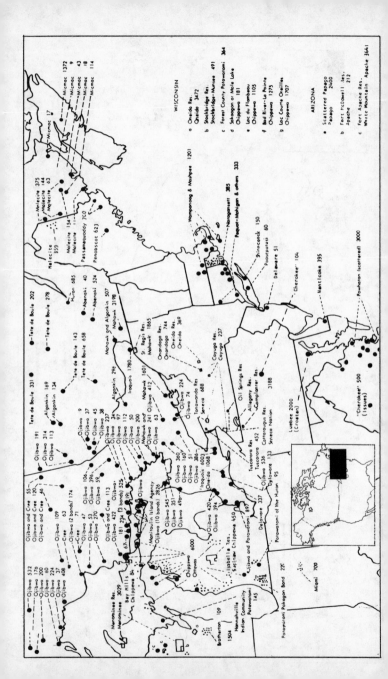

WISCONSIN

o Oneida Res.
   Oneida 3472
b Stockbridge Res.
   Stockbridge-Munsee 491
c Forest County Potawatomi 364
d Sabaogon or Mole Lake
   Chippewa 181
e Lac du Flambeau
   Chippewa 1105
f Bad River–La Pointe
   Chippewa 1275
g Lac Courte Oreilles
   Chippewa 1707

ARIZONA

• Scattered Papago
   Papago 2400
b Fort McDowell Res.
   Apache 212
c Fort Apache Res.
   White Mountain Apache 3641

Micmac 1372
Micmac 9
Micmac 43
Micmac 18
Micmac 114
Micmac 17

Malecite 375
Malecite 144
Malecite 63
Malecite 154
Malecite 11
Malecite 359
Passamaquoddy 760
Penobscot 623

Huron 685
Abenaki 40
Abenaki 524

Tete de Boule 202
Tete de Boule 278
Tete de Boule 331
Tete de Boule 143
Tete de Boule 658

Algonkin 169
Algonkin 134
Algonkin 296
Algonkin 97
Algonkin 112

Wampanoag & Mashpee 1201
Narragansett 385
Pequot–Mohigan & others 333
Shinnecock 150
Poosepatuck 60
Delaware 51

Cherokee 104
Nanticoke 395
Powhatan (scattered) 3000

Ojibwa 191
Ojibwa 314
Ojibwa 113
Ojibwa 9
Ojibwa 37
Ojibwa 45
Ojibwa 38
Ojibwa 237
Ojibwa 34
Ojibwa 97
Ojibwa 50
Ojibwa 200
Ojibwa 63
Ojibwa 224
Ojibwa 74

Mohawk and Algonkin 507
Mohawk 3198
Mohawk 160
Mohawk 241
Mohawk 412
Iroquois 1780
St. Regis Res.
Onondaga 744
Onondaga Res.
Oneida Res.
Oneida 369
Cayuga Res.
Cayuga 237
Oil Springs Res.
Allegany Res.
Complanter Res. 3188
Tonawanda Res.
Seneca 688

Lumbee 2000
(Croatan)

'Cherokee' 500
(Issues)

Ojibwa and Cree 55
Ojibwa and Cree 120
Ojibwa and Cree 44
Ojibwa (2 bands) 174
Ojibwa 109
Cree 71
Cree 63
Ojibwa 47
Ojibwa 53
Ojibwa 270
Ojibwa 398
Ojibwa 58
Ojibwa 113
Ojibwa 422
Ojibwa 545
Ojibwa 351
Ojibwa 49e
Ojibwa 420
Ojibwa 394

Ojibwa 532
Ojibwa 306
Ojibwa 300
Ojibwa 60
Ojibwa 37
Ojibwa 224
Ojibwa 608

Ojibwa 106
Ojibwa 360
Ojibwa 160
Ojibwa 386
Oneida 6003
Iroquois 1068
Oneida 6003

Tuscarora Res.
Tuscarora 452
Cattaraugus Res.
Seneca Nation 123
Ojibwa 536
Delaware 95

Menominee Res.
Menominee 3029
Bay Mills 84
Chippewa

Manitoulin Island Agency
Ojibwa (10 bands) 2826

Chippewa
Ottawas

Brotherton 1504

Hannahville Indian Community
Potawatomi 145

Isabella Res.
Saginaw Chippewa 450
Ojibwa and Potawatomi 897

Ojibwa 6000

Dejware 337

Potawatomi of the Huron

Potawatomi Pokagon Band 22K

Miami 700

Potawatomi 169

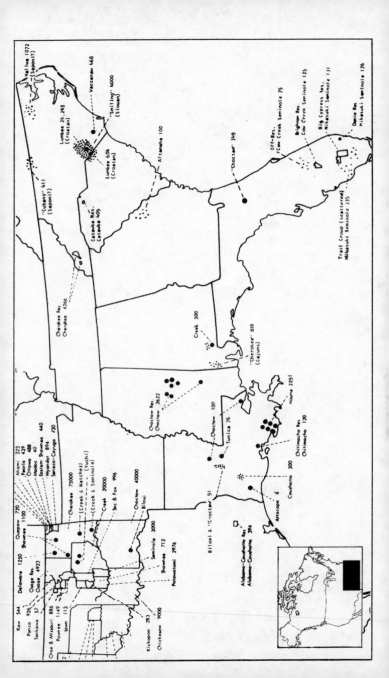

Some other books published by Penguins and Pelicans are described on the following pages.

THE SACRED PIPE

Black Elk's Account of the
Seven Rites of the Oglala Sioux

Recorded and edited by Joseph Epes Brown

A unique account of the ancient religion of the Sioux
Indians. Black Elk was the only qualified priest still alive
when he gave the material in this book to Joseph Epes
Brown during the latter's stay at Pine Ridge Reservation
in South Dakota. Beginning with White Buffalo Cow
Woman's first visit to the Sioux to give them the sacred
pipe, he discusses the seven rites, which were disclosed to
the Sioux through visions. He takes the reader through
the sun dance, the purification rite, the "keeping of the
soul," and the other ceremonies, showing how the Sioux
have come to terms with God, nature, and their fellow
men.

THE CHICANOS

Mexican American Voices
Edited by Ed Ludwig and James Santibanez

An anthology of writings by and about Mexican Americans. The editors have chosen fiction, poems, and articles. Together, their selections form a realistic picture of Chicano life in the United States today. Included are reminiscences—pleasant and unpleasant—of Mexican American childhood; accounts of Chicanos in the American school system; reports on strikes by Chicano workers . . . and poems and stories that reflect the hard realities of poverty and alienation. Among the contributors: Cesar Chavez on the California grape strike; Joan Baez on her experiences as a Mexican American; and José Alvarez on the Chicano and the law. Edward W. Ludwig and James Santibanez are both at San José State College, San José, California.

WHITE OVER BLACK

Winthrop D. Jordan

This monumental work explores the origin and development of white attitudes toward the Negro in America from the sixteenth century through the early years of the Republic. The Englishmen in Jamestown who greeted the first Negro slaves had already acquired attitudes toward the Negro — from tradition, from religion, from earlier European contacts with Africans. Professor Jordan studies these attitudes and traces the ways in which they grew to create a cruel and tragic dichotomy — the twin concepts of "liberty and justice for all" and "the white man's country." Winthrop D. Jordan is associate professor of history at the University of California at Berkeley. *White Over Black* has received Phi Beta Kappa's Ralph Waldo Emerson Award and is the 1969 winner of the National Book Award in history and biography.

CONFRONTATION: BLACK AND WHITE

Lerone Bennett, Jr.

A descriptive analysis of the Negro revolt in America, its origins, history, and implications for the future. Drawing on his vast knowledge of Negro history, his awareness of Negro sociological problems in the contemporary world, the author gives a clear evaluation of the present situation and brings the reader face to face with many hidden and sometimes uncomfortable truths about racial conflict. Mr. Bennett is Senior Editor of *Ebony*. Among his other books are *The Negro Mood; What Manner of Man: A Biography of Martin Luther King, Jr.;* and *Before the Mayflower: A History of the Negro in America, 1619-1964.*

PENGUIN MODERN SOCIOLOGY READINGS

This series offers essential Readings over the whole range of thinking and research, both classical and contemporary, in sociology and social anthropology.

SOCIAL INEQUALITY

Edited by André Béteille

Social inequality has always been one of the major preoccupations of sociology — largely, perhaps, because of the strong moral commitment which many sociologists bring to their work.

Professor Béteille has tried to steer his selection between, on the one hand, philosophical speculation on the moral basis of equality, and on the other, an overconcern with the technique of analysis of stratification. The result is a fascinating blend of sociology and social anthropology that looks at stratification along class, caste and racial lines in a wide range of different societies. Professor André Béteille is Professor of Sociology at the University of Delhi.

WHITE OVER BLACK

Winthrop D. Jordan

This monumental work explores the origin and development of white attitudes toward the Negro in America
from the sixteenth century through the early years of
the Republic. The Englishmen in Jamestown who greeted
the first Negro slaves had already acquired attitudes
toward the Negro — from tradition, from religion, from
earlier European contacts with Africans. Professor Jordan
studies these attitudes and traces the ways in which they
grew to create a cruel and tragic dichotomy — the twin
concepts of "liberty and justice for all" and "the white
man's country." Winthrop D. Jordan is associate professor
of history at the University of California at Berkeley.
White Over Black has received Phi Beta Kappa's Ralph
Waldo Emerson Award and is the 1969 winner of the
National Book Award in history and biography.

CONFRONTATION: BLACK AND WHITE

Lerone Bennett, Jr.

A descriptive analysis of the Negro revolt in America, its origins, history, and implications for the future. Drawing on his vast knowledge of Negro history, his awareness of Negro sociological problems in the contemporary world, the author gives a clear evaluation of the present situation and brings the reader face to face with many hidden and sometimes uncomfortable truths about racial conflict. Mr. Bennett is Senior Editor of *Ebony*. Among his other books are *The Negro Mood; What Manner of Man: A Biography of Martin Luther King, Jr.;* and *Before the Mayflower: A History of the Negro in America, 1619-1964*.

PENGUIN MODERN SOCIOLOGY READINGS

This series offers essential Readings over the whole range of thinking and research, both classical and contemporary, in sociology and social anthropology.

SOCIAL INEQUALITY

Edited by André Béteille

Social inequality has always been one of the major pre-occupations of sociology — largely, perhaps, because of the strong moral commitment which many sociologists bring to their work.

Professor Béteille has tried to steer his selection between, on the one hand, philosophical speculation on the moral basis of equality, and on the other, an over-concern with the technique of analysis of stratification. The result is a fascinating blend of sociology and social anthropology that looks at stratification along class, caste and racial lines in a wide range of different societies. Professor André Béteille is Professor of Sociology at the University of Delhi.